917.304
O.U.R

Our
Native American
Heritage

EXPLORE AMERICA

Our
Native American
Heritage

Reader's Digest

THE READER'S DIGEST ASSOCIATION, INC.
Pleasantville, New York / Montreal

Our Native American Heritage was created and produced by St. Remy Press.

STAFF FOR OUR NATIVE AMERICAN HERITAGE
Series Editor: Elizabeth Cameron
Art Director: Chantal Bilodeau
Editor: Alfred LeMaitre
Assistant Editor: Neale McDevitt
Photo Researcher: Geneviève Monette
Cartography: Hélène Dion, Anne-Marie Lemay, David Widgington
Research Editor: Robert B. Ronald
Researcher: Jennifer Meltzer
Contributing Researcher: Joan McKenna
Copy Editor: Judy Yelon
Index: Christine Jacobs
System Coordinator: Éric Beaulieu
Technical Support: Mathieu Raymond-Beaubien, Jean Sirois
Scanner Operators: Martin Francoeur, Sara Grynspan

ST. REMY STAFF
PRESIDENT, CHIEF EXECUTIVE OFFICER: Fernand Lecoq
PRESIDENT, CHIEF OPERATING OFFICER: Pierre Léveillé
VICE PRESIDENT, FINANCE: Natalie Watanabe
MANAGING EDITOR: Carolyn Jackson
MANAGING ART DIRECTOR: Diane Denoncourt
PRODUCTION MANAGER: Michelle Turbide

Writers: David Dunbar—The Six Nations
Rod Gragg—Hunters of the Plains
George Hardeen—The Navajo Nation
Kim Heacox—People of the Arctic
Beth Hege—The Nez Perce
Jim Henderson—Indian Territory
Rose Houk—Mesa Verde
Steven Krolak—The Pacific Northwest
Brad Lepper—Moundbuilders of the Ohio Valley
Margaret Locklair—Cherokee Country

Contributing Writers: Adriana Barton, Fiona Gilsenan, Enza Micheletti, Armand Thomas

READER'S DIGEST STAFF
Series Editor: Gayla Visalli
Editor: Jill Maynard
Art Director: Joel Musler
Art Editor: Nancy Mace

READER'S DIGEST GENERAL BOOKS
Editor-in-Chief, Books and Home
Entertainment: Barbara J. Morgan
Editor, U.S. General Books: David Palmer
Executive Editor: Gayla Visalli
Editorial Director: Jane Polley
Art Director: Joel Musler
Research Director: Laurel A. Gilbride

Opening photographs
Cover: White House, Canyon de Chelly National Monument, Arizona
Back Cover: Haida totem, Museum of Anthropology, British Columbia
Page 2: Kuzitrin River, Bering Land Bridge National Preserve, Alaska
Page 5: Navajo weaving, Hubbell Trading Post, Arizona

The credits and acknowledgments that appear on page 144 are hereby made a part of this copyright page.

Copyright © 1996 The Reader's Digest Association, Inc.
Copyright © 1996 The Reader's Digest Association (Canada) Ltd.
Copyright © 1996 Reader's Digest Association Far East Ltd.
Philippine Copyright 1996 Reader's Digest Association Far East Ltd.

Library of Congress Cataloging in Publication Data

Our Native American Heritage.
          p.   cm.—(Explore America)
     Includes index.
     ISBN 0-89577-867-X
     1. Indians of North America.   2. United States—Guidebooks.
     I. Reader's Digest Association.   II. Series.
     E77.089   1996
     917.304'929—dc20   96-907

READER'S DIGEST and the Pegasus logo are registered trademarks of The Reader's Digest Association, Inc.

Printed in the United States of America

CONTENTS

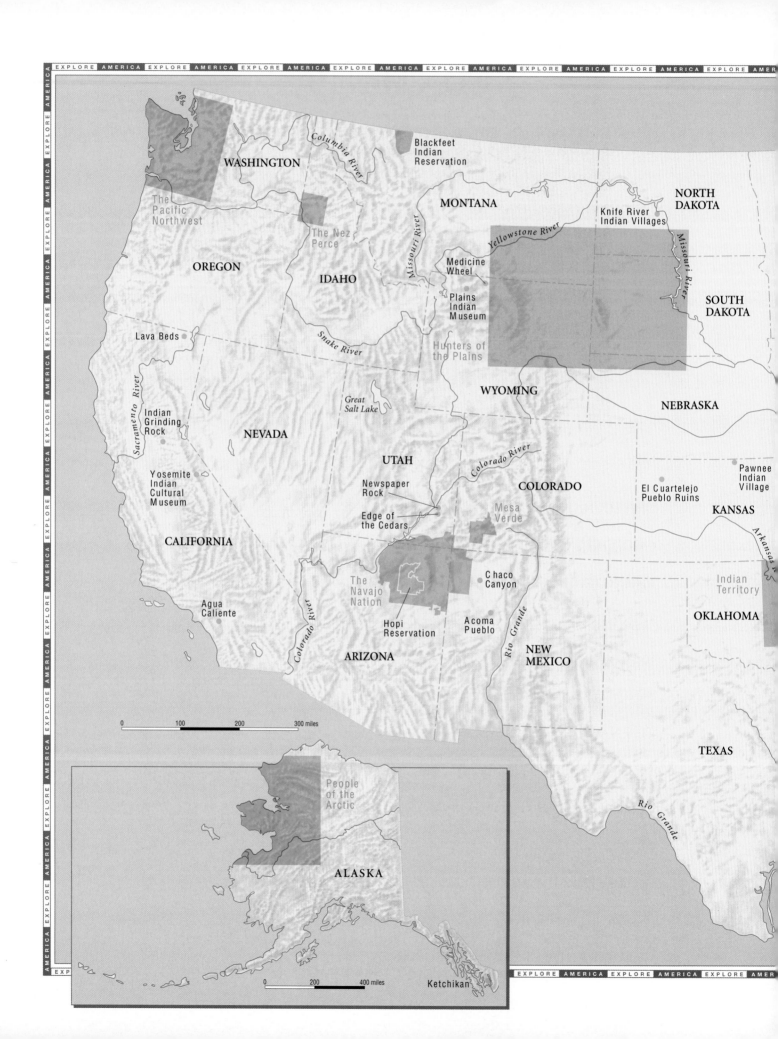

WASHINGTON

Columbia River

Blackfeet
Indian
Reservation

MONTANA

NORTH
DAKOTA

Knife River
Indian Villages

The Pacific
Northwest

OREGON

The Nez
Perce

IDAHO

Missouri River

Yellowstone River

Medicine
Wheel

Plains
Indian
Museum

Missouri River

SOUTH
DAKOTA

Lava Beds

Snake River

Hunters of
the Plains

WYOMING

NEBRASKA

Great
Salt Lake

Sacramento River

Indian
Grinding
Rock

NEVADA

UTAH

Colorado River

COLORADO

El Cuartelejo
Pueblo Ruins

Pawnee
Indian
Village

KANSAS

Arkansas R.

Yosemite
Indian
Cultural
Museum

Newspaper
Rock

Mesa
Verde

Edge of
the Cedars

CALIFORNIA

Chaco
Canyon

Indian
Territory

Agua
Caliente

Colorado River

The
Navajo
Nation

Acoma
Pueblo

Rio Grande

OKLAHOMA

Hopi
Reservation

ARIZONA

NEW
MEXICO

0   100   200   300 miles

TEXAS

Rio Grande

People
of the
Arctic

ALASKA

0   200   400 miles

Ketchikan

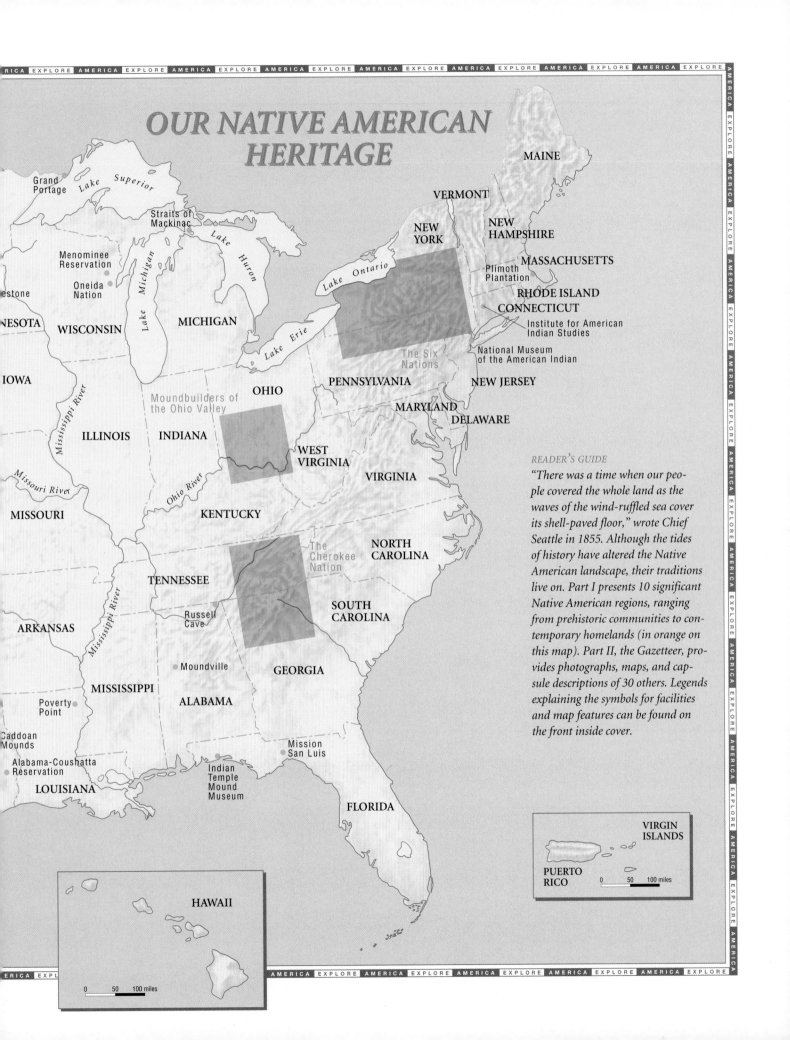

OUR NATIVE AMERICAN HERITAGE

MAINE

Grand Portage

Lake Superior

VERMONT

NEW YORK

NEW HAMPSHIRE

Straits of Mackinac

Lake Huron

MASSACHUSETTS

Menominee Reservation

Plimoth Plantation

Oneida Nation

Lake Ontario

RHODE ISLAND

CONNECTICUT

estone

NESOTA

WISCONSIN

Lake Michigan

MICHIGAN

Institute for American Indian Studies

Lake Erie

The Six Nations

National Museum of the American Indian

IOWA

PENNSYLVANIA

NEW JERSEY

Moundbuilders of the Ohio Valley

OHIO

MARYLAND

ILLINOIS

INDIANA

WEST VIRGINIA

DELAWARE

Mississippi River

Missouri River

VIRGINIA

MISSOURI

KENTUCKY

The Cherokee Nation

NORTH CAROLINA

ARKANSAS

TENNESSEE

Russell Cave

SOUTH CAROLINA

Mississippi River

Moundville

GEORGIA

Caddoan Mounds

MISSISSIPPI

ALABAMA

Alabama-Coushatta Reservation

Poverty Point

Mission San Luis

LOUISIANA

Indian Temple Mound Museum

FLORIDA

HAWAII

0   50   100 miles

READER'S GUIDE

"There was a time when our people covered the whole land as the waves of the wind-ruffled sea cover its shell-paved floor," wrote Chief Seattle in 1855. Although the tides of history have altered the Native American landscape, their traditions live on. Part I presents 10 significant Native American regions, ranging from prehistoric communities to contemporary homelands (in orange on this map). Part II, the Gazetteer, provides photographs, maps, and capsule descriptions of 30 others. Legends explaining the symbols for facilities and map features can be found on the front inside cover.

VIRGIN ISLANDS

PUERTO RICO

0   50   100 miles

THE SIX NATIONS

*Skilled in the arts of diplomacy
as well as war, the Iroquois
confederacy ruled the Northeast.*

When it was completed in 1960, the New York State Thruway was hailed as an engineering marvel for its sweeping interchanges and absence of traffic lights. For the Albany to Buffalo section, however, Thruway surveyors couldn't improve on a centuries-old woodland footpath that once linked Iroquois-speaking tribes south of Lake Ontario. Today Buffalo-bound Thruway motorists follow the same route as warriors and couriers into the heartland of what was once the territory of the Iroquois. Beyond the hum of the tires it is still possible to hear echoes of the tribes' stormy, storied past in museums, historic sites, battlefields, place names, and legend-haunted lakes and glens.

For centuries, the forests and hills of what is now upstate New York were the battleground of the Haudenosaunee (pronounced *hoo-dee-noh-SHAWN-nee*), or "People of the Longhouse." They later came to be known by the name of Iroquois. Before white contact, their warfare took the form of ritual as well as deadly combat, pro-

Johnson Hall, above, was built between 1763 and 1774 by Sir William Johnson, an influential government Indian agent. He was widely respected by the Iroquois for his skill and fairness in negotiation. The clapboards that cover the two-story house, which is now a state historic site, were cut to resemble stone blocks.

ADIRONDACK SUMMIT

Overleaf: From the summit of Giant Mountain, the view of Mount Marcy and its surrounding peaks offers a glorious slice of Adirondack scenery. Iroquois hunters roamed the forests of these mountains, located on the eastern edge of their homeland, in search of game.

viding young warriors with the opportunity to prove their valor and win tribal status on stealthy commando raids.

Centuries of unremitting wars and blood feuds divided and weakened the Iroquois. Then, sometime between A.D. 1350 and A.D. 1600, the Iroquois ended this state of siege by developing a remarkable political system that linked five tribes—the Mohawk, Oneida, Onondaga, Cayuga, and Seneca—into what became known as the League of the Five Nations. The rules governing the alliance became known as the Great League of Peace. Between 1712 and 1723 approximately 500 Iroquois-speaking Tuscarora, hounded out of their homeland in North Carolina, moved north to live among the Oneida. They were soon recognized as the sixth Iroquois nation.

The Great League of Peace could be likened to a longhouse, the distinctive communal structure central to Iroquois village life. Just as many Iroquois families shared a longhouse, each with its own fire, so the nations that formed the confederacy lived together as a single household, each managing its internal affairs and convening to reach consensus on intertribal issues. The Iroquois system of government held Holland, France, and England at bay for more than a century until the American Revolution dealt a shattering blow to the Iroquois.

Wampum belts served as symbols of covenants and as records of great historic events of Iroquois independence. Except by special request, visitors to the Indian galleries in the New York State Museum in Albany never see the institution's priceless collection of wampum belts. These white-and-purple-beaded strips, some of which have been returned to Native American communities, were used as currency during the fur-trade period and were highly prized as personal ornaments. The Hiawatha belt, which was returned to the Onondaga, commemorates the founding of the

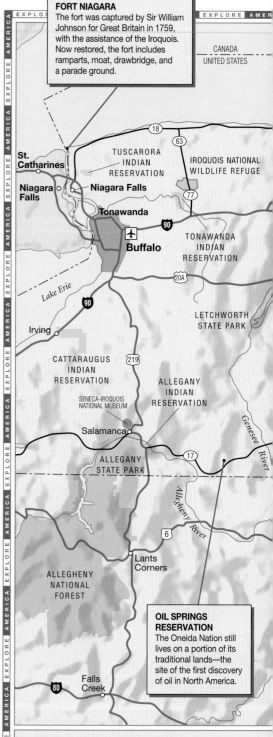

FORT NIAGARA
The fort was captured by Sir William Johnson for Great Britain in 1759, with the assistance of the Iroquois. Now restored, the fort includes ramparts, moat, drawbridge, and a parade ground.

OIL SPRINGS RESERVATION
The Oneida Nation still lives on a portion of its traditional lands—the site of the first discovery of oil in North America.

INFORMATION FOR VISITORS

Interstate 90, part of the New York Thruway, connects Albany and Buffalo. Hwys. 390 and 81 provide access to the Finger Lakes area. Airports at Albany, Syracuse, Rochester, and Buffalo are served by regularly scheduled flights. There is regular Amtrak service to Rochester and Syracuse. Numerous state parks in the region offer plentiful opportunities for camping, hiking, and picnicking. Summertime events include the Iroquois Indian Festival at Cobleskill, held

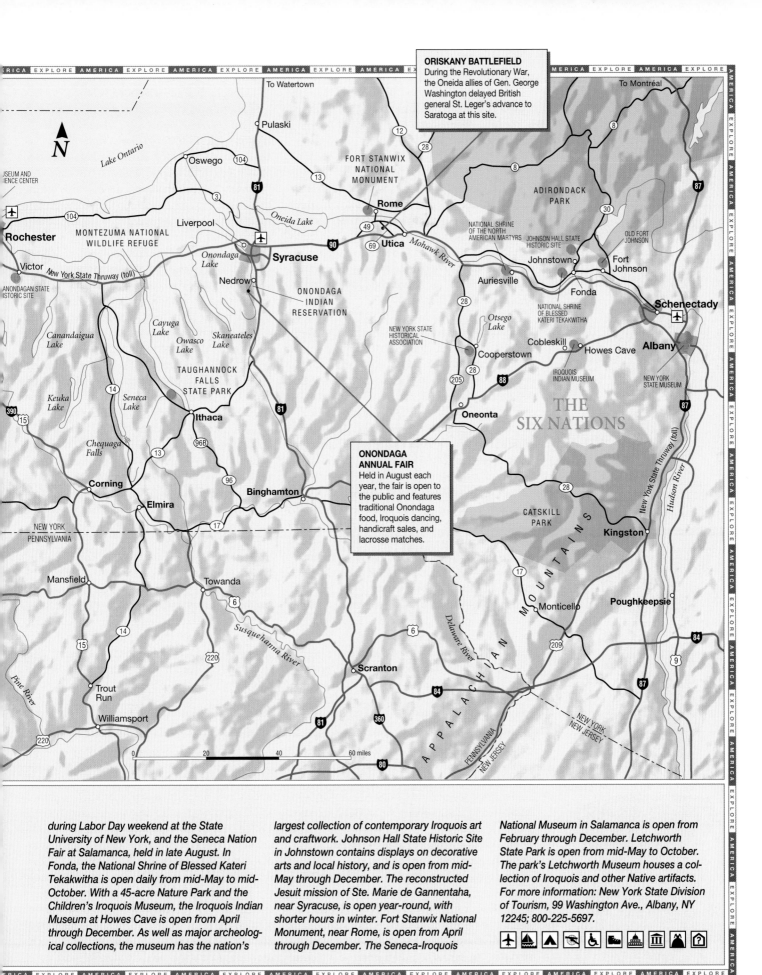

N

To Watertown

ORISKANY BATTLEFIELD
During the Revolutionary War, the Oneida allies of Gen. George Washington delayed British general St. Leger's advance to Saratoga at this site.

To Montréal

Lake Ontario

Pulaski

12

28

8

To Montréal

8

Oswego

104

13

FORT STANWIX NATIONAL MONUMENT

ADIRONDACK PARK

30

87

USEUM AND IENCE CENTER

81

3

Liverpool

Oneida Lake

Rome

49

NATIONAL SHRINE OF THE NORTH AMERICAN MARTYRS

JOHNSON HALL STATE HISTORIC SITE

OLD FORT JOHNSON

104

Rochester

MONTEZUMA NATIONAL WILDLIFE REFUGE

90

69

Utica

Mohawk River

Johnstown

Fort Johnson

Victor

New York State Thruway (toll)

Onondaga Lake

Syracuse

Auriesville

Fonda

Schenectady

ANONDAGAN STATE HISTORIC SITE

Nedrow

ONONDAGA INDIAN RESERVATION

NATIONAL SHRINE OF BLESSED KATERI TEKAKWITHA

Albany

Cayuga Lake

Canandaigua Lake

Owasco Lake

Skaneateles Lake

28

Otsego Lake

Cobleskill

Howes Cave

NEW YORK STATE HISTORICAL ASSOCIATION

NEW YORK STATE MUSEUM

Keuka Lake

Seneca Lake

TAUGHANNOCK FALLS STATE PARK

205

28

Cooperstown

IROQUOIS INDIAN MUSEUM

THE SIX NATIONS

390

14

88

87

15

Ithaca

81

96B

Oneonta

Chequaga Falls

13

96

New York State Thruway (toll)

ONONDAGA ANNUAL FAIR
Held in August each year, the fair is open to the public and features traditional Onondaga food, Iroquois dancing, handicraft sales, and lacrosse matches.

Hudson River

Corning

Binghamton

CATSKILL PARK

Kingston

Elmira

NEW YORK PENNSYLVANIA

17

28

Poughkeepsie

Mansfield

Towanda

Monticello

17

6

Susquehanna River

15

14

6

Delaware River

84

220

Scranton

209

87

Pine River

Trout Run

84

A P P A L A C H I A N   M O U N T A I N S

9

Williamsport

81

360

PENNSYLVANIA NEW JERSEY

NEW YORK NEW JERSEY

220

80

0   20   40   60 miles

during Labor Day weekend at the State University of New York, and the Seneca Nation Fair at Salamanca, held in late August. In Fonda, the National Shrine of Blessed Kateri Tekakwitha is open daily from mid-May to mid-October. With a 45-acre Nature Park and the Children's Iroquois Museum, the Iroquois Indian Museum at Howes Cave is open from April through December. As well as major archeological collections, the museum has the nation's

largest collection of contemporary Iroquois art and craftwork. Johnson Hall State Historic Site in Johnstown contains displays on decorative arts and local history, and is open from mid-May through December. The reconstructed Jesuit mission of Ste. Marie de Gannentaha, near Syracuse, is open year-round, with shorter hours in winter. Fort Stanwix National Monument, near Rome, is open from April through December. The Seneca-Iroquois

National Museum in Salamanca is open from February through December. Letchworth State Park is open from mid-May to October. The park's Letchworth Museum houses a collection of Iroquois and other Native artifacts. *For more information: New York State Division of Tourism, 99 Washington Ave., Albany, NY 12245; 800-225-5697.*

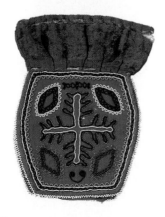

confederacy and serves as its constitution. In the middle of the belt, the centrally located Onondaga nation is depicted as the Great Tree of Peace, flanked by white squares that represent the other members of the league.

ALONG THE MOHAWK

The Mohawk River has a gentle valley, which was a much-contested corridor through the Appalachians between the Hudson River and the Great Lakes. In the town of Fort Johnson stands Old Fort Johnson, a Georgian residence built in 1749 by Sir William Johnson and fortified in 1755. The house contains period furniture and Indian artifacts.

The largest landowner in the Mohawk Valley and an active trader, Johnson learned to speak Iroquois and, when among the Indians, adopted their customs and dress. His reputation for fair dealings stood him in good stead after he was appointed superintendent of Indian Affairs north of the Ohio River in 1756. As many as 1,000 Iroquois camped and parlayed at Old Fort Johnson during Sir William's councils. He helped enlist crucial Iroquois support in Britain's campaign to oust the French from North America.

In the spring of 1643, Jesuit father Isaac Jogues established a mission in the Mohawk village of Gandaouague (now Auriesville). By the fall of 1646 the Frenchman's hosts had turned against him and a lay missionary named Jean de La Lande, blaming them for a caterpillar infestation of their corn; both Jogues and La Lande were slain. The National Shrine of the North American Martyrs in Auriesville honors Jogues, La Lande, and René Goupil, a lay brother killed in 1644 or 1645 for teaching Mohawk children the sign of the cross.

A white marble statue on the shrine's grounds honors Blessed Kateri Tekakwitha, a Mohawk woman born in Gandaouague a decade after Jogues' death. A smallpox epidemic in 1659–60 left the four-year-old Kateri orphaned, pockmarked, and nearly blind. She was taken in by an uncle and grew up in a village eight miles east of Gandaouague, near present-day Fonda, where she was baptized at age 20 on Easter Sunday in 1676. Persecuted by traditionalist Mohawks, Kateri fled north to the St. Francis Xavier Indian mission on the St. Lawrence River, opposite Montreal, Quebec, where she died four years later.

At the 178-acre National Shrine of Blessed Kateri Tekakwitha, located near Fonda, a 200-year-old barn houses a museum with Iroquois artifacts; upstairs, St. Peter's Chapel commemorates the "Lily of the Mohawks" with a statue and stained-glass windows. On the hill behind the barn is the site of Caughnawaga, the only fully excavated Iroquois village in the nation. Stakes indicate the location of 12 longhouses and a wooden palisade.

In Johnstown, a few miles north of Fonda, stands Johnson Hall State Historic Site, a large frame house built in 1763–74 by Sir William Johnson as a successor to his Georgian home in Fort Johnson. Joseph Brant, the renowned Mohawk chief who fought for the British against the colonists during the American Revolution, was a frequent guest here in his youth. Brant's sister, Molly, became Johnson's common-law wife.

Each Labor Day, festivities are sponsored by the Iroquois Indian Museum at Howes Cave. Visitors watch musicians, dancers, potters, and other craftsmen practice their venerable arts and can dine on traditional Iroquois food. The museum's design evokes the longhouse, and exhibits chronicle Iroquois history up to the present.

In 1768 Sir William Johnson sent out wampum belts inviting the Six Nations and other tribes to a council at Fort Stanwix, an elaborate star-shaped redoubt located in present-day Rome. That autumn Johnson came up the Mohawk River with 20 boatloads of presents and met with some 3,000 Indians at the fort—one of the greatest such assemblages in the continent's history. Under the terms of the Treaty of Fort Stanwix, the Iroquois ceded part of their land in return for formal British recognition of their sovereignty over land that was not yet coveted by white settlers.

After the Revolutionary War, American and Native representatives convened at the fort. The ensuing treaty dealt harshly with the Iroquois who had collaborated with the British but established peace terms with the Oneida and Tuscarora tribes, who had sided with the Americans during the war. The confederacy ceded vast tracts of ancestral lands to the new republic, however, which then were distributed to veterans of the war.

PEOPLE OF THE LONGHOUSE

In the symbolic longhouse that was composed of the Six Nations, the Mohawks were known as the Keepers of the Eastern Door. They lived in uneasy coexistence first with the Dutch, and then with English traders at Fort Orange (now Albany). To the west of the Mohawks lay the land of the Oneida, "younger brothers" in the confederacy, along with the Cayuga and the Tuscarora. All that is left of the original 5 million to 6 million acres of Oneida land are 32 acres west of Utica, where the tribe has built a contemporary longhouse. Farther west lay the territory of the Onondaga, Keepers of the Central Fire in the symbolic longhouse. The Onondaga chief served as *Tadodaho*—a kind of moderator—for the 50 coequal sachems, or peace chiefs, who met annually at the confederacy's Grand Council on the shores of Onondaga Lake.

After the Revolutionary War, only the Onondaga retained a substantial portion of their homeland—a 7,000-acre reservation south of the city of Syracuse. In the village of Nedrow, on the Onondaga Reservation, stands a council house—a one-story log building with a cast-iron stove that serves as the sacred fire. Nearby is the grave of Handsome Lake, a Seneca medicine man and sachem who preached a new moral code of faith and temperance known to the Iroquois as *Gaiwiio*, or the Good Word. His teachings became the foundation of the Longhouse religion, which is still practiced by many Iroquois.

Visitors are taken back to 1657 at Ste. Marie de Gannentaha, a re-created Jesuit mission in the Syracuse suburb of Liverpool. Gannentaha was the Iroquois name for what is now Onondaga Lake. Within the palisades of the log fort, located in Onondaga Lake Park, costumed staff demonstrate blacksmithing, carpentry, cooking, farming, and other daily activities of the period.

THE FINGER LAKES

Beyond Syracuse Interstate 90 rolls north of the Finger Lakes, a region of gorges, wooded glens, lakeside vineyards, and waterfalls. Indian mythology relates that the long, narrow lakes are the imprint of the Great Spirit's hand. The Cayuga, who once called this land their home, have been entirely dispossessed and now are divided among the Seneca-Cayuga Reservation in Oklahoma, the Six Nations Reserve in southwestern Ontario, and the Cattaraugus Reservation south of Buffalo.

Taughannock Falls, among the loftiest cataracts east of the Rockies, plunges 215 feet into a gorge on the west bank of Cayuga Lake, 12 miles north of Ithaca. According to Indian legend, the falls were named for a Delaware chief who was thrown over the brink by Cayuga warriors. A less gruesome explanation holds that Taughannock is an Iroquois word that means "great falls in the woods."

At the head of Cayuga Lake lies Montezuma Marsh. For centuries the forests and rich wetlands of Montezuma, now a national wildlife refuge, sustained the Cayuga, who hunted geese, ducks, swans, deer, and muskrats.

The Seneca were the Keepers of the Western Door in the symbolic longhouse. During the colonial era, the Seneca were the most numerous tribe of the confederacy, with a population greater than all the other nations combined. Their territory extended all the way from Lake Ontario south to the Alleghenies, and from Seneca Lake to the west-

Vineyards attest to the fertility of the Finger Lakes region. The Iroquois raised corn, beans, and squash in fields cleared from surrounding forests.

ern watershed of the Genesee River. Today the Seneca Nation holds title to three reservations in western New York State—Allegheny, Cattaraugus, and Oil Springs. The Tonawanda band of Seneca, a separate community of Seneca with its own tribal government, has a reservation near Akron, New York. This was the birthplace and home of Gen. Ely S. Parker, a Seneca sachem who, as Gen. Ulysses S. Grant's secretary during the Civil War, drafted the articles of surrender signed at Appomattox. Parker later became the first Native American to become commissioner of Indian Affairs. The largest Seneca reservation—Allegheny—is in the southwestern corner of the state along the Allegheny River. The Seneca-Iroquois National Museum in

Salamanca—the only city in the nation located entirely on leased Indian land—contains exhibits on the history of the Seneca Nation, as well as contemporary arts and crafts. Among its collection of wampum belts are the personal condolence belt of Chief Cornplanter, the Five Nations Alliance Belt, and a group of belts recovered from Seneca sites in the Genesee Valley.

Seneca Lake was held in special reverence by the tribe. The Seneca believed that supernatural drums spoke from its depths to send them to war. These legends of "death drums" may be based on the rumbling sounds created by natural gas escaping from rifts in the lake bed.

At the southern end of the lake, Shequaga Falls cascades down a ledge 156 feet above the main street of Montour Falls. The town was named for Catherine Montour, a white Canadian captive who eventually became matriarch of her adoptive Seneca clan. Legend has it that the Seneca orator Red Jacket pitted his vocal powers against the falls' thunder.

West of Seneca Lake, in the town of Victor, archeologists have uncovered a major 17th-century Seneca village called Ganondagan, as well as its palisaded granary. Three self-guiding trails that wind through this state historic site explain the medicinal and spiritual significance of various plants to the Seneca, their tribal customs and beliefs, and the natural features of Fort Hill, where the granary was located. From this elevation, looking south on a clear day, it is possible to see Bare Hill on the western shore of Canandaigua Lake—the legendary birthplace of the Seneca, whose name means "People of the Great Hill."

The Genesee River rises in northern Pennsylvania and flows through a valley patterned with orchards, meadows, and grain fields. At the river's mouth, in Rochester, the Museum and Science Center houses a major collection of Iroquois artifacts, including 50 beautiful hair combs that date from prehistoric times to the 19th century. An exhibit titled "At the Western Door" uses six tableaux to outline four centuries of contact between the Seneca and the Europeans in the Genesee Valley.

Some 40 miles upstream from Rochester, the Genesee River plunges over three major waterfalls as it courses through a sinuous gorge 17 miles long and nearly 600 feet deep. In 1859 Buffalo philanthropist William Pryor Letchworth began buying up land on either side of the "Grand Canyon of the East" to protect the gorge from development. Letchworth donated his holdings to New York State in 1910, which became Letchworth State Park.

A museum overlooking the Middle Falls on the Genesee contains Letchworth's extensive collection of Iroquois artifacts. On a ridge behind the museum at the Seneca Council Grounds are the grave and statue of Mary Jemison. She was first captured by the Shawnee in 1758 and then given to the Seneca. Jemison became famous as the "White Woman of the Genesee." Twice married to Seneca warriors, she wielded considerable power among her adopted people and was granted her own reservation in the Genesee Valley. Nearby is a log cabin Jemison built for her daughter, Nancy. In 1872 Letchworth restored the old Seneca council house and invited the descendants of Cornplanter, Red Jacket, Mary Jemison, and other Iroquois notables to kindle one last council fire.

"Our fathers loved their nation and were proud of its renown," the grandson of Mohawk Indian chief Joseph Brant told the final conclave. "But both have passed away forever. Follow the sun in its course from the Hudson to Niagara, and you will see palefaces as thick as leaves in the wood, but only here and there a solitary Iroquois." Yet here, to this day, brave echoes of the Six Nations persist.

LOG LEGISLATURE
The Seneca Council House, above, was moved from Canada to present-day Letchworth State Park by William P. Letchworth. At a meeting held here in 1872, the Buffalo philanthropist was adopted by the Seneca, who named him "Man Who Always Does the Right Thing."

A RIVER'S MIGHT
Bounded by steep rock walls, the Genesee River tumbles through the Middle and Upper falls of Letchworth State Park, left, on its way north to Lake Ontario.

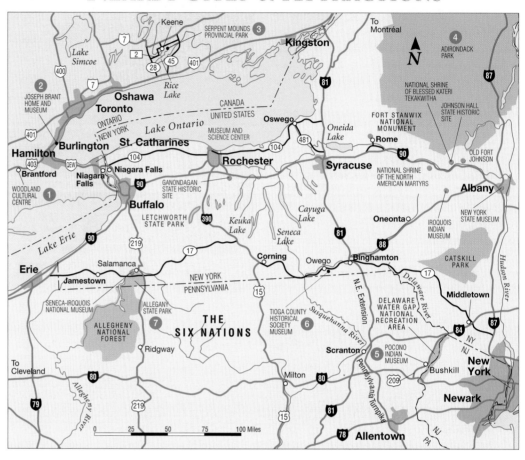

A modern-day artist at Woodland Cultural Centre, above, demonstrates the ancient art of making medicine masks. The main features of the mask are carved directly into the tree before the block is separated from its trunk.

① WOODLAND CULTURAL CENTRE, ONTARIO

Jointly operated by six Native bands, the center gives visitors a unique glimpse into the history of the Eastern Woodland Indians, tracing their story from prehistoric times to the present. The museum houses archeological exhibits of the Middle Woodland Period, wampum displays, and a full-size replica of a 19th-century longhouse interior. Artifacts include birchbark baskets, Iroquoian pipes, false-face masks, stone carvings, and a medicine-man mural. An Indian Hall of Fame is also featured. The center also features special exhibits of contemporary North American Indian art. The Snowsnake Tournament, in which beautifully crafted poles resembling javelins are hurled across the snow, is held the first Saturday in November. Located at 184 Mohawk St. in Brantford.

② JOSEPH BRANT HOME AND MUSEUM, ONTARIO

Lionized in England and reviled in the United States, Joseph Brant—whose traditional name of Thayendanegea means "Two Sticks of Wood Bound Together"—was one of the most compelling Mohawk leaders of the 18th century. An educated gentleman who translated the Bible into Mohawk, Brant also led the warriors of the Six Nations in attacks against American colonists. The museum is a reconstruction of the two-story house that stood

on the edge of Wellington Square, Burlington's historic center, where Brant spent the last five years of his colorful life. Several of the galleries contain Brant's personal possessions, including a medal awarded to him by King George III and a full-length painting of Brant done by the renowned English portrait painter George Romney. In addition to Brant memorabilia, historical exhibits focus on traditional Iroquois life. On display is an original mural of an Iroquois longhouse painted by Native artist Bill Powless, as well as an extensive costume gallery. Located at 1240 North Shore Blvd. in Burlington.

③ SERPENT MOUNDS PROVINCIAL PARK, ONTARIO

Buried among groves of venerable oak trees on the northern shore of Rice Lake are the remains of a people who inhabited this region approximately 2,000 years ago. Thought to be the final resting place of the members of the Point Peninsula culture, Serpent Mounds is the only mound burial complex in Canada. Eight of the earthen tombs are of a simple oval design; the ninth zigzags for 200 feet, giving it a shape similar to Ohio's famed Serpent Mound. Although excavations have helped shed light on the people who lived here, some mysteries still remain. Why, for example, were domestic dogs entombed alongside individuals? And how did conch shells from the Gulf of Mexico, more than 1,000 miles away, come to be interred in the mounds? Situated in a provincial park, the mounds are accessible via a walking trail that winds its way through the site. A visitor center provides information on the history of Serpent Mounds and the people buried within. Located on Hwy. 3 south of Keene.

A solitary canoe, above, lies moored in one of the many lakes in Adirondack Park. Bass, trout, pike, and landlocked salmon lure many fishermen to the region.

4 ADIRONDACK PARK, NEW YORK

Roughly the size of Vermont, Adirondack Park is a 9,000-square-mile patchwork of public and private lands, making it the largest wilderness in the continental United States. A paradise of lush forests, pristine lakes, rushing rivers, and mountain peaks, the park boasts 2,000 miles of hiking trails, 2,300 lakes, and 46 peaks that tower 4,000 feet above sea level. During the summer and fall, visitors can enjoy hiking, canoeing, camping, fishing, and horseback riding; downhill and cross-country skiers flock to the park during the winter months. A 140-mile-long canoe route links Old Forge Lake in the southwest area of the park with Tupper Lake and Saranac Lake in the north-central region. A 146-mile hiking trail runs between Lake Placid and Northville. Interpretive centers, located at Paul Smiths and at Newcomb on Rich Lake, offer educational programs for visitors. Every February Saranac Lake hosts a winter carnival, complete with ice palaces. Located 45 miles north of Albany on Hwy. 87.

5 POCONO INDIAN MUSEUM, PENNSYLVANIA

Inhabitants of present-day Pennsylvania since 10,000 B.C., the Delaware tribe was all but forced out within a century following their initial contact with Europeans in 1609. Located in a two-story, 19th-century house, the Pocono Indian Museum traces the rise and fall of the once-proud nation. A reconstructed village, dating from 10,000 B.C., gives visitors an idea of what a Delaware campsite looked like. Also on display are ancient projectile points, cutting tools, and 10,000-year-old stone knives that were found within a 20-mile radius of the museum. The collection includes 1,000-year-old pottery and scrapers that were used to cut meat from animals. A miniature village depicts the tribe's life 800 years

ago, complete with wigwams, a food storage pit, and dugout canoes. The museum also houses portraits of famous Native Americans, such as Sitting Bull, and a robe made from the skin of a buffalo that was shot by Theodore Roosevelt. Located on Hwy. 209 in Bushkill.

6 TIOGA COUNTY HISTORICAL SOCIETY MUSEUM, NEW YORK

Centuries ago, tribes such as the Oneida, Onondaga, and Susquehannock were drawn to southern New York State because of the abundance of game and fish along the Susquehanna River, as well as in smaller rivers and creeks. Recently the region has attracted archeologists interested in unearthing fragments of the state's rich Native American heritage. Many of the most impressive finds are displayed by the Tioga County Historical Society, whose wide-ranging collection includes a rare Clovis fluted point made by the region's earliest nomadic people and hunting points of the Iroquois. Examples of stone tools, including those used for fishing, implement making, and agriculture, are on exhibit. Thousands of pottery shards, as well some intact pots, are also on display. Located at 110 Front St. in Owego.

7 ALLEGANY STATE PARK, NEW YORK

Nestled in the bend of the Allegheny River and flanked on the west and northeast by the Allegany Indian Reservation, this is New York's largest state park. With some 70 miles of spring-fed mountain streams and dozens of woodland trails, Allegany State Park is a natural playground for outdoor enthusiasts. Visitors can enjoy hiking, boating, and some of the best lake and stream fishing in the region. There are year-round camping facilities and abundant opportunities to observe the park's wildlife, including deer, wild turkeys, and black bears. One resident species of particular interest to naturalists is an aquatic salamander called the giant hellbender, which is a nocturnal creature. On the park's northern boundary lies the city of Salamanca; to the south is Pennsylvania's 470,000-acre Allegheny National Forest. Located east of Jamestown on Hwy. 17.

Encompassing a region of great natural beauty, Allegany State Park, left, also includes part of the Allegany Indian Reservation. The reservation contains the Seneca-Iroquois National Museum, which features displays on the history and culture of the Seneca.

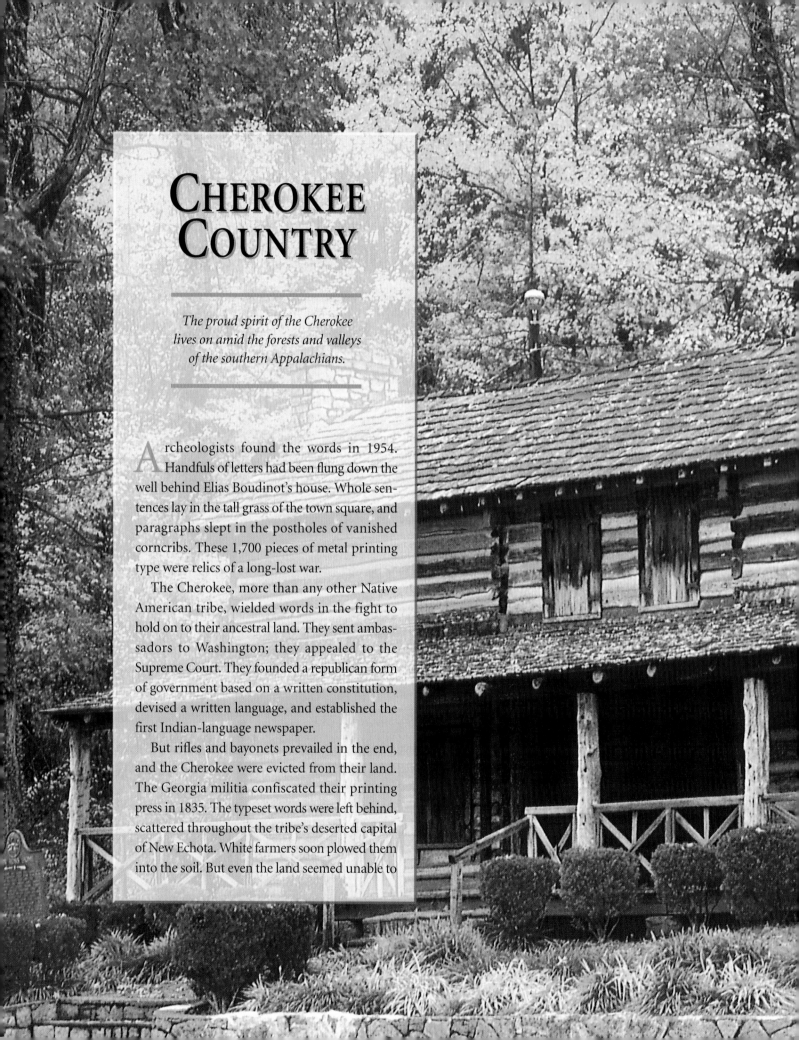

CHEROKEE COUNTRY

*The proud spirit of the Cherokee
lives on amid the forests and valleys
of the southern Appalachians.*

Archeologists found the words in 1954. Handfuls of letters had been flung down the well behind Elias Boudinot's house. Whole sentences lay in the tall grass of the town square, and paragraphs slept in the postholes of vanished corncribs. These 1,700 pieces of metal printing type were relics of a long-lost war.

The Cherokee, more than any other Native American tribe, wielded words in the fight to hold on to their ancestral land. They sent ambassadors to Washington; they appealed to the Supreme Court. They founded a republican form of government based on a written constitution, devised a written language, and established the first Indian-language newspaper.

But rifles and bayonets prevailed in the end, and the Cherokee were evicted from their land. The Georgia militia confiscated their printing press in 1835. The typeset words were left behind, scattered throughout the tribe's deserted capital of New Echota. White farmers soon plowed them into the soil. But even the land seemed unable to

Overleaf: A two-story log cabin, located outside Chattanooga, Tennessee, is now a memorial to John Ross, the greatest of all Cherokee chiefs. The house was built in 1797 by Ross' maternal grandfather, John McDonald.

LIVING CRAFT

A contemporary carver in Oconaluftee Indian Village, below, fashions masks, bowls, and other items that reflect the Cherokee relationship with their woodland environment.

HOT OFF THE PRESS

Visitors to the print shop at New Echota State Historic Site, right, can see pages of the Cherokee Phoenix *inked and pulled from the press. Above the fireplace hangs a portrait of Sequoyah, inventor of the Cherokee alphabet.*

digest the impassioned arguments of a people known as Cherokee.

Against all odds, the Eastern band of the Cherokee has clung to a magnificent scrap of its homeland. Since the 1930's, when the Blue Ridge Parkway was built at its doorstep, the tribe has welcomed visitors to the mountains of North Carolina. By drawing a fat oval on the road map—with the widest points at Cherokee, North Carolina, and Chattanooga, Tennessee—motorists can chart a course to numerous tribal sites in four to five days' driving time, without ever leaving sight of the hills.

The Cherokee people always had an eye for the land. At the dawn of the colonial era, their villages were clustered along the headwaters of rivers on both sides of the southern Appalachians. The Lower Towns occupied what would become northern Georgia and the Piedmont of South Carolina. The Middle Towns covered western North Carolina. The Overhill, or Upper Towns, lay in what is now eastern Tennessee.

It was a lush, fertile country of green valleys and foothills, rising into steep, tree-covered mountains sliced by rivers and waterfalls. Today parts of this homeland make up the Great Smoky Mountains National Park, the most popular destination in the national park system.

In 1539-41 the gold-hungry Spanish explorer Hernando DeSoto cut a swath of bloodshed and destruction through the Southeast. Somehow the Cherokee encounter with DeSoto proved peaceful, and they escaped the ravages of the European diseases he brought with him. As epidemics deci-

mated Indian populations around them, the Cherokee apparently became more numerous, spreading out from the mountains into the rich farmland of the valleys and claiming 43,000 square miles of hunting ground. In time, the Cherokee became one of the five dominant tribes in the Southeast. At 25,000 strong, they were probably also the most numerous. They called themselves the Principal People.

White traders who ventured into Cherokee country in the late 1600's met a warm reception, and quickly inducted the tribe into the deerskin trade. Missionaries, a Quaker botanist, and agents of the king of England likewise enjoyed the hospitality of the Cherokee, and noted their generosity. They reported that if tribesmen fell into poverty, for example, the men of their village organized a ceremonial dance in which each dancer brought goods to be shared with the poor. Generations of Cherokee women kept a pot of *connahanee*—a soupy dish of cracked corn—on the family hearth, to be shared with travelers and family alike.

By language, the tribe appeared to be distantly related to the northern Iroquois, although the Upper, Middle, and Lower towns spoke three distinct languages. The Cherokee lived in permanent villages, their homes constructed of woven saplings grouted with mud and covered in bark or mats. Villages were located near water, and protected from enemies by a log palisade. The most important building was the council house, which could hold up to 500 people. Each family had a summer home open to the fresh air, and a cone-shaped win-

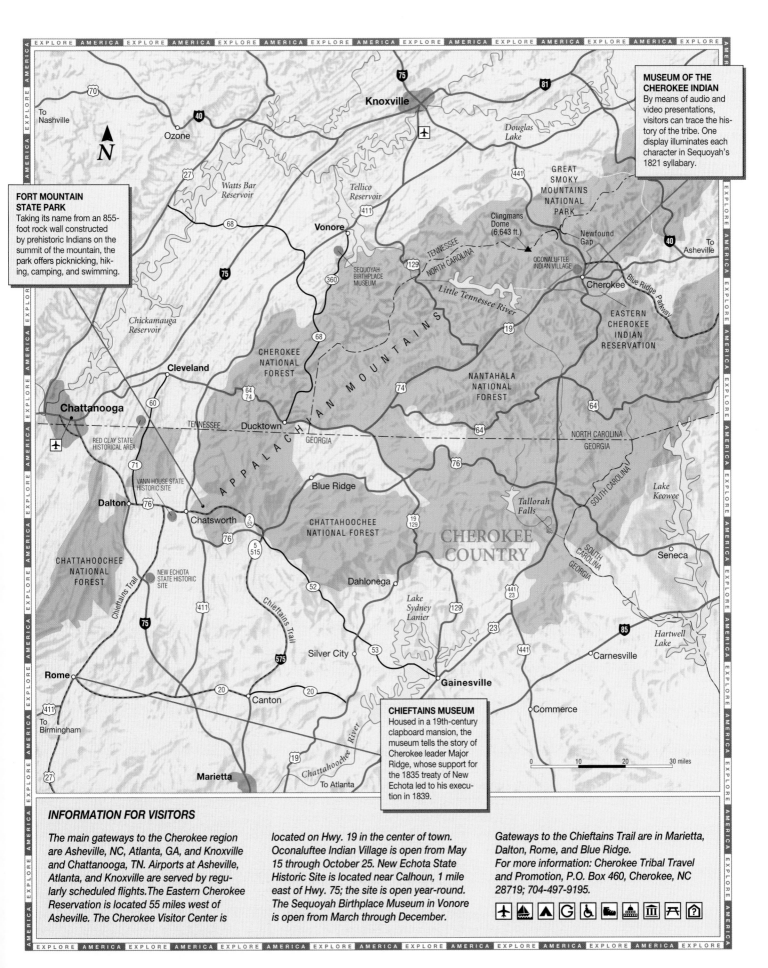

MUSEUM OF THE CHEROKEE INDIAN
By means of audio and video presentations, visitors can trace the history of the tribe. One display illuminates each character in Sequoyah's 1821 syllabary.

FORT MOUNTAIN STATE PARK
Taking its name from an 855-foot rock wall constructed by prehistoric Indians on the summit of the mountain, the park offers picnicking, hiking, camping, and swimming.

To Nashville

Ozone

Knoxville

Watts Bar Reservoir

Douglas Lake

GREAT SMOKY MOUNTAINS NATIONAL PARK

To Asheville

Tellico Reservoir

Vonore

Clingmans Dome (6,643 ft.)

Newfound Gap

TENNESSEE
NORTH CAROLINA

SEQUOYAH BIRTHPLACE MUSEUM

OCONALUFTEE INDIAN VILLAGE

Little Tennessee River

Cherokee

Blue Ridge Parkway

EASTERN CHEROKEE INDIAN RESERVATION

Chickamauga Reservoir

Cleveland

CHEROKEE NATIONAL FOREST

NANTAHALA NATIONAL FOREST

Chattanooga

TENNESSEE
GEORGIA

Ducktown

NORTH CAROLINA
GEORGIA

Red Clay State Historical Area

Vann House State Historic Site

Dalton

Chatsworth

Blue Ridge

CHATTAHOOCHEE NATIONAL FOREST

Tallorah Falls

SOUTH CAROLINA

Lake Keowee

SOUTH CAROLINA
GEORGIA

CHEROKEE COUNTRY

Seneca

CHATTAHOOCHEE NATIONAL FOREST

NEW ECHOTA STATE HISTORIC SITE

Chieftains Trail

Dahlonega

Lake Sydney Lanier

Hartwell Lake

Carnesville

Rome

Canton

Silver City

Gainesville

Commerce

To Birmingham

Marietta

Chattahoochee River

To Atlanta

CHIEFTAINS MUSEUM
Housed in a 19th-century clapboard mansion, the museum tells the story of Cherokee leader Major Ridge, whose support for the 1835 treaty of New Echota led to his execution in 1839.

0   10   20   30 miles

INFORMATION FOR VISITORS

The main gateways to the Cherokee region are Asheville, NC, Atlanta, GA, and Knoxville and Chattanooga, TN. Airports at Asheville, Atlanta, and Knoxville are served by regularly scheduled flights. The Eastern Cherokee Reservation is located 55 miles west of Asheville. The Cherokee Visitor Center is

located on Hwy. 19 in the center of town. Oconaluftee Indian Village is open from May 15 through October 25. New Echota State Historic Site is located near Calhoun, 1 mile east of Hwy. 75; the site is open year-round. The Sequoyah Birthplace Museum in Vonore is open from March through December.

Gateways to the Chieftains Trail are in Marietta, Dalton, Rome, and Blue Ridge.
For more information: Cherokee Tribal Travel and Promotion, P.O. Box 460, Cherokee, NC 28719; 704-497-9195.

The vicissitudes of Cherokee history are mirrored in the time-worn face of this Cherokee elder, above.

ter home, or sweathouse. The members of this society traced their lineage through their mothers. Women looked after the plots of corn, beans, and squash, while men hunted, fished, and went to war.

European visitors took special note of the Cherokee affinity for war. As in most tribes, Cherokee men gained status by becoming warriors, although raids were usually precipitated by a vendetta against the neighboring Creek and Choctaw rather than by a quest for more territory. The Cherokee believed that the spirits of their fallen warriors could not enter "the darkening land" unless they were avenged, and one tribesman defined war as "our beloved occupation."

It was this side of the Cherokee disposition—plus their rapid addiction to guns, alcohol, and trade goods—that unscrupulous Europeans learned to exploit. Both the French and English discovered that it was all too easy to pit one faction against another for their own gain.

As early as 1684, the Cherokee entered into treaties with the English government. From the beginning these treaties recognized the tribe as a sovereign nation, with the authority to govern its people and its borders. Ignoring that fact, waves of white settlers pressed into Cherokee land, sparking skirmishes and sometimes fierce fighting. During the next 135 years, having signed 28 treaties that were consistently broken, the tribe saw its land holdings reduced by more than 90 percent.

Meanwhile, overreliance on the fur trade had undermined the traditional Cherokee culture. By the 1730's Cherokee men had adopted lace-trimmed shirts and European broadcoats, although two decades would pass before they gave up the breechcloth for trousers, which they considered to be effeminate. A smallpox epidemic struck in 1738, killing nearly half the tribe. The survivors continued to adopt aspects of the colonial lifestyle, giving up their wattle-and-daub lodges for log cabins.

VILLAGE LIFE

Today visitors can better grasp this period of tribal life, as it teetered on the brink of sweeping change, by visiting the Oconaluftee Indian Village, located just outside the commercial clamor of Cherokee, North Carolina. After a guided tour, visitors may take a closer look at handwork and crafts demonstrations by men and women with such surnames as Wolf, Crow, Owl, Locust, Reed, and Walkingstick. Here a guide inserts a thistle-tailed dart into a blowgun made from a length of river cane. A quick puff on the other end of the blowgun sends the dart hurtling into a nearby tree. The scent of burning wood marks the spot where a huge poplar tree is slowly being hollowed out into a dugout canoe.

Beside a shallow stream filled with lively trout, two women are finger-weaving belts and sashes, manipulating up to 200 strands of yarn. While their sisters weave baskets, design beadwork, and mold pots, the men carve ceremonial masks and demonstrate the use of a small crossbow drill with an arrowhead drill bit.

Inside the dim, seven-sided Council House, with its rising tiers of log benches, and at the ceremonial stomping ground, guides explain the customs and beliefs that shaped the lives of their ancestors. At the base of the mountain is the outstanding Museum of the Cherokee Indian, and across the street is the Qualla Arts and Crafts Co-op, where authentic Cherokee crafts are for sale.

Hostilities between the Cherokee and settlers sharpened during the Revolutionary War. When one faction of the tribe sided with the British, colonists ferociously attacked Cherokee towns. By the time the Cherokee sued for peace, they had lost 5 million acres of prime hunting grounds.

The postwar years, however, saw increasing intermarriage between the Cherokee and settlers of English, Scottish, and Irish descent. These unions produced a new generation of leaders—some of them only one-eighth Cherokee—who would champion the rights of the tribe all the way to the White House and the halls of Congress.

The tribe's conversion from a hunting to an agricultural economy was spurred by the U.S. government's "civilization" program. Federal agents provided plows, looms, and spinning wheels; mills and blacksmith shops were opened and schools were set up for children. By 1800 the average Cherokee was living much as his white neighbors did. A growing middle class lived in comfortable log homes, with fenced farms and pens of livestock. Prosperous Cherokee used African slaves to work cotton plantations. Several of their mansions can be toured today as part of Georgia's Chieftains Trail driving tour.

During the War of 1812, when the United States and Great Britain went to war over British demands to search American ships for Royal Navy deserters in the Atlantic Ocean, the Cherokee took the

MORNING MAGIC
The haze that gives the Smoky Mountains their name turns dawn into a meditative movement in a visual symphony.

Prized by Cherokee hunters, wild turkeys, such as the one above, were once widespread throughout the East.

American side. In spite of the tribe's loyalty, Andrew Jackson soon campaigned for the presidency on a platform based on the relocation of all Native Americans west of the Mississippi.

SEQUOYAH'S ALPHABET

Between the end of the war and Andrew Jackson's Indian Removal Act of 1830, the Cherokee Nation enjoyed a brief but glorious golden age. In part, that progress was credited to the genius of a crippled silversmith named Sequoyah.

Sequoyah, whose name means "Pig's Foot" in his native language, was the son of a Cherokee mother and a white father who deserted him in infancy. He was crippled from childhood, although the deformity apparently was not severe, and he grew to become a talented craftsman.

Sequoyah devoted 12 years of his life to developing a system for writing the Cherokee language. Early on he abandoned the idea of creating a symbol for a whole sentence, and also concluded there were too many words in the Cherokee language to assign a symbol per word. Sequoyah's wife resented his time-consuming passion, and at one point threw his work into the fire.

Eventually Sequoyah broke down the language into 86 syllables, assigning each a symbol—some resembling English letters, some resembling Greek, and some of his own invention. His daughter learned her syllabary quickly, and in 1821 helped her father give a convincing demonstration that won the endorsement of skeptical tribal leaders. Sequoyah went down in history as the only man to have single-handedly devised a written language.

The novelty of preserving thoughts in writing was reflected in the reaction of a tribal elder named Big Rattling Gourd. Like generations of his ancestors, he had committed anything important to memory. But after listening to Sequoyah read a statement in court, Big Rattling Gourd paid him a visit to report that he "had not slept all night for thinking of the wonder." He said the act of writing surpassed anything he "could have conceived possible for the power of man to accomplish."

Big Rattling Gourd asked Sequoyah if he could write anything he chose, or only particular things. His host explained that he could write anything, provided it was in Cherokee. That was apparently what the elder had hoped. Big Rattling Gourd said he could remember speeches made by former chiefs. If he were to repeat them, could Sequoyah record them? Sequoyah not only could, but did.

His syllabary was easy to learn, and within a year following his first demonstration, the Cherokee Nation was largely literate. On an island overlooking the Tellico Reservoir in the Little Tennessee River Valley, the Sequoyah Birthplace Museum devotes considerable attention to the museum's namesake and the story of his syllabary.

Once owned by Cherokee leader James Vann, the Vann Tavern, right, was moved to New Echota in 1955 to save the structure from inundation caused by the construction of a dam.

In 1825, with U.S. efforts under way to remove the Creeks from Georgia, the Cherokee laid out a forward-looking new capital near Calhoun, Georgia. They called this field of dreams New Echota. Today it is a state historic site that is best visited in the late afternoon, when the setting sun turns it golden and wistful.

The town flourished briefly for only seven years, from 1825 to 1832. Here the Cherokee established a republican form of government. They adopted a written constitution, doing what even the U.S. government had never done: they declared themselves a Christian nation. Under the direction of editor Elias Boudinot, a Cherokee who adopted the name of a U.S. statesman, they established the first Indian-language printing press, publishing religious books and a weekly newspaper called the *Cherokee Phoenix.*

New Echota has been partially reconstructed. The two-story Council House features tall glass windows and a chimney—a world apart from the dim, smoke-filled, seven-sided structures of the traditional villages. This was Congress in miniature: a bicameral legislature, with one house that met upstairs and the other downstairs. A bill had to pass both houses to become law.

Inside the Supreme Court building there is an elevated bench where three justices sat. Here they sentenced the guilty to be fined, whipped, or hanged but not jailed, since the Cherokee Nation had no prison system.

Several other buildings have been moved to the site, including two log dwellings and the Vann Tavern, built about 1805. Worcester House, the one original building on the property, served as a Presbyterian mission station and was the home of missionary Samuel A. Worcester.

From New Echota, principal chief John Ross ruled over a nation of successful farmers. The land was owned by all the people. Each Cherokee farmer was permitted to clear and cultivate as much land as he wanted, as long as he stayed a quarter-mile away from his nearest neighbor. By 1826 Cherokee farmers were growing so much cotton that there was plenty to export.

GOLD FEVER

In October 1828, a blacksmith named Benjamin Parks was hunting deer on Cherokee land when he stumbled on a rock that started the first American gold rush. This was "easy gold," an exceptionally pure type that lay on top of the ground—the kind DeSoto had been seeking during the 1500's. Years later, Parks recalled, "The news got abroad and such excitement you never saw. It seemed within a few days as if the whole world must have heard of it. . . .They came afoot, on horseback and in wagons, acting more like crazy men than anything else."

This chance discovery of gold was to have grave and lasting consequences for the Cherokee. For many years the state of Georgia had been pushing to have all Native Americans removed from within its boundaries. By bribery, deceit, and coercion the Choctaw and the Creek already had been forced out—with great loss of life. At this time the Georgia legislature passed an oppressive code of laws aimed squarely at the Cherokee. They were forbidden to mine gold on their own land, to testify in court against a white man, or to assemble for any purpose. In fact, all of the Cherokee laws were declared null and void.

SILENCED THUNDER

Cherokee legend held that warriors who ventured into the sheer-walled gorge of Tallulah Falls, above, never returned. Located within Georgia's Chattahoochee National Forest, the waterfall attracted fashionable vacationers during the 19th century. When the river was harnessed for hydroelectric power, the torrent was reduced to today's trickle.

The Cherokee Supreme Court building, right, at New Echota State Historic Site is a reconstruction of the original 1829 structure. After the tribe was forcibly removed to Oklahoma, the original buildings of the Cherokee capital were torn down and the land plowed under.

Now a quiet woodland pool, the Blue Hole, above, was the heart of the Cherokee camp at Red Clay, Tennessee, during the dark days of the tribe's struggle to hold on to its homeland.

claim them. All across northern Georgia, strangers announced themselves the new owners of Cherokee property. The situation was ripe for violence, yet the Cherokee held the peace.

Many years later, Benjamin Parks told a reporter, "The Indians were all around when I came, and I have eaten conee-banee [*connahanee*] with them many a time. . . .We always treated them right and they did the same by us. Their agriculture was rude but they were improving all the time and would have gotten on all right if they had been left alone."

Forbidden to assemble at New Echota, the Cherokee shifted their capital to Tennessee in 1832, to a narrow valley now known as the Red Clay State Historical Area. Its landmark—the Blue Hole— looks shallow enough to wade in but is actually 15 feet deep, fed by an underground spring. The Blue Hole provided drinking water for the 11 council meetings held here during the next six frustrating years. Principal chief John Ross never wavered in his efforts to hold on to the Cherokee eastern lands. The tribe even enlisted the backing of former Indian fighters Davy Crockett and Sam Houston and numerous congressmen, including Henry Clay and Daniel Webster.

The town of Dahlonega in Georgia documents this sad period of Cherokee history. The Dahlonega Gold Museum is located in a red-brick courthouse surrounded by 19th-century storefronts. Exhibits and a film presentation help visitors understand the fever that gripped the miners as they tunneled into the mountainside when the easy gold was gone. The vein proved to be so rich that the U.S. government established a branch mint here in 1838. It is heartbreaking to contemplate a wooden barrel that stands on the museum's ground floor. From one side of northern Georgia to the other, the Cherokee land was reduced to the size of lottery slips, drawn from this barrel and others, and placed in the hands of winners who paid an $18 fee to

THE TRAIL OF TEARS

From Washington, President Andrew Jackson tried to induce the Cherokee to leave by offering them several million dollars and replacement lands in the West. "If you will not protect us in the East," replied Ross, "how can we believe that you will protect us in the West?" John Marshall, the chief justice of the U.S. Supreme Court, wrote: "The acts of Georgia are repugnant to the Constitution." Jackson retorted,

the federal government agreed to hold the tribe's 56,000-acre reservation in trust. In 1866 a North Carolina statute—approved by Washington—granted the remaining Cherokee permission to remain within the state. The total of 56,572 acres now held in trust for the Cherokee by the U.S. government lies scattered over five North Carolina counties, consisting of 52 tracts contained in 30 separate parcels of land.

Today the town of Cherokee, North Carolina, is the headquarters of the reservation, which is also known as the Qualla Boundary. The economy of the Cherokee reservation is based mainly on tourism, and the tribe owns or operates numerous enterprises, including its own cable television company. It is the matchless scenery that entices most visitors to the reservation, where among the peaks and hollows of the Great Smoky Mountains some 10,000 Cherokee live today, telling and retelling their story.

HILLTOP DRAMA
The Mountainside Theatre, below, outside Cherokee, North Carolina, is the venue for the famous outdoor drama Unto These Hills. *Telling the story of the Cherokee and of the small band that took refuge in the mountains of North Carolina during the Trail of Tears period, the pageant plays to packed houses every summer.*

"John Marshall has made his decision, now let him enforce it."

There is a peacefulness about Red Clay, even as visitors learn of late-night council meetings, marked by fervent prayer and speeches. The interpretive center profiles the principal players of the period, including the members of the Ridge faction who, in 1835, signed away the nation's land in return for $5 million and land in the West.

Approximately 16,000 Cherokee—almost the entire tribe—signed petitions denouncing the treaty. Nevertheless, in 1837 the Cherokee people were told by the U.S. government that they would soon have to leave their eastern lands, voluntarily or involuntarily. Federal troops swooped down upon the nation the following year and herded almost all the Cherokee into 13 hastily erected concentration camps.

Between 12,000 and 17,000 Cherokee were captured, and an estimated 4,000 of them perished in the camps and on the land and water routes to Oklahoma that became known as the Trail of Tears. Under the command of Gen. Winfield Scott, 7,000 soldiers and volunteers escorted the Cherokee west on foot and in wagons, steamers, and keel boats. Today, with the cooperation of the eastern and western Cherokee tribes and several state governments, the National Park Service is developing markers and exhibits along the route. Those who travel its 800-mile length have to imagine a grave marker every two-tenths of a mile to grasp the loss of life.

And yet at least 1,000 Cherokee escaped into the mountains in North Carolina. A settler named Will Thomas was adopted by the tribe, and he bought land for them in a piecemeal fashion. Eventually

MOUNTAINSIDE THEATRE
HOME OF HISTORICAL OUTDOOR DRAMA
"Unto These Hills"
EPIC PORTRAYAL OF HISTORY OF THE EASTERN BAND OF CHEROKEE

The Drama opened mid-June thru late August July 1, 1950, and is presented each year with average annual attendance of 100,000. Built by Cherokee stone masons and United States G.I. labor the Theatre is located on land where Cherokee history was written. The entrance was rebuilt in 1987.

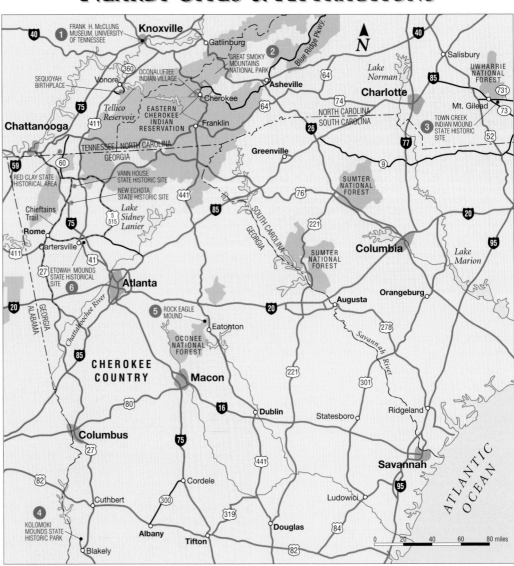

Myrtle Point in Great Smoky Mountains National Park, above, overlooks the highest peaks in the eastern United States.

① FRANK H. MCCLUNG MUSEUM, UNIVERSITY OF TENNESSEE

Showcasing Tennessee's history, art, and geology, the museum contains major archeological collections and some of the finest Native American artifacts in the Southeast. A permanent exhibit recounts the story of the state's Native Americans from the arrival of the first inhabitants during the last ice age to the removal of the Cherokee and other Southeastern tribes in 1838. Artifacts, photographs, and drawings present their cultural history. Significant pieces on display include a 32-foot Cherokee dugout canoe that dates from the 1700's, a spectacular cache of ceremonial flaked stone objects, 600-year-old engraved shell gorgets, and a wide array of pipes, pots, and other everyday implements. There are also permanent exhibits on the fossil history of Tennessee and early medical practices in the state, as well as displays on ancient Egypt, decorative arts, and human evolution. Located on Circle Park at the University of Tennessee, Knoxville campus.

② GREAT SMOKY MOUNTAINS NATIONAL PARK, TENNESSEE/NORTH CAROLINA

Native Americans lived in the shadow of the Great Smoky Mountains until the early 1800's and named the region the "place of the blue smoke" because of the haze that envelops these ancient peaks. Designated an International Biosphere Reserve in 1976, the park preserves 800 square miles of mountainous terrain and a diverse range of flora and fauna. There are 1,570 species of flowering plants, more than 200 bird species, 60 species of mammals, and 48 different kinds of freshwater fish. Scattered throughout the park, restored historic structures, including barns and log cabins, hark back to a time when only the most hardy individuals could survive in this rugged wilderness. Today drivers can meander through the park along one of three major routes: the Little River Road, the Newfound Gap Road, or the Blue Ridge Parkway. Soaring to a height of 6,643 feet, Clingmans Dome is the highest mountain in the park. At the summit, an observation tower provides spectacular views of the surrounding mountains. There are more than 800 miles of hiking trails within

the park. Roaring Fork, Big Creek, Oconaluftee River, and Hazel Creek offer excellent fishing for rainbow and brown trout. The park has two visitor centers: one located 2 miles north of Cherokee, North Carolina, on Hwy. 441; the other 2 miles south of Gatlinburg, Tennessee, on Hwy. 441.

3 TOWN CREEK INDIAN MOUND STATE HISTORIC SITE, NORTH CAROLINA

In the 13th century, the Indians of the Pee Dee River established a ceremonial center located on a bluff overlooking the Town Creek and Little River. The center was used for political, religious, and social functions. The site includes an earthen mound, approximately 12 feet in height and about 100 feet square. A major temple on top of the mound, a minor temple, a priest's house, and a stockade have been reconstructed. Many burial sites have been located in the area, and one of the burial huts has been rebuilt. A visitor center provides an introductory slide program, as well as an exhibit area that features displays interpreting the daily life of the Creek Indians at Town Creek. Located 5.5 miles east of Mt. Gilead between Hwys. 73 and 731.

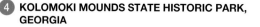

4 KOLOMOKI MOUNDS STATE HISTORIC PARK, GEORGIA

A complex of seven mounds dating from the 12th and 13th centuries, the park includes a great temple mound, two burial mounds, and four ceremonial mounds whose specific functions are still not understood. The mounds can be seen easily from the park road, and a mile-long walking trail allows visitors to get a closer look at some of them. Steps set into the steep side of the great mound enable visitors to climb to its 56-foot-high platform. A museum interprets the cultural history of the Kolomoki people and displays a partially excavated burial mound with skeleton replicas and artifacts. Other exhibits focus on house and mound construction and pottery making. Located 6 miles north of Blakely off Hwy. 27.

5 ROCK EAGLE MOUND, GEORGIA

Constructed of milky quartz rocks and boulders of varying sizes, this effigy mound depicting a great bird with outstretched wings rises 10 feet above the surrounding terrain. The mound measures 102 feet from head to tail and 120 feet from wingtip to wingtip. The mound appears to have been used for religious purposes. A small pointed granite tool located at the site has led archeologists to estimate that the effigy is about 2,000 years old. An observation tower offers visitors a bird's-eye view of the mound. Located on the grounds of Rock Eagle 4-H Club Center, 9 miles north of Eatonton off Hwy. 441.

6 ETOWAH MOUNDS STATE HISTORICAL SITE, GEORGIA

Comprising three large mounds, three smaller ones, and two open squares, this site was home to several thousand Native Americans, who inhabited the region more than 400 years ago. Located on the Etowah River, the site is bounded on the east, north, and southwest by a ditch and two quarries known as borrow pits. Archeologists believe that the ditch and pits served as defensive obstacles that protected Etowah from attack. A palisade of upright logs surrounded the town and central plaza. The two largest mounds, which served as temple platform mounds, have not been excavated, but a burial mound has been completely excavated and restored. A museum exhibits many of the artifacts removed from the burial mound, including two marble effigies of human beings, each weighing approximately 120 pounds. Located southeast of Cartersville off Hwy. 75.

A 12-foot-high stockade surrounds Town Creek Indian Mound, left. A reconstructed ceremonial center is located within the stockade.

The well-preserved earthworks at Etowah Mounds, below, served as platforms and temples, as well as burial sites for noble members of the community. Artifacts found at the site include human statues and decorated sheets of mica.

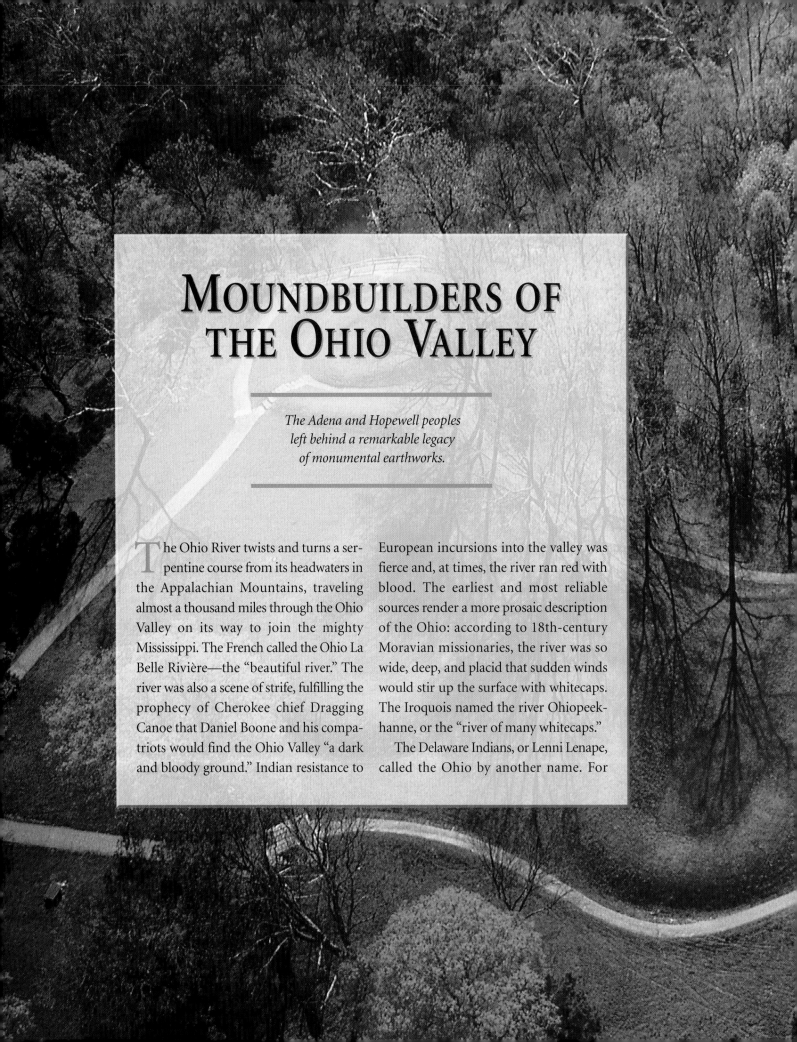

MOUNDBUILDERS OF THE OHIO VALLEY

*The Adena and Hopewell peoples
left behind a remarkable legacy
of monumental earthworks.*

The Ohio River twists and turns a serpentine course from its headwaters in the Appalachian Mountains, traveling almost a thousand miles through the Ohio Valley on its way to join the mighty Mississippi. The French called the Ohio La Belle Rivière—the "beautiful river." The river was also a scene of strife, fulfilling the prophecy of Cherokee chief Dragging Canoe that Daniel Boone and his compatriots would find the Ohio Valley "a dark and bloody ground." Indian resistance to European incursions into the valley was fierce and, at times, the river ran red with blood. The earliest and most reliable sources render a more prosaic description of the Ohio: according to 18th-century Moravian missionaries, the river was so wide, deep, and placid that sudden winds would stir up the surface with whitecaps. The Iroquois named the river Ohiopeekhanne, or the "river of many whitecaps."

The Delaware Indians, or Lenni Lenape, called the Ohio by another name. For

these people it was the river of the *Alligewi*, or Moundbuilders. The Delawares named the river for the people who built the more than 10,000 mounds that dot the Ohio Valley, who also became the source of the name for one of the Ohio River's main tributaries—the Allegheny.

The Ohio Valley was home to a succession of vibrant cultures that created gigantic mounds and earthworks. Nineteenth-century amateur scientists who explored the region believed that the Indian tribes of the Ohio Country were too few and too savage to have built anything so grand. They postulated that the works were constructed by lost civilizations, including Hebrews, Celts, Scythians, and "Hindoos."

Today the identity of the Moundbuilders is no longer a mystery. Two hundred years of exploration have established that it was the ancestors of today's Native Americans who built the mounds. Although the archeological lens cannot precisely identify the particular contemporary tribe that is their heir, it does provide a clear view of times past by examining patterns of change in the intriguing tools, art, architecture, burial practices, and food

remains left behind by these vanished peoples. By unlocking their secrets, archeologists have identified two major moundbuilder cultures: the Adena and the Hopewell. They constructed conical burial mounds and earthworks in geometric forms, as well as earthen enclosures surrounding the tops of hills. The last prehistoric Mississippian cultures that inhabited the central Mississippi River Valley and its tributaries also built mounds, although these were primarily pyramidal platforms for buildings rather than conical mounds covering graves.

THE ADENA
HEARTLAND

The Adena were the first people to build burial mounds in the Ohio Valley. Their heartland was situated between the modern-day cities of Pittsburgh and Louisville; their sites date from 800 B.C. to A.D. 1000. Adena cemeteries were often large rounded mounds built on the tops of hills or on high terraces overlooking the river valleys. The largest remaining Adena mound is Grave Creek Mound, located in Moundsville, West Virginia. This 62-foot-high conical earthwork was erected on a plateau above the

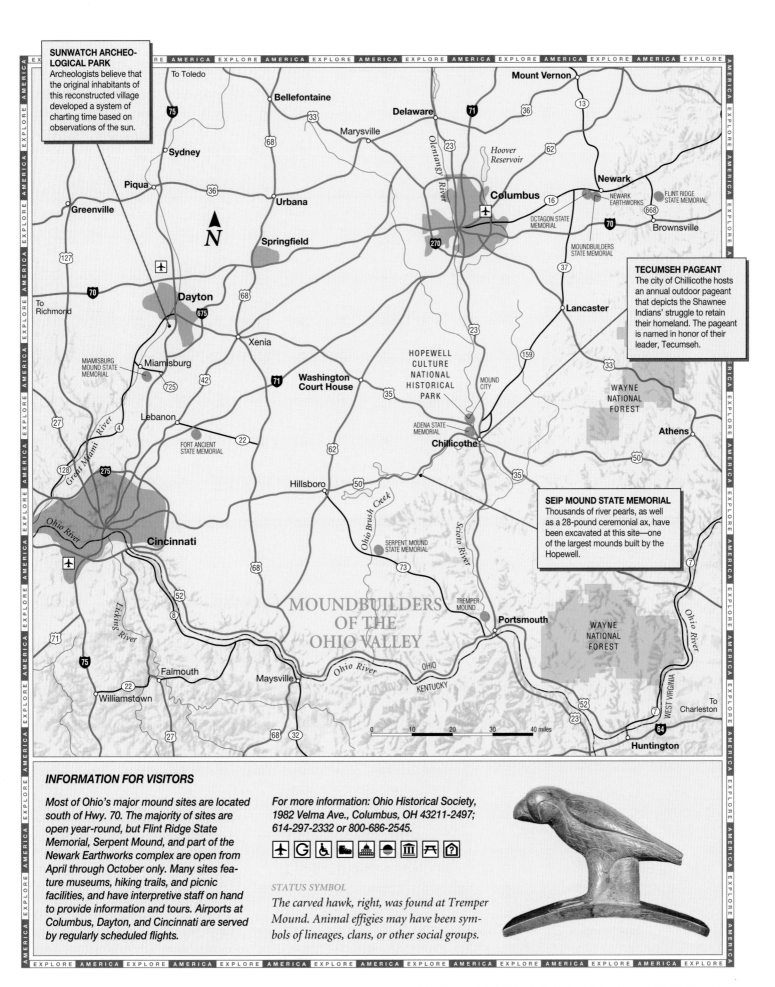

SUNWATCH ARCHEO-LOGICAL PARK
Archeologists believe that the original inhabitants of this reconstructed village developed a system of charting time based on observations of the sun.

To Toledo

Mount Vernon

Bellefontaine

Delaware

Marysville

Olentangy River

Sydney

Piqua

Urbana

Greenville

Dayton

Springfield

Xenia

Lebanon

Miamisburg

MIAMISBURG MOUND STATE MEMORIAL

To Richmond

Great Miami River

Washington Court House

Hillsboro

Fort Ancient State Memorial

Columbus

Newark

NEWARK EARTHWORKS

FLINT RIDGE STATE MEMORIAL

OCTAGON STATE MEMORIAL

Brownsville

MOUNDBUILDERS STATE MEMORIAL

Lancaster

Hoover Reservoir

TECUMSEH PAGEANT
The city of Chillicothe hosts an annual outdoor pageant that depicts the Shawnee Indians' struggle to retain their homeland. The pageant is named in honor of their leader, Tecumseh.

WAYNE NATIONAL FOREST

Athens

HOPEWELL CULTURE NATIONAL HISTORICAL PARK

MOUND CITY

ADENA STATE MEMORIAL

Chillicothe

Scioto River

Ohio Brush Creek

SERPENT MOUND STATE MEMORIAL

SEIP MOUND STATE MEMORIAL
Thousands of river pearls, as well as a 28-pound ceremonial ax, have been excavated at this site—one of the largest mounds built by the Hopewell.

Cincinnati

Licking River

Ohio River

MOUNDBUILDERS OF THE OHIO VALLEY

TREMPER MOUND

Portsmouth

WAYNE NATIONAL FOREST

Ohio River

Falmouth

Maysville

OHIO

KENTUCKY

Williamstown

WEST VIRGINIA

Ohio River

To Charleston

Huntington

0   10   20   30   40 miles

INFORMATION FOR VISITORS

Most of Ohio's major mound sites are located south of Hwy. 70. The majority of sites are open year-round, but Flint Ridge State Memorial, Serpent Mound, and part of the Newark Earthworks complex are open from April through October only. Many sites feature museums, hiking trails, and picnic facilities, and have interpretive staff on hand to provide information and tours. Airports at Columbus, Dayton, and Cincinnati are served by regularly scheduled flights.

For more information: Ohio Historical Society, 1982 Velma Ave., Columbus, OH 43211-2497; 614-297-2332 or 800-686-2545.

STATUS SYMBOL
The carved hawk, right, was found at Tremper Mound. Animal effigies may have been symbols of lineages, clans, or other social groups.

Ohio River Valley. The largest Adena monument in the state, with a circumference of 1,000 feet, this ceremonial complex of earthworks and smaller mounds dates to about 150 B.C. A museum at the site displays exhibits relating to Adena culture.

The origins of moundbuilding in the Ohio Valley coincide with the growth of sedentary communities, farming, and pottery-making in the Adena culture. The construction of large burial mounds in prominent locations may have served as a way of marking the boundaries of a group's territory. A fixed territory was important to this community of hunters, farmers, and fishermen because they had to manage their land to ensure that the soil did not become exhausted and that game animals were not overhunted. The ceremonies and rituals relating to the burial of group members served to strengthen the ties that bound each of these communities together.

Adena burial mounds also furnish evidence of bonds with distant groups. Artifacts buried with some prominent individuals included ornaments fashioned from copper. Copper is not native to the Ohio Valley and was probably imported from the faraway Lake Superior area. These rare and valuable possessions were status symbols that pointed to the owner's privileged access to the resources of a broader community. The social and trading links that the Adena established through the exchange of materials such as copper also could be counted on to supply more essential needs such as food in times of local crop failure.

ANCIENT ART

A talon of a bird, above, cut from a thin sheet of mica about 1,800 years ago, was found at the Hopewell Mound Group in Ross County, Ohio. It may have been used in ceremonies or as a badge denoting the status of a prominent Hopewellian.

HOPEWELL TREASURES

The Hopewell culture, which began about 100 B.C. and continued to thrive until A.D. 400, generated new and more elaborate forms of mound and earthwork construction, and further developed art and rituals that were originated by the Adena culture. The Hopewell also expanded the trade network, extending their influence far beyond the Ohio Valley. Societies from the lower Missouri River to the Appalachian Mountains and from the Great Lakes to the Gulf of Mexico adopted many of the elements of Hopewell culture and exchanged a wide array of exotic raw materials, including copper and mica from the southern Appalachians and obsidian from the Rocky Mountains. The Hopewell continued to build mounds over burial sites and erected increasingly elaborate earthen ceremonial enclosures.

Unfortunately, very little of the architectural splendor of the Hopewell remains unravaged by the passage of time. Perhaps the two best places to see Hopewell earthworks in a nearly pristine state are the Moundbuilders State Memorial in Newark, Ohio, and Fort Ancient State Memorial, located along the Little Miami River near Lebanon in Warren County, Ohio.

Fort Ancient is a three-and-a-half-mile-long series of earthen walls enclosing an area of about 100 acres, including a bluff that rises 275 feet above the Great Miami River Valley. Archeologists once thought it was a Moundbuilder fort, but now conclude it was a huge ceremonial center. The scale of the walls is difficult for visitors to appreciate fully because the entire enclosure winds through the rich upland forests of southwestern Ohio and cannot be seen from one spot. There is a splendid view

of the Miami Valley from the North Overlook, where the site's system of trails connects to the National North Country Scenic Trail. A museum at the site features exhibits on Ohio's Native American cultures, archeology, and history.

At Newark, set amidst the houses, streets, and shops of a bustling blue-collar town, lie the remnants of the largest set of geometric earthworks ever built: they originally covered an area of more than four square miles. Two major sections are preserved in two parks located about a mile from each other. Moundbuilders State Memorial comprises an earthwork called the Great Circle, which is a wall 15 feet high and 1,200 feet in diameter. A ditch, or moat, inside the circle makes the walls appear more imposing. At the center, surrounded by venerable oak trees, is a cluster of mounds that an imaginative antiquarian identified as an eagle

LINKS WITH THE PAST
Octagon State Memorial includes the meticulously manicured greens of the Moundbuilders Country Club, above. These ancient earthworks and mounds, enclosing an area of 50 acres, were erected by the Hopewell culture.

SYMBOL OF A STATE
Often sighted in the forests of the Ohio Valley, the cardinal is Ohio's state bird. Shown at left is the female of the species; the male displays the more familiar bright red plumage.

A six-inch carved figurine of a shaman or medicine man dressed as a bear, below, displays the talents of a Hopewell artisan. Human figures were molded from clay or carved from stone and ivory.

VERDANT NECROPOLIS

Cloaked in vivid green, the 23 burial mounds at Mound City, right, are physical records of Hopewell burial rituals. Cremated bodies and ceremonial objects were placed in excavated basins and then covered with dirt.

effigy. Although it is called Eagle Mound, few scholars believe that it was intended to represent a bird. A small museum at the site presents exhibits showcasing the art of prehistoric Woodland cultures.

Walking beneath the canopy of trees within the Great Circle, visitors can almost forget the hustle and bustle of the city that surrounds this island of ancient grandeur. That illusion is not possible at Newark's other preserved Hopewellian enclosure. Octagon State Memorial consists of a circular embankment, only slightly smaller than the Great Circle, that is connected to a 44-acre octagonal enclosure by a short segment of parallel walls. The greens and fairways of Moundbuilders Country Club were already established on the site when this magnificent earthwork was donated to the Ohio Historical Society. Today a network of paved golf-cart paths winds its way around the site—in some places climbing up and over the embankment walls. In recent years archeologists have determined that the parallel walls connecting the circle and the octagon are aligned to the northernmost rising of the moon in its complicated 18.6-year cycle of risings and settings.

A PRIZED POSSESSION

Flint Ridge State Memorial is a beautiful natural area and archeological park located 10 miles southeast of Newark. There are no dramatic cliffs of shining flint here, as its name implies. Instead, miles of trails wind through an upland forest linking hundreds of prehistoric flint mines. A museum at the site has been built around a typical quarry pit, which has been restored to its original appearance.

Flint from this area was highly prized by Ohio's Native peoples because of its high quality and spectacular colors. Although used by virtually every prehistoric culture in the Ohio Valley, flint was of special importance to the Hopewell people. Archeologists have identified numerous artifacts crafted from this flint at sites at the outer reaches of the Hopewell world. It is unknown whether these were objects exchanged by Hopewellian traders or tokens obtained by pilgrims at sites located near the quarry. But it is no coincidence that the largest Hopewell ceremonial and major trading center— the Newark earthworks—is built near this seven-mile-long deposit of rainbow-colored flint.

Although the earthwork complex at Newark was the largest set of geometric enclosures in the Hopewell world, it pales in comparison with the profusion of separate mounds and enclosures on the broad terraces of the Scioto River Valley above and below the modern-day town of Chillicothe. One of the most remarkable of these sites is commonly known as Mound City, and that is exactly

what it appears to be—a city made up of mounds. A 13-acre almost-square enclosure contains 23 mounds of varying shapes and sizes. The National Park Service operates the site as Hopewell Culture National Historical Park. It includes restored mounds, and an interpretive center displaying many artifacts found within the mounds.

SERPENT'S TALE

Perhaps the most renowned of Ohio's profusion of earthworks is Serpent Mound. Animal effigy mounds are extremely rare in the Ohio Valley, but the Great Serpent Mound has yet another claim to fame: it is the world's largest serpent effigy. From its coiled tail to the tip of its head, the mound stretches 1,348 feet along a rocky promontory more than 100 feet

above Ohio Brush Creek. Walking beside its coils, visitors can feel the power of this ancient icon. The monumental geometry of Newark or the maze of walls at Fort Ancient might be puzzling, but Serpent Mound is readily identified as a snake. This recognizability beguiles many visitors into a false sense of intimacy with the mound's creators. No one really knows why the serpent was laid out here or what the giant effigy represented to the society that built it. A museum at the site presents what is known of the mound and the prehistoric cultures of the Ohio Valley.

Archeologists long believed that the Great Serpent Mound was built by the Adena people. Recently, however, charcoal recovered from the bowels of the serpent yielded a radiocarbon date of A.D. 1070, suggesting that Ohio's most famous mound was built by the prehistoric Fort Ancient people. Further research is needed to confirm that date.

The mounds and enclosures of the Ohio Valley are the vestiges of some of America's most enigmatic cultures. Such monumental achievements are usually a hallmark of more complex civilizations. Neither the Adena nor the Hopewell had kings or even chiefs to compel the labor of commoners. They neither lived in cities, nor produced large surpluses of crops. Nevertheless, Hopewellian astronomers understood the cyclical dance of the sun and moon; their architects and engineers envisioned and designed earthworks of mythic proportions and mathematical precision; they sculpted gigantic earthen birds and beasts; and their leaders somehow marshaled the will of the people to execute these grand designs.

QUARRY RICHES
Flint from the quarry at Flint Ridge, above, was treasured by Ohio's prehistoric peoples. They extracted and chipped this multihued silica into tools and utensils, and also used it as a trading commodity. A museum at the Flint Ridge site describes the geology of the region and the techniques used to craft the flint into objects.

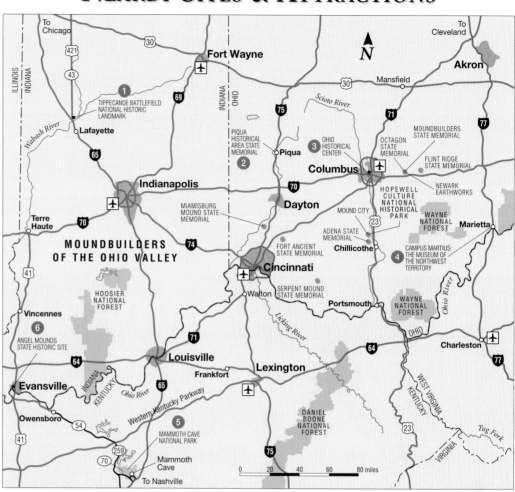

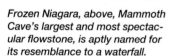

Frozen Niagara, above, Mammoth Cave's largest and most spectacular flowstone, is aptly named for its resemblance to a waterfall.

1 TIPPECANOE BATTLEFIELD NATIONAL HISTORIC LANDMARK, INDIANA

Tippecanoe was a thriving Indian trading post in the 1700's, but was razed in 1791 by U.S. soldiers under orders to disperse its inhabitants. In 1808 a new village called Prophet's Town was founded near the site by two Shawnee brothers, Tecumseh and Tenskatawa, who hoped that it would become the capital of a great Indian confederacy. The village also became a training center for Indian warriors. In 1811 an expedition led by the governor of Indiana Territory, William Henry Harrison, burned Prophet's Town to the ground. An 85-foot marble obelisk marks the site of his encampment, and interpretive markers explain the battle. A visitor center houses a museum, which displays artifacts and a map that traces troop movements. The battlefield itself is surrounded by scenic woods and marshland. Located 7 miles north of Lafayette off Hwy. 43.

2 PIQUA HISTORICAL AREA STATE MEMORIAL, OHIO

Presenting an overview of 2,000 years of Ohio's Native and pioneer history, this historical park includes the Col. John Johnston Farm, the Historic Indian Museum, a prehistoric Indian mound, and

the *General Harrison,* a 70-foot replica of a canal boat. The farmland and restored two-story homestead of federal Indian agent Johnston illustrate his keen interest in agriculture. A ring-shaped mound earthwork, located on the farm, is thought to have been constructed about 2,000 years ago by people of the Adena culture and used for ceremonial purposes. The Historic Indian Museum, built to resemble the blockhouse style of Fort Piqua, exhibits beadwork, pipes, canoes, and weapons of the Native American tribes that inhabited the region from the 17th century to the 19th century. Visitors can view a restored mile-long section of the Miami and Erie Canal and enjoy a ride aboard the *General Harrison.* Located at 9845 North Hardin Rd. in Piqua.

3 OHIO HISTORICAL CENTER, OHIO

The richness of the history of Ohio prior to the advent of European settlement comes to life at the state's premier heritage showcase. The center's three main galleries house exhibits on the archeology, history, and natural history of the state. In the archeology gallery, special emphasis is given to the mound-building Adena and Hopewell peoples. On display are many objects from Ohio's mound sites, including flint tools, pottery, exotic ceremonial tools crafted from obsidian, claws and hands made from mica, and a variety of copper cutout objects used as ornaments. A moose, giant beaver, and complete mastodon skeleton are among the remains of ice-age fauna on display at the center. Located at the 17th Ave. exit off Hwy. 71 in Columbus.

4 CAMPUS MARTIUS: THE MUSEUM OF THE NORTHWEST TERRITORY, OHIO

Campus Martius (Latin for "field of mars") was a civilian fortification built between 1788 and 1790 to protect Marietta, the first organized American settlement in the Northwest Territory of the United States. The fortification later became the seat of the territorial government from 1788 to 1795, and provided protection for settlers during the Ohio Indian Wars, which took place from 1791 to 1794. One of the highlights of the museum is the home belonging to Rufus Putnam, the superintendent of the land company responsible for settling Marietta. This simple plank structure, standing in its original location, is the only surviving dwelling of the first Campus Martius fortification. Also on the site is the Ohio Company Land Office, where land deeds were allotted for the Ohio Company Purchase. Some of the earliest maps of the Northwest Territory were made here. The museum also displays tools, decorative arts, furnishings, agricultural implements, and Native American artifacts. Adjoining the museum is the Ohio River Museum, which recounts the history of the river and the boats that plied its length from the days of the fur traders to present times. Located at Second and Washington Sts. in Marietta.

5 MAMMOTH CAVE NATIONAL PARK, KENTUCKY

Beneath the wooded surface of the Kentucky Plateau lies one of the world's longest and most elaborate cave systems. Established as a national park in 1941, Mammoth Cave has more than 300 miles of passages, domes, pits, and underground rivers that are still being explored. Prehistoric Indians discovered this twisting labyrinth

more than 4,000 years ago. They left behind artifacts and mummies that were preserved by the cave's constant cool temperatures and stable humidity. According to legend, a hunter stumbled across the gaping entrance to the cave in the late 1790's while chasing a bear through the surrounding hills. During the War of 1812, nitrate was discovered in the cave and was mined for use in the manufacture of gunpowder. Led by experienced guides, visitors can today tour 10 miles of passageways year-round. These excursions range from the two-hour Historic Tour—which takes visitors to the remnants of the 19th-century nitrate mining operations—to the six-hour, five-mile Wild Cave Tour, which leads to some of the undeveloped sections of Mammoth Cave. The Frozen Niagara Tour takes visitors to see Mammoth's largest flowstone, which resembles a cascading waterfall. Above ground, 70 miles of scenic trails allow visitors to explore the oak-hickory woodlands and view the park's abundant population of white-tailed deer and wild turkeys. The visitor center is located 2 miles off Hwy. 70.

6 ANGEL MOUNDS STATE HISTORIC SITE, INDIANA

Located on the banks of the Ohio River, Angel Mounds is one of the best-preserved prehistoric Indian settlements in the country. The site, built by people of the Mississippian mound-building culture from about A.D.1300 to A.D. 1500, was occupied for nearly 250 years. The riverside setting was an ideal location for an agricultural people who also hunted and fished. The inhabitants gathered plants and grew corn, squash, pumpkins, beans, and gourds. Originally the town encompassed 103 acres and probably served as an important religious, political, and trade center for people living in the Ohio Valley. A group of 11 mounds functioned as platforms for buildings. Archeologists have reconstructed several winter and summer houses, a roundhouse, a temple, and a section of stockade wall. The interpretive center features a replica of an archeological dig and displays artifacts that have been excavated at the site, including ceramic effigy faces, projectile points, and a variety of bone tools and fishhooks. Located at 8215 Pollack Ave. in Evansville.

The reconstructed stockade at Angel Mounds State Historic Site, above, is made of vertically placed logs covered with wattle and daub.

A statue of Gen. William Henry Harrison, left, stands at the base of the monument at Tippecanoe Battlefield. Harrison led the U.S. infantrymen, Indiana militia, and Kentucky volunteers who fought against the Native American inhabitants of Prophet's Town in 1811.

HUNTERS OF THE PLAINS

Where buffalo once roamed the prairie, brave warriors fought the last of America's Indian wars.

From the vantage point of the weathered rim of South Dakota's Badlands a few miles south of Cactus Flat, dawn breaks orange and dazzling above the distant horizon to reveal a vast and treeless land called the Great Plains. It is a tame land now, churned into farmland by the plow; fenced, dissected by highways, and sown with crossroads, hamlets, and towns. Just a few lifetimes ago, however, the Great Plains sprawled untamed across most of what is now Kansas, Nebraska, North and South Dakota, Oklahoma, and eastern Colorado, Montana, and Wyoming, stretching south into Texas and north into Canada's Western provinces. From horizon to horizon, it was a landlocked ocean of prairie, swept by winds that rolled the buffalo grass like billowing waves. Life-giving rivers sliced across the grasslands like narrow sashes made green by cottonwoods and willows. Mule and white-tailed deer, prairie dogs and sharp-tailed grouse, pronghorn antelope and—like a dark shadow on the land—massive herds of buffalo inhabited this

Miles C

Yellowstone River

94

Forsyth

39

To Billings

Tongue River

NORTHERN
CHEYENNE
TRIBAL
MUSEUM

Hardin

Crow
Agency

Lame Deer

212

CROW
INDIAN
RESERVATION

NORTHERN
CHEYENNE
INDIAN
RESERVATION

LITTLE
BIGHORN
BATTLEFIELD
NATIONAL
MONUMENT

CUSTER
NATIONAL
FOREST

Little Bighorn River

90

BIGHORN MOUNTAINS

Sheridan

FORT PHIL
KEARNY STATE
HISTORIC SITE

87

14 **16**

14

Kearny

BIGHORN
NATIONAL FOREST

Powder River

Cloud Peak
(13,165 ft.)

Buffalo

90

16

BIGHORN MOUNTAINS

387

25

To Wind River
Indian Reservation

20 26

Platte Rive

Casper

2

INFORMATION FOR VISITORS

Hwys. 90 and 25 are the main routes through the region. Regularly scheduled flights serve Pierre and Rapid City, SD, and Casper, WY. Little Bighorn Battlefield National Monument is located 18 miles south of Hardin, MT, off Hwy. 90. The site offers guided tours of the battle-

---

HERD INSTINCT

South Dakota's Custer State Park, above, supports a herd of approximately 1,000 bison, commonly known as buffalo. Almost wiped out by hunters during the late 1900's, bison now roam freely in protected areas like this one.

TWILIGHT ON THE PRAIRIE

Overleaf: Immense in its sweep and lonely majesty, the grass-and-sage-covered prairie of central Wyoming was once the domain of Plains hunters such as the Sioux, Cheyenne, and Arapaho.

territory. This was the homeland of the Great Plains Indians and their hunting grounds.

When Europeans entered the Great Plains in the 18th century, the region was peopled by tribes such as the Ojibwa, Blackfoot, Pawnee, and Assiniboine, which were subdivided into many bands speaking many distinct languages. What is now southeastern Montana and northern Wyoming was home to a few major tribes, including the Crow, Northern Cheyenne, and Northern Arapaho, which were dominated by the most numerous and powerful people of the region—the Great Sioux Nation.

HORSE AND BUFFALO

Originally a woodland people, the Sioux were driven from Minnesota and Wisconsin in the 18th century, reaching the Black Hills in approximately 1770. As the tribe migrated to the Plains, three branches emerged: the Santee, Yankton, and Teton. The first treaty that established a territory for the Sioux was signed at Fort Laramie in 1851. Within a few years most Santee were living on reservations; most Yankton Sioux also moved to reservations during the 1860's and 1870's.

The nomadic Teton Sioux wanted no part of reservation life. By 1850 they were 15,000 strong, divided into seven subgroups: Hunkpapa, Oglala, Brule, Two-Kettle, Sans Arc, Blackfoot, and Minneconjou. The Teton were a powerful people, living at the zenith of a golden age created by the buffalo and the horse.

The horse transformed the lifestyle of Plains Indians like the Teton Sioux. Hunting on horseback meant they could kill more buffalo, and more easily outfit themselves with buffalo-hide robes.

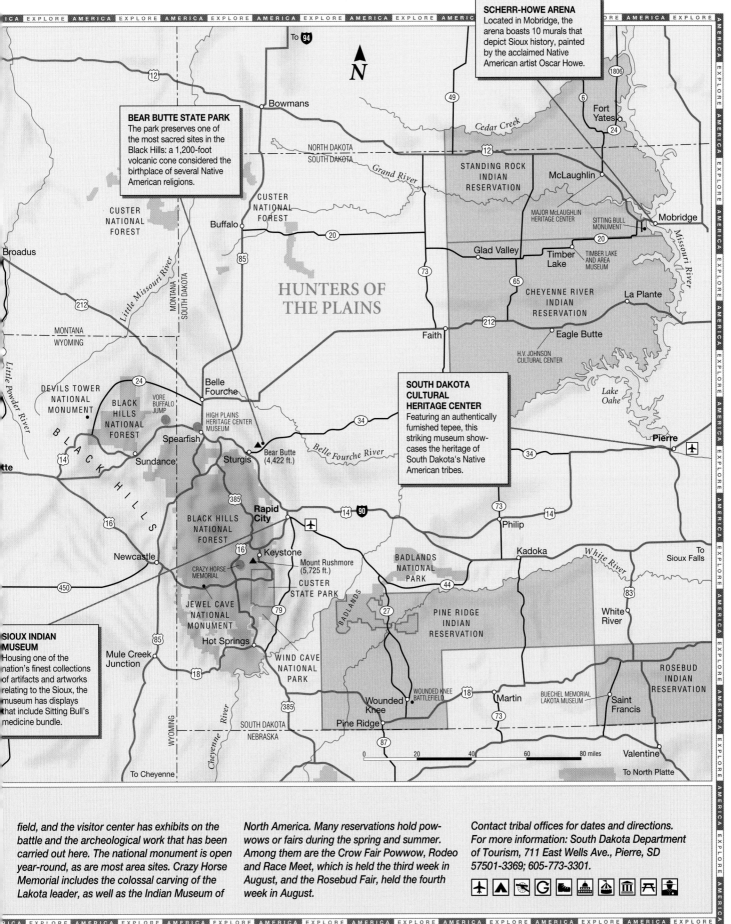

To 94

N

SCHERR-HOWE ARENA
Located in Mobridge, the arena boasts 10 murals that depict Sioux history, painted by the acclaimed Native American artist Oscar Howe.

BEAR BUTTE STATE PARK
The park preserves one of the most sacred sites in the Black Hills: a 1,200-foot volcanic cone considered the birthplace of several Native American religions.

Bowmans

Cedar Creek

Fort Yates

NORTH DAKOTA
SOUTH DAKOTA

Grand River

STANDING ROCK INDIAN RESERVATION

McLaughlin

MAJOR McLAUGHLIN HERITAGE CENTER

SITTING BULL MONUMENT

Mobridge

CUSTER NATIONAL FOREST

Buffalo

Glad Valley

Timber Lake

TIMBER LAKE AND AREA MUSEUM

Missouri River

Broadus

Little Missouri River

MONTANA
SOUTH DAKOTA

HUNTERS OF THE PLAINS

CHEYENNE RIVER INDIAN RESERVATION

Eagle Butte

La Plante

MONTANA
WYOMING

Faith

H.V. JOHNSON CULTURAL CENTER

Lake Oahe

Little Powder River

DEVILS TOWER NATIONAL MONUMENT

BLACK HILLS NATIONAL FOREST

VORE BUFFALO JUMP

Belle Fourche

HIGH PLAINS HERITAGE CENTER MUSEUM

SOUTH DAKOTA CULTURAL HERITAGE CENTER
Featuring an authentically furnished tepee, this striking museum showcases the heritage of South Dakota's Native American tribes.

Pierre

Spearfish

Belle Fourche River

Sundance

Bear Butte (4,422 ft.)

Sturgis

BLACK HILLS

Rapid City

Philip

SIOUX INDIAN MUSEUM
Housing one of the nation's finest collections of artifacts and artworks relating to the Sioux, the museum has displays that include Sitting Bull's medicine bundle.

BLACK HILLS NATIONAL FOREST

Keystone

Mount Rushmore (5,725 ft.)

CRAZY HORSE MEMORIAL

CUSTER STATE PARK

BADLANDS NATIONAL PARK

Kadoka

White River

To Sioux Falls

Newcastle

JEWEL CAVE NATIONAL MONUMENT

BADLANDS

PINE RIDGE INDIAN RESERVATION

White River

Mule Creek Junction

Hot Springs

WIND CAVE NATIONAL PARK

ROSEBUD INDIAN RESERVATION

WOUNDED KNEE BATTLEFIELD

Martin

BUECHEL MEMORIAL LAKOTA MUSEUM

Saint Francis

Wounded Knee

WYOMING

SOUTH DAKOTA
NEBRASKA

Cheyenne River

Pine Ridge

Valentine

To Cheyenne

0   20   40   60   80 miles

To North Platte

field, and the visitor center has exhibits on the battle and the archeological work that has been carried out here. The national monument is open year-round, as are most area sites. Crazy Horse Memorial includes the colossal carving of the Lakota leader, as well as the Indian Museum of

North America. Many reservations hold powwows or fairs during the spring and summer. Among them are the Crow Fair Powwow, Rodeo and Race Meet, which is held the third week in August, and the Rosebud Fair, held the fourth week in August.

Contact tribal offices for dates and directions. For more information: South Dakota Department of Tourism, 711 East Wells Ave., Pierre, SD 57501-3369; 605-773-3301.

Warfare and personal combat were major pursuits of the Sioux and other Plains tribes. The horse enabled their raiding parties to cover long distances, making them formidable foes.

The buffalo was central to the culture of the Plains. Every part of the animal—inside and out—was put to use as clothing, weapons, equipment, tools, toys, and ornaments. Even dried buffalo droppings were used as fuel on the treeless prairie. So abundant was the buffalo that an early 19th-century mountain man allegedly rode alongside a herd for an entire day trying to measure its length, but was unable to reach the head by day's end.

On high ground along streams or rivers, villages of buffalo-hide tepees suddenly would arise and then just as quickly disappear when their nomadic dwellers took a notion to move. The tepee was portable, easily erected and dismantled, able to accommodate a cozy fire in winter, and simple to ventilate in warm weather.

For many Sioux men, a principal rite of manhood was the sun dance, in which the dancers made sacrifices for a specific purpose. Warriors would move rhythmically beneath a center lodge pole for four days and nights without food or drink, blowing bone whistles and requesting guidance from their god, Wakan Tanka. Often participants skewered rawhide thongs through their chest or back muscles, attached the thongs to the center pole, and pulled away until the skewers were ripped

loose. In contrast to their capacity for endurance and self-discipline, the Sioux were an emotionally demonstrative people, given to exultant celebrations and wild outbursts of grief.

Visitors can explore the history of the Sioux at the Sioux Indian Museum in Rapid City, South Dakota, which holds a 5,000-piece collection of Sioux artifacts dating from the mid-19th century. Among its most popular exhibits are a group of 21 mannequins in authentic Sioux dress and a display that explains the uses and influence of the horse. More displays related to the lifeways and culture of the Plains Indians are found at the Peter Norbeck Center in Custer State Park and at the High Plains Heritage Center Museum in nearby

LIVING HISTORY
War paint and feathers worn by a young man, above, in a re-enactment of Custer's Last Stand recall the deadly contest between Plains warriors and cavalry during the Indian wars. The event is part of Little Bighorn Days, held each June in Hardin, Montana.

RUGGED RIDGES
Sunset casts a golden glow over the Badlands, left, a 100-mile geological curiosity that extends across the plains of South Dakota just north of the Pine Ridge Indian Reservation. The eroded remnants of sediments laid down by rivers, this fossil-laden landscape is preserved in 242,755-acre Badlands National Park. The park contains several sites sacred to the Oglala Sioux.

45

Spearfish. At the Crazy Horse Memorial, the Indian Museum of North America presents more than 20,000 artifacts—all donated by Native Americans. About two miles across the Wyoming border at a marked pullout on Highway 90 lies the Vore Buffalo Jump, where Native Americans slaughtered buffalo by driving them over a cliff.

———————
A TIME OF
WAR
———————

Living so deep in the wilderness, the Teton Sioux had little contact with whites until the 19th century. The threat of lost lands seemed distant until the era of Crazy Horse, the great Oglala warrior who vehemently opposed relinquishing traditional Sioux territory to encroaching civilization. "One does not sell the earth upon which the people walk," he is said to have proclaimed. Crazy Horse was born into the Oglala branch of the Teton Sioux about 1842, and grew into manhood at a time of deepening conflict between the Sioux and the white emigrants.

By mid-century growing numbers of settlers were crossing the Plains en route to California and Oregon. Contact between the two cultures was peaceful until 1854, when bloodshed occurred on the North Platte River near Fort Laramie, in what is now eastern Wyoming.

Agents of the U.S. government had persuaded a handful of Sioux chiefs to grant the immigrants travel rights through their lands in 1851. Three years later, as several thousand Brule and Oglala Sioux camped near Fort Laramie to receive government annuities, a stray cow belonging to an immigrant party was butchered by the Sioux. This sparked a confrontation between soldiers and the Sioux, which turned bloody when tense troops opened fire and were massacred by Sioux warriors.

A year later, the army destroyed a Brule village in Nebraska, slaughtering men, women, and children and leaving a legacy of distrust between Anglo-Americans and the Sioux.

Gold was discovered in western Montana in 1862, which increased travel across Sioux land and prompted the development of the Bozeman Trail as a shortcut between Julesburg, Colorado, and Virginia City, Montana. The increased traffic across their traditional hunting grounds in Wyoming disturbed the Sioux, as did reports that reached them in

1863 of the Sioux uprising in Minnesota and the savage massacre of peaceful Cheyenne by Colorado militiamen at Sand Creek. Joined by their Northern Cheyenne and Northern Arapaho allies, Sioux war parties attacked travelers on the Bozeman Trail. The government responded by building forts along the trail and doing battle with the Sioux.

The army established Fort Phil Kearny east of the Bighorn Mountains in northern Wyoming as a keystone of the Bozeman Trail fortifications. The fort boasted 42 structures surrounded by a log palisade, but it was isolated in Sioux hunting grounds and was under almost constant siege.

Red Cloud was an Oglala war leader who led a band of Oglala Sioux in making war against the Bozeman Trail. Twenty years younger than Red Cloud, Crazy Horse also led war parties against the army in what was known as Red Cloud's War. On December 21, 1866, Red Cloud dealt the U.S. Army a shocking defeat called the Fetterman Massacre, in which an 80-man force led by Capt. William J. Fetterman was ambushed and killed.

At an 1868 peace conference held at Fort Laramie, Wyoming, Red Cloud agreed to cease fighting if the army abandoned its Bozeman Trail posts. The treaty negotiated at the meeting provided the Teton Sioux, the Northern Cheyenne, and other allies with a huge, permanent reservation surrounding the Black Hills, whose boundaries the federal government vowed to protect and preserve. In exchange for the right to build a road through Indian territory, the government granted annuities to the Sioux for four years, plus horses and equipment to facilitate farming, and the promise of education for the children of the tribe. Although he was not a chief and led only a portion of the Sioux, Red Cloud did what no other Indian leader had ever done: he won a war with the U.S. government.

Today visitors can drive a route that roughly follows the Bozeman Trail across eastern Wyoming. This is the Plains at its wide-open best, where pronghorn antelope still race across the rolling grasslands. Fort Phil Kearny State Historic Site is located a short distance off Highway 90 between Buffalo and Sheridan and features a small museum and interpretive signs. The fort has not been restored, and the windswept site hints at the isolation young soldiers must have felt as they warred with their Sioux adversaries during the 1860's.

For the next eight years the Yankton and the Santee Sioux struggled to adapt to the white man's world, but Teton leaders like Crazy Horse and Sitting Bull were determined to preserve their people's traditional lifeways. Government attempts to make reservation life more acceptable were marred by frequent cases of incompetence and corruption: promised supplies and rations were inadequate

EVERY PICTURE TELLS A STORY
Serving as a form of calendar, buffalo hides called winter counts were used to record important tribal events each year. The Sioux winter count below would have been rolled and stored between uses. Buffalo robes sometimes bore pictographs of the owner's deeds.

The black-tailed prairie dog, below, was once common throughout the Great Plains. About the size of a cat, the animal lives in "towns" made up of groups of low mounds. Colonies are protected in Badlands National Park, Custer State Park, Wind Cave National Park, and Devils Tower National Monument.

SACRED SITE

The Cheyenne River, left, meanders north and south around the Black Hills, deep in the heart of the Great Plains. This country was sacred to the Sioux, who named these mountains He Sapa—the Black Hills.

and undependable; federal Indian agents were sometimes indifferent or outright dishonest.

The tension smoldering between the Sioux and the U.S. government was finally ignited by reports of large gold deposits in the Black Hills in 1874. Thousands of gold-seekers descended on the beloved mountains of the Sioux, despite attempts by the army to keep them out. The Sioux responded by killing the miners. The government then tried to buy the Black Hills from the Sioux. As gold fever increased, the Sioux and Cheyenne launched raids against settlers living outside Indian lands. In November 1875, the government ordered the Teton Sioux and their allies to return to their reservation by the end of January or face the consequences. When Sitting Bull and other Sioux leaders failed to comply, the government turned to the military. The standoff ended at a site in Montana called Little Bighorn.

Instead of reporting to the reservation as ordered by the federal government, Sitting Bull and a huge gathering of Teton Sioux—joined by the Cheyenne and the Arapaho—had camped on the Little Bighorn River, known as the Greasy Grass to the Indians. They observed their ritual summer sun

dance and held council about the threat from the white government. With perhaps more than 10,000 Indians in attendance, it may have been the largest gathering of Native Americans on the Great Plains.

On June 25, 1876, Gen. George Armstrong Custer and approximately 600 troops of the 7th Cavalry attacked the Indian encampment. By tribal accounts, the battle ended quickly: Custer and his immediate command were wiped out.

TOURING THE REGION

The Battle of the Little Bighorn represented the last stand for the Plains Indians too. In the wake of the battle, the U.S. government took an even harder line against the Sioux, as well as their Cheyenne and Arapaho allies. In December 1875, it again ordered them all to come into reservations by January 30, 1877.

Little Bighorn Battlefield National Monument is administered by the National Park Service. The visitor center features exhibits about this famous battle. Ironically, the site of the greatest Sioux victory is located on what became the reservation of their historic enemy—the Crow—who supplied some of Custer's scouts. The Crow Fair Powwow,

Rodeo, and Race Meet, held the third week in August, is Montana's largest annual Native American celebration.

Highway 212 takes visitors from the Little Bighorn Battlefield National Monument 25 miles east to the Northern Cheyenne Reservation. Farther down Highway 212 at Lame Deer, Cheyenne culture and history is showcased at the Northern Cheyenne Tribal Museum.

Like the Sioux, the Cheyenne migrated from the Minnesota forests to the Great Plains, separating into a northern and a southern group. After the Battle of the Little Bighorn, the Northern Cheyenne were rounded up and sent to a reservation in modern-day Oklahoma. In 1884 they fought their way back to their traditional homeland in Montana and were allowed to remain in the Great Plains, being relocated to the site of their present reservation on the Rosebud and Tongue rivers. In January, May, and July, the Northern Cheyenne celebrate their heritage with a series of public powwows.

The wilds of South Dakota's Standing Rock Reservation, home of the Hunkpapa and Yankton Sioux, contains the birthplace of Sitting Bull. This is where he died at the hands of federal officials who were sent to arrest him in 1890. Sitting Bull was buried at Fort Yates, on the Missouri River, in North Dakota. At the town of McLaughlin, just off Highway 12, exhibits related to the culture of the Standing Rock Sioux and the work of agent James McLaughlin are to be found at the Major McLaughlin Heritage Center. Public powwows are held on the Standing Rock Reservation in June, July, and August. Across the Missouri River from Mobridge, the Sitting Bull Monument overlooks Lake Oahe. In 1953 the chief's relatives had his remains reinterred in a granite memorial.

A sidetrip to the west leads to the Cheyenne River Reservation, home to several bands of the Teton Sioux: the Sans Arc, Two-Kettle, Blackfoot, and Minneconjou. The H. V. Johnston Cultural Center at Eagle Butte features traditional Sioux crafts, and the Timber Lake and Area Museum in nearby Timber Lake displays Sioux artifacts from the Standing Rock Indian Reservation. Powwows are usually scheduled on the reservation in July, August, and September.

Southwest of Pierre, near the Nebraska border, lies the Rosebud Indian Reservation, home of the Brule band of the Teton Sioux. Powwows are held on the reservation in July and August. At nearby Saint Francis is the Buechel Memorial Lakota Museum, which celebrates the Sioux culture with historical exhibits and authentic crafts.

The Pine Ridge Indian Reservation is the home of the Oglala band of the Teton Sioux and the site of Red Cloud's grave. This is also where, on December 29, 1890, the 7th Cavalry tried to disarm a band of Minneconjou under Sioux leader Big Foot, sparking a fusillade of gunfire that killed 25 soldiers and at least 168 Sioux, including women and children.

The battleground is marked but undeveloped. A simple stone monument marks the site of the Indians' mass grave. The massacre at Wounded Knee, as the slaughter came to be known, marked the end of the protracted series of Plains Indian wars. In time, Native Americans like the Oglala adapted to the white man's ways, while seeking to preserve their unique heritage.

No monument on the Great Plains marks the grave of Crazy Horse. On May 6, 1877, the great warrior brought his people to Red Cloud Agency in Nebraska. Promised a reservation in Wyoming, Crazy Horse was instead arrested a few months later. In a scuffle with his guards, he was mortally wounded. His last words were: "Tell the people it is no use to depend on me anymore now." Crazy Horse's grieving parents retrieved his body and secretly buried it somewhere in the Western wilds.

North of Wounded Knee and across the Pine Ridge Reservation lies the Badlands. Here the road is engulfed by windswept pinnacles, gullies, deep canyons, and ragged buttes. In the glory days of the Great Sioux Nation, warriors thundered across this land. Today its silence is an eloquent reminder of the lifeway of a noble people long gone—the hunters of the Great Plains.

RELICS OF THE PLAINS
Beaded moccasins, decorated arrows, woven backrests, and other Blackfoot artifacts, above, are a poignant reminder of the days when this great tribe inhabited the Great Plains.

FEATHERED RIG
A young Native American, left, performs a traditional dance in full regalia.

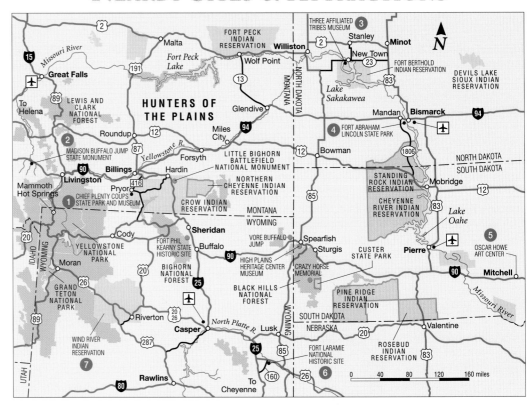

At North Dakota's Fort Abraham Lincoln State Park, a reconstructed Mandan earthlodge, above, hints at the settled lifestyle of this farming people. Mandan earthlodges consisted of a wood framework covered with willow branches and a thick layer of grass and clay.

1 CHIEF PLENTY COUPS STATE PARK AND MUSEUM, MONTANA

The last and greatest leader of the Crow tribe, Chief Plenty Coups helped his people during the difficult transition from the nomadic lifestyle of the Plains to settled life on a federal reservation. His Crow name, Aleck-chea-ahoosh, means "Many Achievements" or "Plenty Coups." Often referred to as Chief of Chiefs for his efforts to preserve the Crow culture through cooperation with whites rather than through warfare, Plenty Coups is buried just outside the park. Land for the park, as well as Plenty Coups' own log house, was deeded to the nation by the chief and his wife in 1928. In his dedication speech, Plenty Coups declared: "This park is not to be a memorial to me, but to the Crow Nation. It is given as a token of my friendship for all people, both red and white." The park is situated within the Crow Reservation. Visitors can view Plenty Coups' house, as well as a museum dedicated to the Crow—the only one of its kind in the nation. Located 35 miles south of Billings and 1 mile west of Pryor off Hwy. 416.

2 MADISON BUFFALO JUMP STATE MONUMENT, MONTANA

In the limestone bluffs along the Madison River stands a spectacular *pishkun*, or buffalo jump—a sheer precipice over which Shoshone, Nez Perce, Flathead, and Pend d'Oreille hunters would stampede buffalo to their deaths and then butcher the carcasses. The Madison site consists of a grazing area, drive lanes made up of low rock piles and brush that formed a funnel to direct the buffalo

toward the cliff, the 30-foot jump, and a slope at the foot of the cliff where crippled animals were killed and butchered. There is also a campsite where various tribes lived for the duration of the jump and carried out the final butchering, drying of meat, and preparation of hides. Interpretive displays—including an artist's sketch of buffalo tumbling over the rimrock—tell the story of the jump. Located 48 miles west of Livingston off Hwy. 90.

3 THREE AFFILIATED TRIBES MUSEUM, NORTH DAKOTA

The museum was established to provide a heritage center for the Mandan, Hidatsa, and Arikara peoples, also known as the Three Affiliated Tribes. It is located on the Fort Berthold Indian Reservation, overlooking massive Lake Sakakawea, a reservoir that was formed by the construction of the Garrison Dam on the Missouri River. The Mandan people lived a settled agricultural life in earthlodge villages at the mouth of the Heart River and later moved to join the Hidatsa at Knife River after a smallpox epidemic decimated their ranks. Because of their skill in farming, the two tribes were known as the Corn Indians. The Arikara were once part of the Pawnee tribe, but migrated north in 1823 after encounters with white militia. The museum displays artifacts, arts, crafts, and historical data related to these Native peoples. Of particular interest to visitors is a unique collection of garden tools, seeds, and foodstuffs. Located on Hwy. 23 in the Four Bears Memorial Park, 4 miles west of New Town.

4 FORT ABRAHAM LINCOLN STATE PARK, NORTH DAKOTA

Within Fort Abraham Lincoln State Park—the site of the army post where George A. Custer was based before the Battle of the Little Bighorn—the reconstructed dwellings of Slant Village bring to life the world of the Mandan people. The On a Slant Village, named for its slope toward the Missouri River, was first occupied in the mid-1600's. With ravines on the northern and southern sides and the river to the east, the site was easy to defend. A palisade and ditch were built on the western side. Shallow depressions are remnants of the original earthlodges, which probably housed 10 to 15 people each. Today several of these domed houses have been reconstructed, including a ceremonial lodge. The park's visitor center displays artifacts and exhibits depicting the lifeways of the Mandan, the Lewis and Clark expedition, and the fur trade. In summer, reenactments of life at the fort and village are presented. Located 4 miles south of Mandan on Hwy. 1806.

5 OSCAR HOWE ART CENTER, SOUTH DAKOTA

Housed in a 1903 former Carnegie Library building, the Oscar Howe Art Center displays the work of the Yanktonai Sioux painter who is renowned as the father of contemporary Native American art. Born on the Crow Creek Indian Reservation, Oscar Howe obtained his art training in Santa Fe in a school that encouraged Native artists to produce work drawing on their tribal beliefs. Howe's linear abstract style used sweeping line, color, and space to interpret his Sioux heritage. The center's Oscar Howe Gallery has more than 20 of the artist's original works on permanent display, as well as Howe's mural designs for Mitchell's famed Corn Palace. Two other galleries are used for temporary exhibits. The mural on the building's interior dome was painted by Howe in 1940. It depicts a prayer for rain and fertility, with the central skylight symbolizing the sun. Located at 119 West Third St. in Mitchell.

6 FORT LARAMIE NATIONAL HISTORIC SITE, WYOMING

Just a half-day's drive from the Black Hills, the 837-acre Fort Laramie National Historic Site is among the largest and perhaps the best restored of the nation's Western army posts. Originally established by fur traders, the site was purchased by the U.S. government in 1849 and soon became an important stop on the Oregon Trail. During the era of the Plains Indian wars, Fort Laramie became one of the most important army posts in Wyoming Territory. Attractions include the officers' quarters, enlisted men's barracks, the sutler's store, and the parade ground. With no furniture, toilet, or light, the jail in the basement of the guardhouse gives visitors an idea as to just how rugged life was in this isolated outpost. The visitor center contains various artifacts, including an 1876 Gatling gun. Located 130 miles southeast of Casper off Hwy. 26, on Hwy. 160.

7 WIND RIVER INDIAN RESERVATION, WYOMING

Located east of the Wind River Mountains, the vast Wind River Indian Reservation contains 3,500 square miles of pristine forests and beautiful alpine areas. Wyoming's only reservation is shared by the Arapaho and Shoshone nations, each with its own culture and language. This magnificent tract of land was originally given to the Shoshone in recognition of their friendliness toward white settlers. Led by their beloved chief Washakie, who headed the tribe for more than 60 years, the Shoshone assisted the U.S. Army in its campaigns against the Sioux and Cheyenne. At the southern end of Wind River is the burial site of Washakie; also buried on the reservation is Sacajawea, the Shoshone woman who served as a guide for the Lewis and Clark expedition. Visitors can hike, hunt, fish, boat, and camp on the reservation; permits for hiking, hunting, and fishing must be obtained from the Wind River Fish and Game Department. Located on Hwy. 26.

Old Bedlam, above, served as Fort Laramie's headquarters, as well as living quarters for bachelor officers. Built in 1849, the two-story structure is the oldest standing military building in Wyoming.

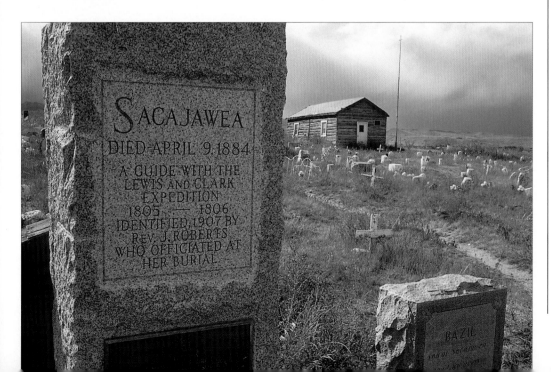

A few miles south of the settlement of Wind River, the monument to Sacajawea, left, commemorates the young woman who guided Lewis and Clark through the West on their journey to the Pacific.

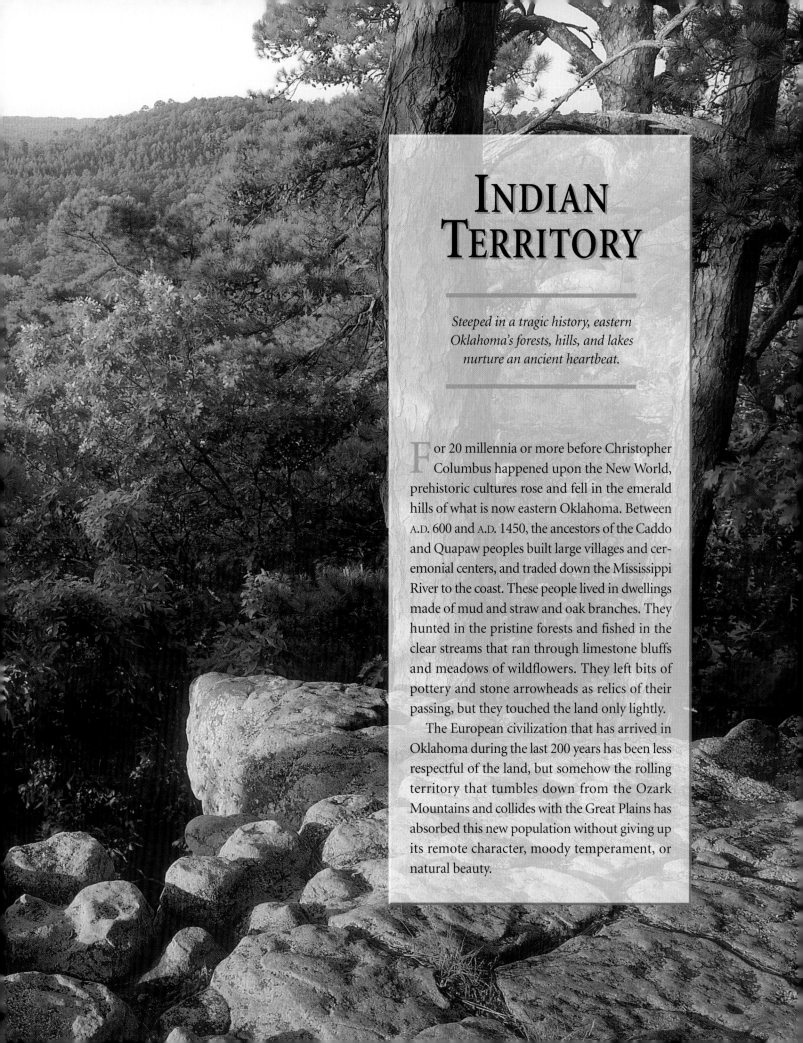

INDIAN TERRITORY

Steeped in a tragic history, eastern Oklahoma's forests, hills, and lakes nurture an ancient heartbeat.

For 20 millennia or more before Christopher Columbus happened upon the New World, prehistoric cultures rose and fell in the emerald hills of what is now eastern Oklahoma. Between A.D. 600 and A.D. 1450, the ancestors of the Caddo and Quapaw peoples built large villages and ceremonial centers, and traded down the Mississippi River to the coast. These people lived in dwellings made of mud and straw and oak branches. They hunted in the pristine forests and fished in the clear streams that ran through limestone bluffs and meadows of wildflowers. They left bits of pottery and stone arrowheads as relics of their passing, but they touched the land only lightly.

The European civilization that has arrived in Oklahoma during the last 200 years has been less respectful of the land, but somehow the rolling territory that tumbles down from the Ozark Mountains and collides with the Great Plains has absorbed this new population without giving up its remote character, moody temperament, or natural beauty.

Spanish gold-seekers came in 1541, followed by the Osage Indians, who migrated from the Ohio Valley into Missouri and Arkansas, and French traders, who paddled up the Mississippi and Arkansas rivers from New Orleans to barter with them. With the growth of the American republic, the tribes of the Southeast—the Cherokee, Chickasaw, Choctaw, Creek, and Seminole—were forcibly removed from their lands east of the Mississippi and relocated here. This was called Indian Territory, an area reserved by the federal government for Native settlement. White settlement was to be prohibited "as long as the grass grows and the water runs." For about half a century, Native peoples governed themselves according to their ancestral laws.

The peace of Indian Territory was shattered in the 1870's, when the railroads arrived in Oklahoma. Hard on the heels of the iron horse came a rush of white settlers, ranchers, farmers, coal miners, and lumbermen, who soon came to outnumber Native American residents. Statehood was granted in 1907, amid the Oklahoma "oil rush," when Congress chose to ignore proposals from the Native peoples to create a Native state named Sequoyah.

In this century, oil prospectors and road- and dam-building engineers have continued to transform the landscape. Airports and highways have been etched into the soil, and great rivers have been made navigable for seagoing cargo ships. But on spring mornings, when threads of cotton-colored haze are woven through the hills and the air is sweet with alfalfa and wild lavender, the land still seems untouched by the hand of man, as though it will forever be possessed by another time.

In the Arbuckle Mountains, a range of low, rounded limestone in the Chickasaw Nation of south-central Oklahoma, mountain goats forage among the red cedar, soapberry, and blackjack oak trees near Turner Falls, where spring-fed Honey Creek cascades down a 77-foot stone bluff.

In the southeastern corner of the state, where the Choctaw settled 160 years ago, black bears, wolves, bobcats, and deer roam the pine forests of the Sans Bois, Jackfork, and Kiamichi mountains. In the upper regions of the Choctaw Nation, rainbow trout thrive in icy streams; farther south, alligators inhabit the warmer, cypress-lined waterways. Within the huge Ouachita National Forest, Talimena Drive (Highway 1) still ranks as one of the nation's most picturesque scenic drives, especially when the roadsides are painted with the blinding hues of autumn colors.

In the Creek and Cherokee lands to the north, pecan trees multiply abundantly along the shores of the Arkansas River. Upland oak, hickory, sycamore, and other hardwood trees grow so densely that they make the hills almost impassable. These forests provided a place of refuge for a string of legendary outlaws—Jesse James, Pretty Boy Floyd, and Ma Barker, among many others—who hid out in the remote hollows, as well as moonshiners, who turned bootleg whiskey into a thriving industry.

With occasional expanses of tallgrass prairie, the region provides a habitat for whitetail deer, buffalo, wild turkeys, bobwhite quails, and mourning doves. Eufaula Lake, Grand Lake O' The Cherokees, and Tenkiller Lake are home to bass, crappie, catfish, walleye, and bream, as well as waterfowl, beavers, and otters.

NATIVE HEARTLAND

Above all, the area has held tightly to its Native American past. Place names such as Pushmataha, Sallisaw, Owasso, Nowata, Tamaha, and Tishomingo are reminders that long before this was the state of Oklahoma—a combination of the Choctaw words *okla* (red) and *homma* (people)—it was Indian Territory. The state remains home to the largest concentration of Native Americans in the nation. For the most part, they reside within a 50-mile radius of downtown Tulsa, where the boundaries of the Creek, Cherokee, and Osage nations intersect. Among public school students in Tulsa, more than 64

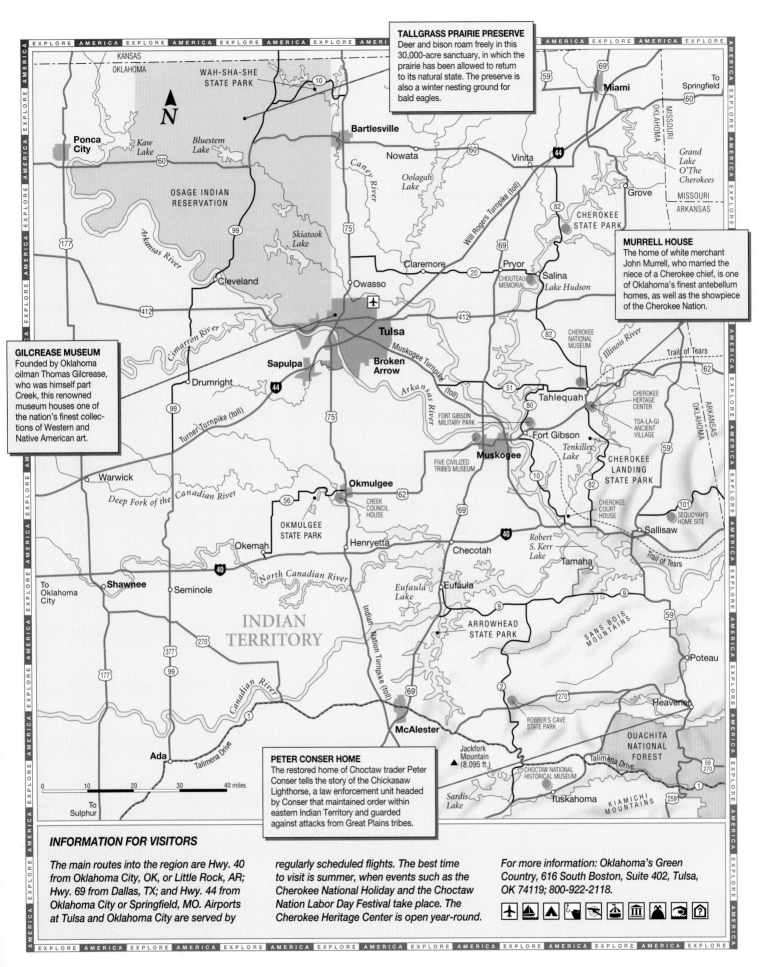

WAH-SHA-SHE
STATE PARK

N

TALLGRASS PRAIRIE PRESERVE
Deer and bison roam freely in this 30,000-acre sanctuary, in which the prairie has been allowed to return to its natural state. The preserve is also a winter nesting ground for bald eagles.

To
Springfield

Miami

MISSOURI
OKLAHOMA

Ponca City

Kaw
Lake

Bluestem
Lake

60

Nowata

60

Vinita

44

Grand
Lake
O'The
Cherokees

Grove

MISSOURI
ARKANSAS

Caney River

Oolagah
Lake

59

CHEROKEE
STATE PARK

82

OSAGE INDIAN
RESERVATION

99

Skiatook
Lake

75

Claremore

20

Pryor

Salina

Lake Hudson

69

CHOUTEAU
MEMORIAL

MURRELL HOUSE
The home of white merchant John Murrell, who married the niece of a Cherokee chief, is one of Oklahoma's finest antebellum homes, as well as the showpiece of the Cherokee Nation.

177

Arkansas River

Cleveland

Owasso

412

82

CHEROKEE
NATIONAL
MUSEUM

Illinois River

Trail of Tears

62

GILCREASE MUSEUM
Founded by Oklahoma oilman Thomas Gilcrease, who was himself part Creek, this renowned museum houses one of the nation's finest collections of Western and Native American art.

412

Tulsa

Muskogee Turnpike (toll)

51

CHEROKEE
HERITAGE
CENTER

ARKANSAS
OKLAHOMA

Cimarron River

Sapulpa

Broken Arrow

80

Tahlequah

TSA-LA-GI
ANCIENT
VILLAGE

Drumright

44

Arkansas River

Fort Gibson
Military Park

Fort Gibson

59

99

75

FIVE CIVILIZED
TRIBES MUSEUM

Muskogee

Tenkiller
Lake

CHEROKEE
LANDING
STATE PARK

Turner Turnpike (toll)

Warwick

Deep Fork of the Canadian River

56

Okmulgee

62

CREEK
COUNCIL
HOUSE

10

CHEROKEE
COURT
HOUSE

101

SEQUOYAH'S
HOME SITE

OKMULGEE
STATE PARK

69

82

Sallisaw

Okemah

Henryetta

Checotah

40

Robert
S. Kerr
Lake

Trail of Tears

Shawnee

40

Seminole

North Canadian River

Tamaha

SANS BOIS
MOUNTAINS

59

To
Oklahoma
City

Eufaula
Lake

Eufaula

9

ARROWHEAD
STATE PARK

9

**INDIAN
TERRITORY**

270

377

Poteau

99

177

Canadian River

Indian Nation Turnpike (toll)

2

270

Heavener

1

69

ROBBER'S CAVE
STATE PARK

Ada

Talimena Drive

McAlester

OUACHITA
NATIONAL
FOREST

59
270

PETER CONSER HOME
The restored home of Choctaw trader Peter Conser tells the story of the Chickasaw Lighthorse, a law enforcement unit headed by Conser that maintained order within eastern Indian Territory and guarded against attacks from Great Plains tribes.

Jackfork
Mountain
(8,095 ft.)

Talimena Drive

1

0   10   20   30   40 miles

CHOCTAW NATIONAL
HISTORICAL MUSEUM

KIAMICHI
MOUNTAINS

59

To
Sulphur

Sardis
Lake

Tuskahoma

INFORMATION FOR VISITORS

The main routes into the region are Hwy. 40 from Oklahoma City, OK, or Little Rock, AR; Hwy. 69 from Dallas, TX; and Hwy. 44 from Oklahoma City or Springfield, MO. Airports at Tulsa and Oklahoma City are served by

regularly scheduled flights. The best time to visit is summer, when events such as the Cherokee National Holiday and the Choctaw Nation Labor Day Festival take place. The Cherokee Heritage Center is open year-round.

For more information: Oklahoma's Green Country, 616 South Boston, Suite 402, Tulsa, OK 74119; 800-922-2118.

Native tribes are represented, each with its own language and culture.

The Southeastern tribes have had the largest impact on the history of the state and on contemporary life here. The Cherokee, Chickasaw, Creek, Choctaw, and Seminole are often called the Five Civilized Tribes (a term used as early as 1876 in official U.S. Indian Office documents) because in their aboriginal lands east of the Mississippi River they had established constitutional governments with three branches—a form of government developed by the Iroquois and later adopted by the United States. They had a very progressive school system and productive farmlands, engaged in industry and commerce, and lived peacefully with their neighbors. The Cherokees even had an alphabet (or syllabary) that allowed them to communicate in writing. The forced removal of these peoples to Indian Territory was a lamentable page in American history.

THE ROAD WEST

Whites had long coveted the traditional Native American territory of the South and Southeast, which abounded in timber, minerals, and fertile topsoil. After the Louisiana Purchase in 1803, the government came under increasing pressure to remove the tribes to lands west of the Mississippi. Pressure quickly turned to violence following the discovery of gold on Cherokee land in Georgia in 1828. Two years later, Pres. Andrew Jackson pushed through Congress a bill to force the tribes west.

Yet the cruelty of the subsequent deportation stung the sensibilities of many whites. "The Red Men must soon leave," thundered Alabama's *Montgomery Advertiser* in the mid-1830's. "They have nothing left on which to subsist. Their property has been taken from them— their stock killed, their farms pillaged—by whom? By white men. By individuals who should have scorned to take such mean advantage of those who were unprotected and defenseless. Such villainy may go unpunished in this world, but the day of retribution will most certainly come."

The first to be relocated were the Choctaw of Mississippi, and their passage foreshadowed the tragedy that would mark the entire relocation process. Under military guard, one contingent of 1,000 people left Mississippi in the fall of 1830; only 88 arrived at the group's final destination of the Kiamichi River in the following spring.

Next were the Chickasaw, who were closely related to the Choctaw, but more warlike and nomadic. Although their habitat was primarily in northern Mississippi, they also claimed—and savagely defended—lands as far north as the Ohio River.

They resisted removal until 1837, when it was estimated that more than 500 of their people died during relocation, mostly from smallpox and malaria.

Greater coercion was required to displace the Creek of Alabama and the Seminole of Florida. The Seminole waged war almost continuously from 1832 to 1842 in a vain effort to protect their homeland. Although they offered less resistance than the Seminole, the Creek nonetheless were rounded up, bound and shackled together, and driven like cattle to Indian Territory. Hundreds died of disease, some committed suicide, and many were murdered by their army guards.

Perhaps most tragic was the removal of the Cherokee, a branch of the Iroquoian family that once claimed a large region of the southern Alleghenies and parts of Virginia, Tennessee,

HORN SPOON

A Choctaw carved spoon, above, is crafted from the horn of a bull. Many among the Five Civilized Tribes turned their attention to cattle ranching after their arrival in Indian Territory.

Georgia, the Carolinas, and Alabama. Of the approximately 15,000 people who were assembled to begin the journey in 1838, more than 4,000 died, either in concentration camps before departure or on the muddy, disease-infected 1,000-mile march that became known in Cherokee lore as Nunahi-Duna-Dlo-Hili-I—"Trail Where They Cried"—or, more familiarly, the Trail of Tears.

Once in their new land, the five tribes were faced with tornadoes, deadly outbreaks of cholera, and many other hardships, but they rebounded from the traumatic resettlement process with remarkable resilience. By 1848 the Choctaw and Chickasaw had, with the help of African-American slave labor, built immense plantations and successfully launched a newspaper printed partly in their native language and partly in English. The Creek pro-

CHEROKEE VILLAGE
The reconstructed dwellings at Tsa-La-Gi Ancient Village, above, present an authentic picture of life in a Cherokee village immediately before the arrival of the white man.

LAKESHORE VIEW
With 130 miles of rocky shoreline, Tenkiller Lake, left, in the heart of the old Cherokee Nation, is one of eastern Oklahoma's most popular recreational lakes. It was created when the waters of the Illinois River were impounded by the construction of a dam.

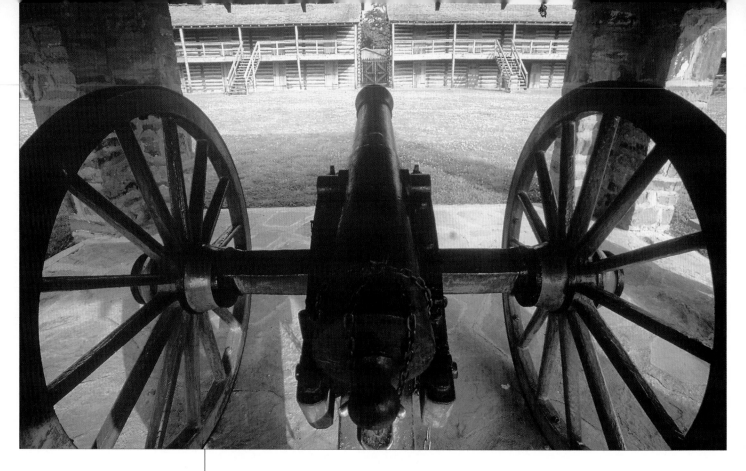

duced bountiful crops of corn and raised herds of livestock, selling the surplus as far away as the West Coast. The Cherokee established an advanced school system, including two seminaries, that was superior to the educational systems of neighboring white settlements. More than a few shrines of that renaissance have survived.

MEN OF LEARNING

The two-story Creek Council House has been restored in downtown Okmulgee on the site where it was originally built in 1878. The building and grounds are listed on the National Register of Historic Places. Here a museum showcases clothing, jewelry, and baskets made by the Creek. In Muskogee the Five Civilized Tribes Museum is housed in the old Union Indian Agency headquarters. Constructed about 1875, the white-columned, two-story sandstone edifice is located at the edge of Honor Heights Park, which explodes each spring with millions of azaleas, tulips, and roses. In its lifetime, the building has served as an orphanage for the children of freedmen, a dance hall, tea room, American Legion office, and veterans' hospital. It is now a repository for the archives and art collection of the Southeastern tribes, as well as for costumes, letters, manuscripts, photographs, carvings, and memorabilia. Also on display are a number of evocative wood carvings by Willard Stone, a Cherokee who, until his death in 1985, was widely considered the greatest Native American sculptor of his time.

Deep in the Cookson Hills, a short drive from Muskogee, the modern-day town of Tahlequah represented the end of the Trail of Tears for the Cherokee. It was here that the tribe, under the astute leadership of John Ross, re-established themselves by setting up a government and publishing a newspaper called the *Cherokee Advocate*. The town still remains the center of tribal culture and government. The Cherokee Supreme Court Building, erected in 1845, is the oldest government building in Oklahoma. It stands across a small square from the Cherokee Capitol Building, which was completed in 1870. The sandstone tribal prison, built in 1874, is now a library. The centerpiece of the Northeastern State University campus is an imposing three-story red-stone building that was erected in 1889 to house the Cherokee National Female Seminary.

Numbering more than 160,000, the Cherokee are the nation's second-largest Native tribe. Their affairs are administered from a modern government complex just south of Tahlequah. But the soul of their tribal history resides at the Cherokee Heritage Center (Tsa-La-Gi), a complex that sprawls over 40 wooded acres near the Illinois River. The center includes a museum, a reconstructed village, an arboretum, and an herb garden. The museum, completed in 1975, is based on the design of a Cherokee longhouse. Its centerpiece is the Ancient Village, a re-created 16th-century Cherokee settlement, where Native Americans demonstrate traditional ways of making pottery, baskets, arrowheads, beadwork, and other handicrafts. Located nearby is Adams Rural Village, a reconstructed frontier town of the 1890's, complete with a general store, school, log church, and two houses. An outdoor amphitheater hosts the *Trail Of Tears* drama nightly in summer. A large wooden statue of Sequoyah, the unschooled silversmith who devised the 86-character Cherokee syllabary in 1820, dominates the interior of the amphitheater. Sequoyah's legacy represents the only alphabet in human history to have been written by one man.

Other figures revered by the Cherokee can be found at the Cherokee National Museum, located adjacent to the theater. The monuments that ring a stone-paved patio pay tribute to men of wisdom and learning. Among them are Robert Latham Owen, a lawyer, financier, and U.S. senator who co-authored the Federal Reserve Act and established the first bank in Oklahoma; Elias Boudinot, editor of the *Cherokee Phoenix* from 1828 to 1832; John Ross, the great chief who guided the tribe through its removal to Indian Territory and subsequent recovery; and Joseph James Clark, who rose to the rank of admiral in the U.S. Navy.

MONUMENTS TO SURVIVAL

Following the Civil War, Indian Territory was cut in half, perhaps in part as punishment for the Southeastern tribes' support of the Confederacy during the conflict. All of the tribes were slaveholders, and a Cherokee brigadier general named Stand Waite was the last Confederate officer to surrender his command—the Cherokee, Creek, Seminole, and Osage Battalion—in a ceremony that took place near Fort Towson on June 23, 1865. But tribal government structures, legal systems, schools, newspapers, and churches continued to be influential long after Oklahoma became a state. As lawmaking entities, however, the tribal governments' powers were severely restricted.

Memories of the beginnings of Indian Territory are to be found throughout the region. On the site of present-day Salina, located on the Grand River, Maj. Jean Pierre Chouteau established a trading post that grew into the first white settlement in Indian Territory. Chouteau convinced 3,000 Osage to relocate here in 1802. Fort Gibson was established in 1824 near the junction of the Grand, Verdigris, and Arkansas rivers, known as the Three

SEAT OF GOVERNMENT
When the Choctaw Nation moved its capital to Tuskahoma in 1884, the tribe built a brick council house, below, in the fashionable Second Empire style. The building served as the center of tribal affairs until 1907. Today it houses the Choctaw National Historical Museum.

Forks. Oklahoma's first military post, Fort Gibson was established to facilitate the relocation of the Southeastern tribes and keep peace in the new territory. Sequoyah's restored log cabin is located near the town of Sallisaw. His hand-forged farming tools are on display inside the log cabin. The Choctaw Council House Historical Museum outside Tuskahoma served as the first political capital of the Choctaw.

Today the tribes have been largely assimilated into contemporary society. Yet it is said that deep in the hills are thousands of full-bloods who still speak their native languages and practice their time-honored customs, as though they—like the land—will continue on through the ages.

MIGHTIER THAN THE SWORD
With quill pen poised, a bronze statue of Sequoyah, left, captures the creative fever that compelled the Cherokee silversmith to create an alphabet for his people. The statue stands on the grounds of Sequoyah's Home Site, outside Sallisaw, where Sequoyah built a log home in 1829.

Nearby Sites & Attractions

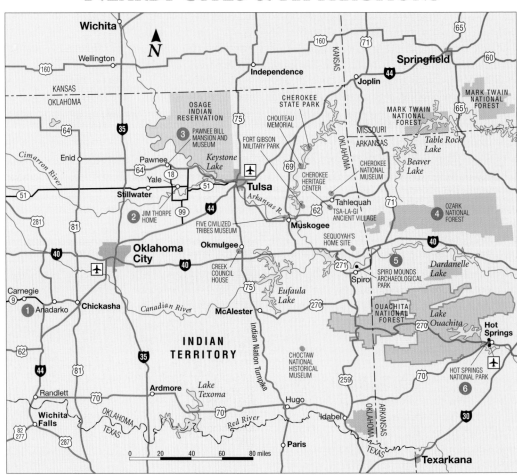

A stained-glass window at Indian City, U.S.A., above, provides a striking tribute to the tribes of the Great Plains.

① ANADARKO, OKLAHOMA

The southwestern Oklahoma town of Anadarko is a major center of Native American culture. Indian City, U.S.A. is a 200-acre outdoor museum that features authentic reconstructions of Navajo, Wichita, Caddo, Kiowa, Chiricahua Apache, and Pueblo villages in beautiful natural surroundings. Tribal members relate how their ancestors lived prior to the arrival of the white man. Visitors can also see their tools, cradles, cooking utensils, weapons, and musical instruments. A herd of buffalo roams on an adjoining 140 acres of land. At Anadarko's National Hall of Fame for Famous American Indians, bronze sculptures immortalize the achievements of famous Indians, including Sauk chief Black Hawk; Sacajawea, the Shoshone woman who guided Lewis and Clark; Sequoyah, the inventor of the Cherokee alphabet; Sioux chief Sitting Bull; and Massassoit, the Wampanoag chief who negotiated a peace treaty with the Pilgrims of Plymouth Colony in 1621. Also located in Anadarko, the Southern Plains Indian Museum showcases the works of Native American artists and craftsmen from across the nation. A permanent exhibition gallery presents the historic arts of the Native peoples of Oklahoma, as well as traditional costumes of the Southern Plains Indians. Located 56 miles southwest of Oklahoma City, at the junction of Hwys. 62 and 281.

② JIM THORPE HOME, OKLAHOMA

Once called the world's greatest athlete, Jim Thorpe was born in 1887 on Sauk and Fox tribal lands near Prague, Oklahoma. While Thorpe was attending the Carlisle Institute, an Indian school in Pennsylvania, his athletic prowess caught the attention of the school coach, Glenn Warner. Coached by Warner, Thorpe won both the decathlon and pentathlon at the 1912 Olympic Games in Stockholm, Sweden—the only athlete in history to have achieved this feat. Thorpe was forced to return his medals when it was revealed that he had played two seasons of semipro-fessional baseball. (His records were reinstated in 1983.) In 1917 he purchased a small home in Yale, where he lived with his wife until 1923. Now owned by the Oklahoma Historical Society, the modest two-bedroom bungalow contains some of the Thorpes' original furniture. Visitors can see the 27 track and field awards won by Thorpe during his days at the Carlisle Institute, as well as other memorabilia from the athlete's life. Located at 706 East Boston in Yale.

③ PAWNEE BILL MANSION AND MUSEUM, OKLAHOMA

Fascinated by the West since childhood, Gordon W. Lillie—better known as Pawnee Bill—came to Indian Territory in 1875 and became a teacher among the

5 SPIRO MOUNDS ARCHAEOLOGICAL PARK, OKLAHOMA

The 140-acre site encompasses 12 mounds—one burial mound, nine house mounds, and two platform mounds—yielding evidence of a local Indian culture that flourished in the region from A.D. 600 to A.D. 1450. Many of the artifacts unearthed here resemble items found at Moundville, Alabama, and Etowah, Georgia. Beautifully crafted items found buried with the wealthy include engraved conch shells. Only the elite lived at the site, but an extensive city of 7,500 to 10,000 inhabitants surrounded the mounds. It is thought that the demise of Spiro began about A.D. 1300, during a period of severe drought. By about A.D. 1450, its inhabitants probably moved westward in search of more arable lands. Two walking trails take visitors through the mound complex. Located 7 miles northeast of Spiro off Hwy. 271.

6 HOT SPRINGS NATIONAL PARK, ARKANSAS

Fed by 47 hot springs, the waters of this national park have been renowned for their therapeutic properties since the days when Native American hunters designated the area as sacred ground. Legend held that the Great Spirit resided in the waters, and the rising steam was his breath. In fact, the steam is created when rainwater seeps through cracks in the bedrock and is heated by the earth's internal furnace. The mineral-rich water then rises back to the surface through faults in the sandstone. When it reaches the surface, the average temperature of the water is 143°F. During the early 1900's, the town of Hot Springs became a fashionable resort, and several grand bathhouses were built along the town's Central Avenue. Today only one of these is still operational. One of the most elegant—a 77-room bathhouse containing 22 rooms with period furnishings—now serves as the park's visitor center. There are 26 miles of nature trails and a promenade that enables visitors to glimpse some of the region's geological and botanical features. Located in Hot Springs on Hwy. 7.

Flowering dogwood, left, lends a delicate touch of spring to Ozark National Forest.

No longer open to the public, the Ozark is one of many bathhouses and hotels that grace Central Avenue—better known as Bathhouse Row—in the western Arkansas spa town of Hot Springs.

Pawnee. He later joined Buffalo Bill's Wild West Show before starting his own. Eventually the two productions combined and toured the world as "The Two Bills' Show." Visitors may tour the entertainer's 1910 mansion, as well as the log cabin in which he previously lived. There is also a blacksmith shop, a goldfish pond, an Indian flower shrine, and a three-story barn in which Pawnee Bill housed his herd of Scottish shorthorn cattle. A large billboard on display in the barn depicts many acts from the Wild West show. Horrified at the slaughter of the buffalo, Pawnee Bill became the champion of these great beasts and once owned one of the largest private buffalo herds in the world. Visitors can drive through an on-site pasture and see buffalo, elk, and longhorns grazing. Located west of Pawnee on Hwy. 64.

4 OZARK NATIONAL FOREST, ARKANSAS

One of Arkansas' premier recreation areas, Ozark National Forest covers more than 1 million acres, mostly in the Ozark Mountains. Hardwood trees occupy 65 percent of the total area, with oak and hickory predominating. The forest offers some of the state's most scenic drives, as well as camping, canoeing, and kayaking. Together with the neighboring St. Francis National Forest, Ozark National Forest contains 200 miles of hiking trails, including a portion of the 160-mile Ozark Highlands Trail. At Alum Cove Natural Bridge Recreation Area, a one-mile nature trail guides visitors to a spectacular 120-foot-long natural arch. The Sylamore Ranger District includes Blanchard Springs Caverns, one of the nation's most spectacular cave systems. In summer visitors can tour this natural wonder. Near Mount Magazine—the highest point in Arkansas—Cove Lake offers camping, swimming, fishing, and boating. Located in northwestern Arkansas off Hwy 40.

MESA VERDE

The sandstone canyons of south-western Colorado open up the lost world of the ancient Anasazi.

The clean, fresh scent of piñon and sagebrush fills the air. Fat lizards dart under rocks. Towering rain clouds darken the blue sky of late summer as two glossy black ravens rise up from the cliffs. Below them, nestled perfectly into the glorious sweep of a sandstone alcove, stands an elegant stone dwelling.

In every part of the wondrous Four Corners region of the Southwest can be found the homes of the Ancestral Pueblos—better known as the Anasazi—a prehistoric people who also inhaled the intoxicating perfume of dampened sagebrush and greeted summer clouds with joy for the rains they bestowed.

On the northern frontier of their homeland in southwestern Colorado stands the high green tableland called Mesa Verde, which soars 2,000 feet above the Montezuma Valley. In most of the fingerlike canyons that incise the mesa are stone dwellings that are among the most stunning examples of prehistoric architecture in the world.

Among some 600 cliff dwellings that have been recorded in Mesa Verde National Park are Cliff Palace, Spruce Tree House, Long House, Balcony

WALL PAINTINGS

Well-preserved painted designs incorporating geometric patterns, right, adorn the interior walls of Cliff Palace's four-story section.

COLORFUL CORNUCOPIA

Originally domesticated in Mexico from a tropical grass, corn—such as the varieties seen below—was a vital crop for Mesa Verde farmers, as it is still for Pueblo Indians. Ancestral Pueblo farmers developed strains that would mature in the region's 155-day growing season.

TWILIGHT PALACE

Overleaf: Cliff Palace still retains all of the grandeur and mystery beheld by two ranchers named Richard Wetherill and Charlie Mason, who discovered it in December 1888.

House, and Step House, to name only a few. The dwellings fit organically into the natural contours of the caves that blend harmoniously with the glowing tan sandstone cliffs. The ancient homes are vacant and silent now: no longer do children play along the edges of the cliffs nor women hum as they grind corn. Neither do men prepare for the deer hunt, nor elders tell stories by winter firelight. Yet the homes of the Ancestral Pueblos, in Mesa Verde National Park and throughout the Four Corners region, have yielded exquisite ceramics, woven textiles, tools, and ceremonial sites that reveal much about this mysterious ancient culture.

As awe-inspiring and romantic as the ruins of Mesa Verde appear today, a trip down into them quickly confirms that their inhabitants enjoyed few creature comforts. Using blocks of buff- and cream-colored sandstone, the Ancestral Pueblos laid up walls, chinked them with mud and stones, and supported them with wooden beams, many of which can still be seen. Just like modern visitors, the Mesa Verdeans probably also had to stoop to pass through the T-shaped doorways to their homes. Inside was a hearth in the middle of the floor and the ubiquitous *metates*—rock troughs where corn was worked into meal by hand. Interior walls, in places blackened by soot, provide evidence that fires were likely kept burning day and night during the winter months. This small living space also served as a bedroom, with nothing more than a woven juniper mat or soft turkey feather blanket spread on the stone or mud floor.

When the weather was good, many day-to-day activities could be carried out on the rooftops, plazas, and courtyards: smoothing moist coils of clay on a new water jar, stringing squash to dry in the summer sun, or tanning a hide. In their spare time, the Ancestral Pueblos outlined their hand-prints in red ocher on the sandstone walls, as if they knew that someday someone would come to search for signs of human existence here.

SEASONAL HARVESTERS To the Mesa Verdeans, the world must have appeared exceedingly vertical. From their canyon homes, they climbed up to fields on the mesa using wooden ladders and hand- and toeholds carefully chipped into the cliff walls. In spring they went down into the canyon bottoms to gather fresh greens, and in autumn they went back up to the mesas to harvest edible piñon nuts and acorns.

By about A.D. 500, the Ancestral Pueblos had turned their attention to agriculture. In Mesa Verde and throughout the northern San Juan country, they began to coax corn, beans, and squash from land that receives only about 18 inches of precipitation each year.

Mesa Verde farmers sited their fields at the mouths of gullies, on terraces, and on mesas. To

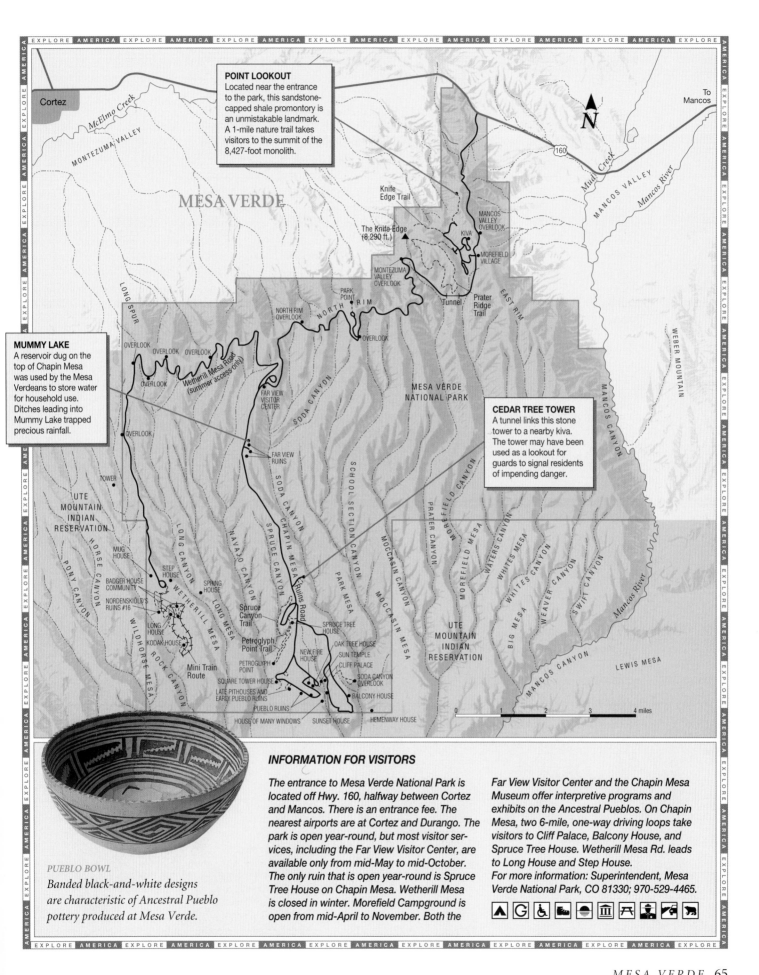

Cortez

To Mancos

MESA VERDE

McElmo Creek

MONTEZUMA VALLEY

Mud Creek

Mancos Creek

MANCOS VALLEY

Mancos River

POINT LOOKOUT
Located near the entrance to the park, this sandstone-capped shale promontory is an unmistakable landmark. A 1-mile nature trail takes visitors to the summit of the 8,427-foot monolith.

Knife Edge Trail

The Knife Edge (8,290 ft.)

KIVA

MANCOS VALLEY OVERLOOK

MOREFIELD VILLAGE

MONTEZUMA VALLEY OVERLOOK

PARK POINT

NORTH RIM

Tunnel

Prater Ridge Trail

EAST RIM

LONG SPUR

NORTH RIM OVERLOOK

OVERLOOK

MUMMY LAKE
A reservoir dug on the top of Chapin Mesa was used by the Mesa Verdeans to store water for household use. Ditches leading into Mummy Lake trapped precious rainfall.

OVERLOOK OVERLOOK OVERLOOK

OVERLOOK

Wetherill Mesa Road (summer access only)

FAR VIEW VISITOR CENTER

SODA CANYON

MESA VERDE NATIONAL PARK

WEBER MOUNTAIN

MANCOS CANYON

CEDAR TREE TOWER
A tunnel links this stone tower to a nearby kiva. The tower may have been used as a lookout for guards to signal residents of impending danger.

OVERLOOK

FAR VIEW RUINS

SODA CANYON

CHAPIN MESA

SCHOOL SECTION CANYON

MOREFIELD CANYON

PRATER CANYON

MOREFIELD MESA

WATERS CANYON

WHITES MESA

TOWER

UTE MOUNTAIN INDIAN RESERVATION

HORSE CANYON

PONY CANYON

MUG HOUSE

LONG CANYON

WETHERILL MESA

NAVAJO CANYON

LONG MESA

SPRUCE CANYON

Ruins Road

PARK MESA

MOCCASIN CANYON

MOCCASIN MESA

WHITES CANYON

BIG MESA

WEAVER CANYON

SWIFT CANYON

Mancos River

STEP HOUSE

BADGER HOUSE COMMUNITY

NORDENSKIOLD'S RUINS #16

SPRING HOUSE

LONG HOUSE

KODAK HOUSE

WILDHORSE ROCK CANYON

Mini Train Route

Spruce Canyon Trail

Petroglyph Point Trail

PETROGLYPH POINT

NEW FIRE HOUSE

SPRUCE TREE HOUSE

OAK TREE HOUSE

SUN TEMPLE

CLIFF PALACE

UTE MOUNTAIN INDIAN RESERVATION

LEWIS MESA

SQUARE TOWER HOUSE

LATE PITHOUSES AND EARLY PUEBLO RUINS

PUEBLO RUINS

HOUSE OF MANY WINDOWS

SUNSET HOUSE

SODA CANYON OVERLOOK

BALCONY HOUSE

HEMENWAY HOUSE

0   1   2   3   4 miles

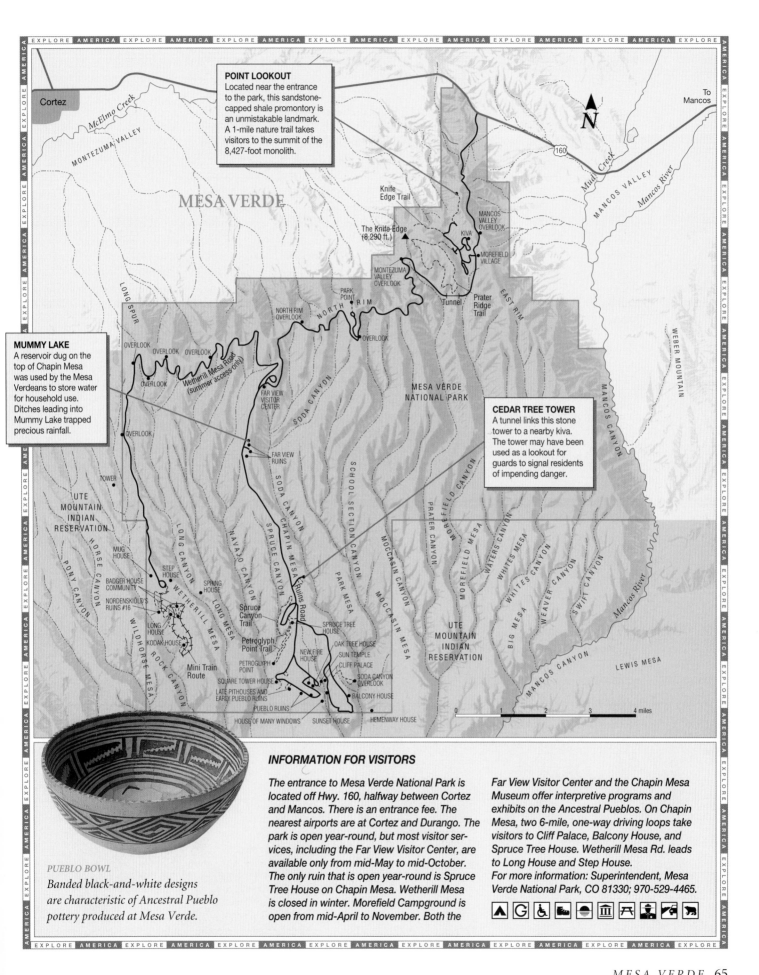

PUEBLO BOWL
Banded black-and-white designs are characteristic of Ancestral Pueblo pottery produced at Mesa Verde.

INFORMATION FOR VISITORS

The entrance to Mesa Verde National Park is located off Hwy. 160, halfway between Cortez and Mancos. There is an entrance fee. The nearest airports are at Cortez and Durango. The park is open year-round, but most visitor services, including the Far View Visitor Center, are available only from mid-May to mid-October. The only ruin that is open year-round is Spruce Tree House on Chapin Mesa. Wetherill Mesa is closed in winter. Morefield Campground is open from mid-April to November. Both the Far View Visitor Center and the Chapin Mesa Museum offer interpretive programs and exhibits on the Ancestral Pueblos. On Chapin Mesa, two 6-mile, one-way driving loops take visitors to Cliff Palace, Balcony House, and Spruce Tree House. Wetherill Mesa Rd. leads to Long House and Step House.

For more information: Superintendent, Mesa Verde National Park, CO 81330; 970-529-4465.

nudge nature, they constructed dams on nearly every small drainage to harness moisture, which they used to irrigate their fields. Mummy Lake and a large structure at Far View both suggest that the Mesa Verdeans even constructed reservoirs to ensure a steady supply of water.

Much of the land was cleared for farming. The primary crop that they raised was corn. Seeds of corn had gradually passed northward from Mexico—where the plant was first domesticated from a tropical grass—until a strain arrived that could mature in the 155-day growing season on the frontier north of the San Juan River.

The agricultural life demanded that the Ancestral Pueblos stay home in order to produce enough food to fill empty stomachs through long, bitter winters. Nearly every cliff dwelling at Mesa Verde had an upper row of rooms where grain was stored. Stone slabs secured the openings of these granaries to keep out raiding rodents. The ever-present possibility of crop failure through drought, freeze, or pestilence could mean devastation for the entire community. Thus, both population and prosperity ebbed and flowed in direct relationship to the fortunes of crops.

DISCOVERY AND EXPLORATION

It was nearly five centuries after the mysterious disappearance of the Mesa Verdeans before Europeans even came close to the site. In 1776, on a difficult journey from Santa Fe, two Spanish Franciscan priests named Francisco Atanasia Domínguez and Silvestre Vélez de Escalante camped near the mesa but did not enter the canyons, where the prehistoric ruins lay. Almost a century later, in 1874 a miner named John Moss led government photographer William Henry Jackson up the mesa. Jackson photographed what is now called Two-Story House, providing the first documentation of a Mesa Verde site.

In the 1870's silver was discovered in the nearby San Juan Mountains. Many people flocked to the region, eager to strike it rich. Among them were

TIMELESS TOWER
Built into a rock overhang, the four-story stone tower at Square Tower House, below, is the tallest structure at Mesa Verde. The tower was part of an apartment complex totaling 80 rooms.

Benjamin Wetherill and his family. Although Wetherill did not not make a fortune from silver, he and his family found treasures of another kind. It was they who put Mesa Verde on the map.

The Wetherills homesteaded the Alamo Ranch along the Mancos River, just under the bulwark of Mesa Verde. They were on good terms with the local Ute Indians, who told them tales of houses built in the shelter of cliffs in the area. In winter they ran their cattle on pastures by the river. Tracking strays up a canyon during a snowstorm in December 1888, Benjamin Wetherill's eldest son, Richard, together with his brother-in-law, Charlie Mason, caught sight of a stone dwelling in a fine state of preservation. Richard named it Cliff Palace, now known to be the largest cliff dwelling in Mesa Verde, with 217 rooms.

In *The Professor's House,* author Willa Cather fashions the novel's main character, Tom Outland, after Richard Wetherill. As Outland describes his discovery: "It was more like sculpture than anything else. I knew at once that I had come upon

the city of some extinct civilization, hidden away in this inaccessible mesa for centuries, preserved in the dry air and almost perpetual sunlight . . . guarded by the cliffs and the river and the desert."

The Wetherills and Mason soon located nearby Spruce Tree House and Square Tower House, which fired their imaginations. They spent as much time as possible exploring Mesa Verde, uncovering its cliff dwellings in a rush of discovery. They scrambled up the cliffs, probably with the aid of the same hand- and toeholds that the Ancestral Pueblos had pecked into the rock. Once in the ruins, they plunged their shovels into the dusty floors and trash middens, removing pots, arrowpoints, and yucca cords untouched by human hands for almost six centuries. Eager to share their discovery with the rest of the world, the Wetherills took visitors and reporters through the ruins and sold many of the precious artifacts that they had

found. They also assembled a collection of pottery, baskets, and other objects found at the ruins and toured the country. From public exhibits of the "curiosities" and "relics" that they had gathered, word spread quickly about the treasures that lay hidden in Mesa Verde.

In 1891 the Wetherills guided young Gustaf Nordenskiold into Mesa Verde. So captivated was the Swedish scholar that he decided to investigate further. He dug in the dwellings, photographed them, and collected innumerable artifacts, which he promptly shipped back to Sweden. His collections eventually ended up in the National Museum in Helsinki, Finland, where they reside to this day. In the remaining three years of his life, Nordenskiold published *The Cliff Dwellers of Mesa Verde,* the first major record of archeological work in the United States. Concerned citizens, meanwhile, were busy forming groups to preserve the ruins for future

SPRUCE TREE HOUSE
A T-shaped doorway at Spruce Tree House, above, reveals the reconstructed roof of a kiva, with a ladder protruding from the entrance. These doorways are common to Ancestral Pueblo cliff dwellings, although archeologists do not fully understand their significance. The gopher snake, left, makes its home in the scrub vegetation of the surrounding canyons.

generations. These initial efforts were spearheaded by *New York Graphic* reporter Virginia Donaghe McClurg and Washington socialite Lucy Peabody. These public-spirited women worked closely with the Ute, on whose tribal lands the cliff dwellings lay. Their efforts were successful: on June 29, 1906, Pres. Theodore Roosevelt signed a bill that designated Mesa Verde as a national park.

Today Mesa Verde is one of the jewels of the national park system, as well as being the only national park created specifically to preserve man-made sites. Yet it only tells the story of the final days of the Ancestral Pueblos.

THE FIRST PEOPLE

The first Ancestral Pueblos, known as the Basketmakers, dug simple but snug homes in the ground called pithouses. They walled and roofed these dwellings with poles, brush, and mud. At Mesa Verde the earliest pithouses were built in the alcoves and date to about A.D. 450. Later pithouses were located on the mesa among the piñon and juniper woodland. Along the Ruins Road in the park, visitors can view a number of pithouses that have been excavated.

The Ancestral Pueblos hunted deer and elk and gathered plants such as beeweed, cattail, prickly pear, and goosefoot. They propelled their hunting spears with an extension called an atlatl, and killed rabbits with wooden throwing sticks before they acquired the bow and arrow. In their beautifully woven yucca baskets, they parched piñon nuts and winnowed grass seeds.

Some baskets were waterproofed with pine pitch so that a woman could carry water back home from a spring. Turkeys were domesticated, and from

their downy feathers the Ancestral Pueblos made footwear and warm blankets.

Pottery was a major innovation. The first pieces were plain gray utensils intended for cooking and storage, sometimes with corrugations pinched in the clay. The people of Mesa Verde later were to achieve a peak of artistic expression with exquisite black-and-white geometric patterns that adorned their mugs, bowls, jars, and ladles.

Pithouse communities grew into homesteads, homesteads into hamlets, and hamlets into villages as the Ancestral Pueblos made a notable transition to the aboveground dwellings that the Spanish dubbed pueblos. The earliest were single-story adjoining rooms that curved around a pithouse. Pithouses evolved into kivas—places of religious significance where the entire village gathered for dances and ceremonies. Mesa Verde kivas have a keyhole shape, and some of the largest cliff dwellings boast a dozen or more of them.

At Mesa Verde and other Ancestral Pueblo communities, some very large kivas were also built. These "great kivas" may have served as gathering places for people from many surrounding villages for especially significant ceremonies. They might have functioned as trade centers as well, where the Mesa Verdeans swapped their own products for cotton, turquoise, and shells from Chaco Canyon to the south, or for items from communities as far west as the Grand Canyon in Arizona and the Virgin River drainage of eastern Nevada

Pueblos grew larger and more elaborate, rising to three or even four stories, with straight walls of finely worked masonry. At Mesa Verde and Hovenweep National Monument, as well as throughout the northern Four Corners region, the pueblos frequently included tall stone towers. These were perhaps used as observatories, where a chief

FAR VIEW

From the edge of the 40-room Far View House on Chapin Mesa, opposite page, the sweeping view takes in Navajo Canyon's East Fork and neighboring mesas. The vegetation that cloaks the area's canyons and mesas gave rise to the name Mesa Verde, which means "green table" in Spanish. Snow bedecks an enigmatic petroglyph, left, carved in stone at Far View House.

WILY COYOTE

Visitors to Mesa Verde National Park often catch sight of coyotes, such as the one at left, which emerge from the piñon and juniper forest in search of mice and rabbits.

Nestled in a rock shelter on Wetherill Mesa, right, Mug House takes its name from a group of pottery vessels tied together with string that was found here. A kiva is visible in the foreground. In addition to mugs, the group that lived at Mug House made narrow-necked jars, bowls, and ladles.

BASKETMAKER'S BOWER

A reconstructed pithouse in Step House, above, offers visitors a glimpse of life during the Basketmaker period. The timber frame was covered by a layer of mud-sheathed branches.

might watch the sun and moon to establish the proper time for planting and religious ceremonies.

Seventy miles to the south of Mesa Verde, Chaco Canyon in northern New Mexico was a major center for the Ancestral Pueblos. Even though these people never possessed the wheel, a complex road system radiates from Chaco. Pilgrims may have walked along these highways to reach this mecca. Even today, a visit to Chaco Canyon—formally known as Chaco Culture National Historical Park—is akin to a pilgrimage, a chance to marvel at the astonishing architecture of "great houses" such as Pueblo Bonito and Chetro Ketl.

The cosmopolitan Chacoans enjoyed a gilded age earlier than did their neighbors to the north. The golden years of Chaco lasted from A.D. 1000 until about A.D. 1140 to A.D. 1150. During that time, this planned community established an elaborate trading and communication network. Multistory houses, each with its own great kiva, were built just before and during this period. The houses were made of blocks of sandstone covered with a thin sandstone veneer. Archeologists estimate that more than 1 million stone blocks were required to build Pueblo Bonito. An elite class may have developed, sustained by the food brought in by farmers from the hinterland. By A.D. 1150, however, Chaco Canyon seems to have lost its preeminent position as a center of religious and commercial activity. No one knows exactly why, although a 50-year drought that began in A.D. 1130 may have been partially responsible.

This idea of retreat, perhaps from invading newcomers, is still offered as an explanation for the withdrawal of the people of Mesa Verde to the alcoves. But scant evidence exists of any warfare at the time. Crowding and depleted resources may have been the deciding factors that drove the people away. What is known for certain is that from A.D. 1275 to A.D. 1300 a prolonged and extensive drought struck the region.

By A.D. 1300 the Ancestral Pueblos were gone from Mesa Verde and the Four Corners region. They headed south and east, ending up at the Hopi mesas in northern Arizona and the pueblos of Zuni, the upper Rio Grande, and other sites in northern New Mexico, where their descendants live to this day. The Hopi do not use the term *Anasazi*, which was coined by archeologists after a Navajo word that means "enemy ancestors." Instead they call their ancestors *hisatsinom* ("the old ones") and express their own ideas about why these people abandoned the Four Corners region: they moved simply because it was time. Prophecies had told them that life had gotten too good, that they had become selfish and thus must leave.

And so today the descendants of the Ancestral Pueblos live on in other lands, still praying to the same sky and the same sun, asking for rain for their corn, for health, and for happiness.

GNARLED NATIVE
The juniper tree, below, thrives throughout Mesa Verde and the Four Corners region. Juniper berries are still used as a tangy flavoring. The tree's shaggy bark was once used to make diapers for Ancestral Pueblo infants.

THE PEOPLE DEPART

For the people of Mesa Verde and their northern San Juan neighbors, the century from A.D. 1000 to A.D. 1100 was a time of maximum precipitation. These must have been halcyon days. In the early 1200's, however, something changed. Most of the Anasazi of Mesa Verde moved en masse to the alcoves beneath the mesas, hidden deep in the heads of the canyons.

One such site from this period was Mug House, one of the most remarkable ruins discovered by Charlie Mason and the Wetherills. "It appeared," wrote Mason, "as though the people had been frightened away with no opportunity to carry anything with them. All seemed to have been left just where it had been used last."

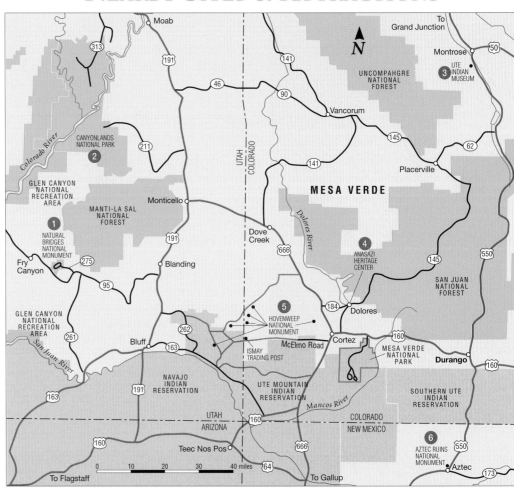

The reconstructed Great Kiva at Aztec Ruins National Monument, above, displays the remarkable engineering skills of the Ancestral Pueblo people.

1 NATURAL BRIDGES NATIONAL MONUMENT, UTAH

In the deep, twisting canyons that carve through this 7,600-acre, high-desert park are three of the world's largest natural bridges. Each of the yellow sandstone bridges represents a different stage in the erosion process—principally carved by running water—that began here some 260 million years ago. The mature, 53-foot-thick Sipapu Bridge spans 268 feet of White Canyon at a height of 220 feet. Also in White Canyon is the youthful Kachina Bridge, 93 feet thick and 204 feet long, named for the ghost dancers depicted in the Hopi rock paintings that adorn it. Armstrong Canyon's 106-foot-high Owachomo Bridge, the oldest span, stretches 180 feet and is just 9 feet thick. Walking trails that link the three bridges pass Ancestral Pueblo cliff dwellings and ruins. Located on Hwy. 275.

2 CANYONLANDS NATIONAL PARK, UTAH

Two mighty rivers meet at the heart of this sprawling, 337,570-acre wilderness of sandstone arches, cliffs, buttes, and spires. In Cataract Canyon, the Colorado River tumbles down 12 miles of rapids, making its waters among the swiftest and most powerful of any river system in the nation. The confluence of the rivers divides the park into three distinct sections. To the north is Island in the Sky, characterized by a towering mesa that overlooks the park. The Needles, an arid landscape of weathered rock formations to the southeast, is named for the predominance of its enormous white-and-red-banded pinnacles. To the west, the Maze is made up of chiseled canyons that can challenge even experienced hikers. Nearby is the Great Gallery, a collection of Native American rock art created more than 2,000 years ago. Located on Hwy. 211 or Hwy. 313, off Hwy. 191.

3 UTE INDIAN MUSEUM, COLORADO

Exhibits, dioramas, and festivals are the main features of the Ute Indian Museum. Situated on what was once the farm of the great Ute chief Ouray, the museum features a monument erected in his honor near the gravesite of his wife, Chipeta. A botanical garden showcases plants used by the Ute tribe for medicinal purposes. Artifacts on exhibit in the museum include ceremonial clothing, feather headresses, beads, and photographs, some of which date back to the 1880's. Dioramas depict crucial events in the tribe's history. September's Native Lifeways Festival allows visitors to enjoy traditional songs and dances, and to sample typical food. An outdoor exhibit commemorates the Franciscan

Anasazi rock paintings on the walls of Horseshoe Canyon in Canyonlands National Park, left, are about 2,000 years old.

priests Francisco Atanasia Domínguez and Silvestre Vélez de Escalante, who were guided by the Ute in their attempt to reach the California missions in 1776. During their journey through Colorado, the priests mapped the area and named many of its rivers, mountains, and valleys. Located 3 miles south of Montrose on Hwy. 550.

4 ANASAZI HERITAGE CENTER, COLORADO

Dedicated to the Ancestral Pueblo (or Anasazi) people, this outstanding museum is an excellent place to learn about the prehistory of the Four Corners region. A visit to the center begins with a film that illustrates the Ancestral Pueblo lifestyle and culture. On display are pottery, tools, and clothing. Other exhibits illustrate the development of the extensive Ancestral Pueblo trade network, and trace the people's evolution from hunters and gatherers to farmers and traders. Hands-on displays include computer simulations of the daily life of the Ancestral Pueblos, as well as their archeological sites. Visitors can grind corn using a mano and metate, or learn how to weave cloth on a traditional loom. A reconstructed pithouse dating to about A.D. 880 is part of a walk-through display. The site also includes a half-mile trail to the Domínguez and Escalante ruins, dwelling complexes that have been excavated and interpreted for visitors. Located 10 miles north of Cortez on Hwy. 184.

5 HOVENWEEP NATIONAL MONUMENT, COLORADO/UTAH

Straddling the Colorado/Utah border, Hovenweep's six ruins are a poignant reminder of the era when the region was a thriving agricultural community. The Ancestral Pueblo inhabitants lived here until about A.D. 1300. Archeologists speculate that climatic changes in about A.D. 1200 forced these people to abandon their valley and mesa farmlands and move to sites in the Hovenweep canyons. In the 19th century, the ruins were given the name of Hovenweep, a Ute word that means "deserted valley." These 700-year-old masonry remains are noted for their square, circular, semicircular, and oval towers. It is believed that the towers were used as lookouts and observation platforms for viewing the night sky. Much of the masonry has disappeared, but many walls remain standing—some of them 20 feet in height. A self-guided hiking trail links the ruins of the Square Tower Group, site of the monument's headquarters, which is located 43 miles west of Cortez on McElmo Rd.

6 AZTEC RUINS NATIONAL MONUMENT, NEW MEXICO

Early Anglo settlers erroneously named this site for the Aztec Indians of Mexico. In fact, the region was inhabited by the Ancestral Pueblos, who built a number of remarkable structures here between A.D. 1106 and A.D.1124. One of the most prominent of these, now known as West Ruin, is a four-story complex of 350 to 400 rooms that once housed as many as 500 people. The pueblo prospered until A.D.1200, when it may have been abandoned. In A.D.1225 residents of Mesa Verde moved here and began repairing the old structures, as well as building new ones. The Great Kiva, used for religious ceremonies, was thoroughly excavated in 1921 and restored in 1934. A trail connects the ruins, and the visitor center displays pottery and tools found on the site. Located 1.5 miles north of Aztec off Hwy. 550.

The elegant shape of a yellow sandstone bridge in Natural Bridges National Monument, below, was created by erosion. The monument contains the largest number of natural bridges in the world.

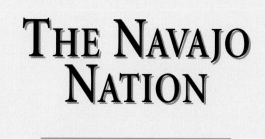

THE NAVAJO NATION

A proud people thrives amid the matchless landscape of the nation's largest reservation.

Navajo Mountain rises huge and imposing, its forested flanks climbing 10,388 feet into a cloudless summer sky. Straddling the Arizona-Utah border, it rears boldly alone on the immense landscape. Like an apparition emerging from the mist, it can easily be seen from as far away as the Hopi mesas or even the Grand Canyon, located 100 miles to the south. Thousands of serpentine pink sandstone canyons—some of them 500 feet deep—disappear at its base like folds in a swirling skirt. They conceal the remnants and ruins of vanished civilizations in their many nooks and crannies, and relate the mountain's 230-million-year geological history.

Navajo Mountain is unconnected to any range, isolated in a sea of unending pink, orange, and white slickrock domes, buttes, and cliffs. The mountain is massive enough to generate its own weather systems. Thunderheads build above it on balmy July afternoons, sending rain down through arroyos and into the Colorado and San Juan river arms of Lake Powell, the natural

FACE OF THE PEOPLE
The long history of the Navajo people appears etched on the facial features of this Navajo elder.

BRONZE BUTTES
Overleaf: A dusting of snow accents the glow of a winter sunset on the West and East Mitten buttes in Monument Valley. The valley's famed eroded buttes, spires, and mesas now lie within Navajo Monument Valley Tribal Park.

boundary of this region of the Navajo people. The Navajo Nation, or Dine' Bikeyah—the "land of the people" in the Navajo language—stretches 27,000 square miles across the states of Arizona, Utah, and New Mexico. It is a wide landscape of rocky plateaus, grassy plains, and statuesque buttes that is drenched in year-round sunshine. According to anthropologists, the Navajo still speak the language of their ancestors, an Athabascan-speaking people who migrated from northern and western Canada in approximately A.D. 1400-1500. Here everything has a sense of timelessness, from the women's traditional hair buns tied low behind the head to the tinkling of a cowbell on the lead sheep grazing with the flock on the open range.

The Navajo way of life was greatly influenced by that of the Pueblo Indians of the Southwest. From the Pueblos, the Navajo learned weaving, sand painting, and farming, and began to settle in agricultural communities. With the arrival of the Spanish in the 17th century, the Navajo acquired sheep, goats, and horses, establishing a pastoral tradition that continues to this day.

Although considered poor on a material and monetary scale, the Navajo people are among the most successful Native peoples on the continent. Although the majority of Indian tribes lost land with the westward expansion of white settlers, the land holdings of the Navajos actually increased in size, until by 1934 their territory encompassed

DINOSAUR TRACKS
A few miles west of Tuba City, footprints left in a mudflat by a dinosaur 180 million years ago are clearly visible. A short road leads off Hwy. 160 to the site.

GLEN CANYON NATIONAL RECREATION AREA

RAINBOW BRIDGE NATIONAL MONUMENT

Lake Powell

Navajo Mountain (10,388 ft.)

Page

Marble Canyon

INSCRIPTION HOUSE TRADING POST

Colorado River

Bitter Springs

NAVAJO INDIAN RESERVATION

Cedar Ridge Trading Post

Wildcat Peak (6,805 ft.)

GRAND CANYON NATIONAL PARK

PAINTED DESERT

Tuba City

Moenkopi

KAIBAB NATIONAL FOREST

Little Colorado River

PAINTED DESERT

WUPATKI NATIONAL MONUMENT

SAN FRANCISCO PEAKS

COCONINO NATIONAL FOREST

Sunrise Trading Post

Flagstaff

INFORMATION FOR VISITORS

Hwy. 40 parallels the southern boundary of the Navajo Reservation. The main north-south routes through the reservation are Hwy. 89, which runs between Flagstaff, Arizona, and Page, Arizona; and Hwy. 666, which runs between Cortez, Colorado, and Gallup, New

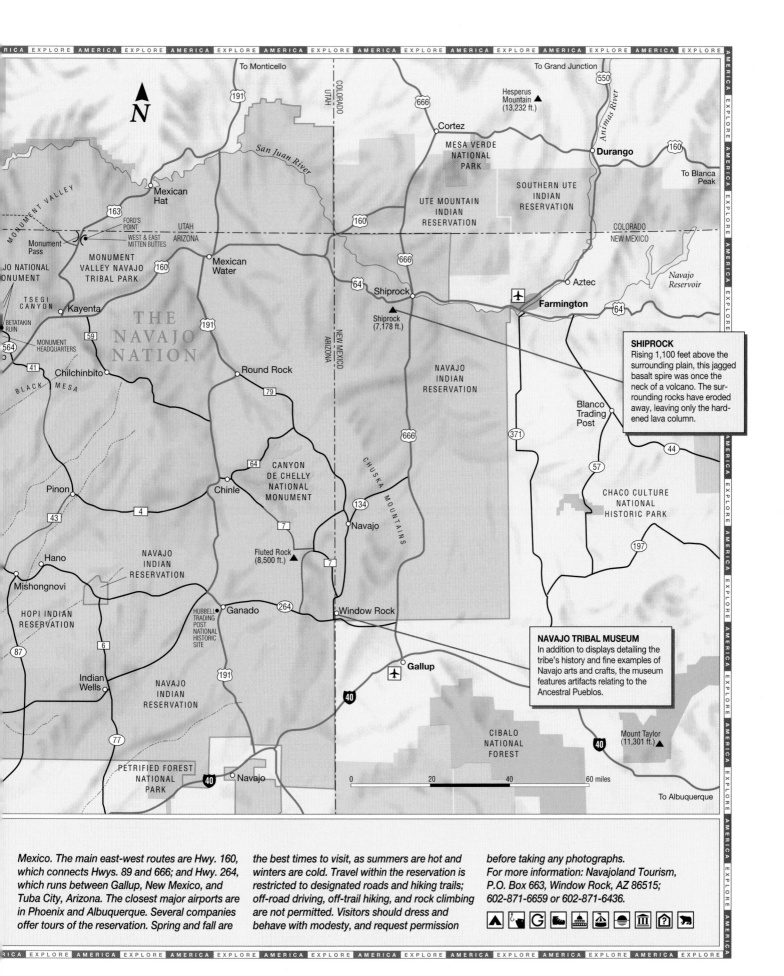

SHIPROCK
Rising 1,100 feet above the surrounding plain, this jagged basalt spire was once the neck of a volcano. The surrounding rocks have eroded away, leaving only the hardened lava column.

NAVAJO TRIBAL MUSEUM
In addition to displays detailing the tribe's history and fine examples of Navajo arts and crafts, the museum features artifacts relating to the Ancestral Pueblos.

Mexico. The main east-west routes are Hwy. 160, which connects Hwys. 89 and 666; and Hwy. 264, which runs between Gallup, New Mexico, and Tuba City, Arizona. The closest major airports are in Phoenix and Albuquerque. Several companies offer tours of the reservation. Spring and fall are the best times to visit, as summers are hot and winters are cold. Travel within the reservation is restricted to designated roads and hiking trails; off-road driving, off-trail hiking, and rock climbing are not permitted. Visitors should dress and behave with modesty, and request permission before taking any photographs.
For more information: Navajoland Tourism, P.O. Box 663, Window Rock, AZ 86515; 602-871-6659 or 602-871-6436.

The domed hogan, right, is a common sight throughout the Navajo Reservation. Made of logs coated with mud, its single entrance always faces east, the direction of the rising sun.

A STUDY IN SILVER
Navajo silversmiths are renowned for the intricacy of their creations, above, many of which incorporate pieces of turquoise into their designs. The necklace features a traditional squash-blossom motif.

almost their entire aboriginal homeland. In the past 130 years, the Navajo population has expanded from 10,000 people living in widely scattered bands to a total of some 250,000 people who can boast of the most highly developed, three-branch tribal government in the country.

Despite the pressures of the dominant society surrounding the Navajo Reservation, the Navajo Nation, like the ancient land, remains intact and little disturbed. Foreign ideas and the mass media have naturally found their way here, and many tribal members have been forced to seek employment off the reservation. But the Navajo have proved able to incorporate change into their culture and to adapt to it in their own way.

Today the mixture of the old and the new is apparent on the reservation. The Navajo still make their finely crafted jewelry and handwoven rugs as they have in the past, but have yielded to modernity in their clothing and in their vehicles. Lifelong residents affectionately observe: "You know you're on the res when you see six people in the front seat of a pickup."

FOUR SACRED MOUNTAINS

The Navajos define their homeland as the land that is bound by four sacred mountains. To the east—the most important of the four cardinal directions to the Navajo—lies Colorado's Blanca Peak, known as the White Shell Mountain. To the south near Grants, New Mexico, is Mount Taylor, or the Turquoise Mountain. To the west at Flagstaff, Arizona, are the San Francisco Peaks, known to the Navajo as the Abalone and Coral mountains. To the north, also in southern Colorado, is Hesperus Mountain, or the Black Jet Mountain. The number four has great symbolic significance for the Navajo. In their culture, there are the four directions, four seasons, first four clans, four ritual songs, and four colors—white, turquoise, yellow, and black—associated with the four sacred mountains.

These mountains also dictate the shape of the hogan—the traditional domed Navajo dwelling—that is still found throughout the reservation. For the Navajo, the hogan represents a link with their past. The old log and mud-covered hogan is less common today as a primary residence for Navajo families, but it is far from forgotten. Although Navajos have adapted their houses to modern building materials and now construct dwellings from lumber, plywood, and even concrete, their homes still have an eight-sided wooden framework with a domed roof and a doorway facing east to greet the dawn. Traditional hogans continue to be used for ceremonial and religious purposes.

At daybreak the Navajo offer their daily prayers to the Holy People, a wide pantheon of deities. Asking for strength, happiness, a good corn crop, many sheep, and all good things in life for himself and his family, a Navajo worshiper dips a thumb and forefinger into a small buckskin pouch and raises an arm in an arc overhead, sprinkling a few powdery grains of sacred corn pollen.

Although easily accessible by highway from Page, Arizona, or the reservation town of Tuba City, Navajo Mountain is located in an isolated area of the Navajo Reservation. The new pavement of the one 30-mile road ends after 15 miles, just past Inscription House Trading Post. From this point it becomes a simple byway, typical of the roads all over the reservation. Out here, Navajo continues to be the dominant language; the only daily news to make it back this far comes from the tribally owned radio station, KTNN.

One of Navajo Mountain's old, two-rut wagon roads runs through sparse stands of piñon and juniper and leads to the dozens of Navajo sheep camps hidden among the rimrocks and alcoves of this most remote region of the reservation. A sheep trail runs to the top of the rocky mesa, affording a spectacular view across the 10-mile distance to the sacred, dome-shaped mountain. Below in a sage-filled valley is the site of the annual celebration known as Navajo Mountain Pioneer Day. The 30-year-old community gathering continues to grow larger every year but holds on to the traditions of a half century ago.

Reservation old-timers congregate at Navajo Mountain Pioneer Day to relive the good old days. This is the only place where visitors will find a dozen or more Navajo cowboys galloping bareback at breakneck speed in race after race between two long rows of spectators. Grandmothers in colorful velveteen, satin, and turquoise fan out along a starting line to dash 25 yards to scoop up prizes of pots and pans at the finish line. Teenage girls grab a thick rope for a dusty tug-of-war. Winners and losers alike share rewards of soda pop.

Navajos hold social gatherings year-round, most of them connected to their religious ceremonies. Some of these include the three-day ceremony called the Nidaa, or squaw dance, which is performed in the summer, and the nine-day winter Yei Be Chei—a healing ceremony in which masked dancers make an appearance. Navajo Mountain Pioneer Day has become the unofficial start of a series of Navajo fairs and festivals that stretches on through October. The large Navajo towns, like Shiprock, Chinle, and Tuba City, all play host to old-fashioned country fairs. Here Navajo silver-and-turquoise jewelry, sand paintings, and baskets

HOME ON THE RANGE
Sheep farming is a Navajo tradition that dates back to the 17th century. The animals are a source of food, and their wool is used to make the famed Navajo rugs.

are sold from the tailgates of pickup trucks at half the trading post prices, and Pueblo Indians from Santo Domingo Pueblo in neighboring New Mexico drive over with vans full of their round, fresh-baked oven bread.

DAYS AT THE FAIR

The seasonal climax occurs in the second week of September, when the Navajo Nation Fair takes place in Window Rock, the Navajo capital city located in the southeastern corner of the reservation. Touted as the largest annual gathering of Native Americans in the world, the tribal fair draws approximately 100,000 atten-dees for each of its four days. A new Miss Navajo Nation is crowned, politicians ranging from U.S. senators to county assessors seek votes, and country-and-western stars play to adoring crowds. The fair claims to have the biggest powwow, the largest Native American rodeo, the biggest tribal parade, the biggest fry bread contest, and the most monumental traffic jams of the whole Navajo year.

Here, as in other areas far from the few highways that cross the reservation, Navajo life is little changed from generations past, with the exception of the ubiquitous pickup truck. Sheep still provide the foundation of the family livelihood. The art of weaving continues to be passed on from one gen-

CEREMONIAL FAN
The beautifully crafted red-tail hawk fan, above, is a sacred instrument used in prayer ceremonies.

CANYON CROP
Mists cloak the ancient rocks of Tsegi Canyon at daybreak. The cornfield in the background is evidence of the ability of Navajo farmers to coax crops from the arid land.

eration to the next. Wood is still used for cooking and heating, and water is still hauled from the windmill in barrels. Traditional taboos, such as marrying within one's clan, telling certain stories outside their season, or burning wood that has been struck by lightning, are strictly adhered to.

STORY OF CREATION

Something mystical resides here, too. In the Navajo language, Navajo Mountain is known as Naatsis'aan, or "It sits there protecting them from the enemy." It is also referred to as Head of Earth. In Navajo lore, the immense Black Mesa—the reservation's largest land formation—represents the body of a female figure, whose feet are the Chuska Mountains to the east of Canyon de Chelly.

It is on top of Naatsis'aan where the Hero Twins of the Navajo people—Monster Slayer and Child Born of Water—were born. In the Navajo creation story, the people had migrated through three previous worlds, each time becoming corrupted before the world was destroyed. Now they had arrived at the fourth, called the Glittering World, which was inhabited by Alien Giants. To make the world safe for the five-fingered Earth Surface People, the twins traveled on a rainbow to visit their father, the Sun, to ask him for weapons of lightning bolts to slay the monster enemies, who roamed the land killing and eating the people. Once dead, the giant bodies of these heinous monsters turned to stone, and today are seen as the mesas, plateaus, and eroded rock formations that are strewn fantastically across their homeland.

Navajo Mountain was once the homeland of the prehistoric Anasazi, who built cliff dwellings and granaries in the caves around it. Only a century ago, it was a place of last refuge for the Navajo. After the United States acquired possession of the Southwest from Mexico in 1848, intermittent warfare broke out between the Navajo and the white settlers who had begun to enter the region. In 1863 the U.S. Army decided to permanently subdue the Navajo. Under Col. Kit Carson, troops destroyed herds and burned cornfields. Some 8,000 Navajos—women, children, and the elderly—were indiscriminately rounded up and forced to march some 400 miles on the infamous Long Walk to New Mexico's arid Bosque Redondo reservation, where they endured four years of squalid resettlement. One-third died or were killed along the way; others died from homesickness and disease once they arrived. Only a few Navajo managed to escaped the disaster by taking refuge in the Grand Canyon or the land around Navajo Mountain. For that reason, each time they speak its name, they offer thanks to the mountain for its protection.

But this distant corner of the Navajo land has long been visited by friendly outsiders, because it provides the only land access to the famed Rainbow Bridge. At 270 feet in length, the sandstone arch is the largest natural bridge in the world. Both Theodore Roosevelt and Zane Grey made the overland trip here on horseback in 1913, traveling 150 miles from Flagstaff to Kayenta, and another 75 miles through the mysterious Monument Valley to the mountain.

MONUMENT VALLEY

Grey used this region for the settings of stories such as *The Rainbow Trail* and *Riders of the Purple Sage.* Arriving at Monument Valley, a place the Navajo call the "valley of standing up rock," Grey beheld sheet lightning flashing to the north. Mesmerized by the scenery, he described the landscape as "colossal shafts and buttes of rock, magnificently sculpted, standing isolated and aloof, dark, weird, lonely," in eerie silhouettes. "Dawn, with the desert sunrise, changed Monument Valley," he later wrote. "It was hard for me to realize that those monuments were not the works of man. The great valley must have been a plateau of red rock from which the softer strata

SAND PAINTING
Originally created during the traditional healing ceremonies, sand paintings are composed of fine, earth-colored pigments trickled through the artist's fingers onto a base of clean and flattened sand. The paintings most commonly depict spirit figures, animals, and plants, as shown in The Shawl Dancer, *above.*

had eroded, leaving the gentle league-long slopes marked here and there by upstanding pillars and columns of singular shape and beauty."

Perhaps the most famous landscape in the whole of the Southwest, Monument Valley's dramatic, eroded sandstone pillars and flat-topped buttes have been immortalized in such films as *Stagecoach, My Darling Clementine, The Searchers,* and *She Wore a Yellow Ribbon,* as well as countless other films and advertisements. In fact, one of the park's most scenic overlooks—Ford's Point—takes its name from film director John Ford, who favored it as a camera position.

The natural monuments within the valley bear descriptive names, such as Full Moon Arch, Hidden Bridge, Honeymoon Arch, the Three Sisters, and El Capitan—a 1,400-foot-high rock spire that is the remnant of volcanic activity. The Navajo call it A-gath-la, or "the place of the scraping of hides," because it is here that sheep are shorn. El Capitan is also the site of powwows and other celebrations. The entire valley is part of Monument Valley Navajo Tribal Park, established in 1958. Visitors can tour the valley in the company of a Navajo guide. Petroglyphs pecked into the rocks by the Ancestral Pueblos, or Anasazi, still guard their secret meanings, and pictographs—intriguing painted images of figures and designs—remain visible on rock faces today.

Following his visit to Rainbow Bridge, hidden in a canyon behind the mountain, Grey traveled up Tsegi Canyon near Kayenta to the wondrous Ancestral Pueblo towns of Betatakin and Keet Seel. Together they are known today as Navajo National Monument. With 135 rooms, Betatakin, or "ledge house," and Keet Seel, or "broken pieces of pottery," are the largest prehistoric ruins in Arizona.

Betatakin nestles in an enormous rounded cave that is visible from an overlook at the end of the half-mile Sandal Trail. To visit the ruin, visitors may take a ranger-led guided tour that follows a two-and-a-half-mile-long trail descending 700 feet into the canyon. Keet Seel's 155 rooms are in an excellent state of preservation, but in order to keep them that way no more than 20 people are allowed to tour the site each day.

Some 125 Ancestral Pueblos lived in the fertile canyon for a mere 50 years until A.D. 1300, when they mysteriously departed. Some experts believe that a great flood affecting the whole Southwest led them to abandon thousands of their settlements. Archeological evidence suggests that the depletion of local resources, accompanied by the alkalinization and erosion of the soil, probably led to their departure. But the Hopi, who claim the Ancestral Pueblos as their direct ancestors, maintain that they were simply continuing their great migrations to the Hopi mesas in accordance with their spiritual instructions.

| A LIVING MONUMENT | Today the Hopi live on three mesas, called First, Second, and Third, which comprise their own reservation, situated in the |

very center of the Navajo Reservation. Their stone pueblo homes cluster in 12 villages, most perched atop three huge cliffs on the southern escarpment of Black Mesa, or sitting in the valley below. The style of their rock homes, their clan symbols, and their pottery closely resembles that of the Ancestral Pueblos, as does much of their religious and ceremonial cycle. Many of the old Ancestral Pueblo sites continue to be used as sacred shrines by the Hopi, where offerings of eagle feathers are left during pilgrimages in the quest for rain.

Unlike the Navajo, who do not like to live in towns, the Hopi prefer town life. The village of Moenkopi, founded in the 1870's, contains tidy houses built of red stone and a central plaza where

religious ceremonies are held. On Third Mesa, the Hopi founded the town of Oraibi in the 12th century. Today it is one of the oldest continuously inhabited villages in North America.

Only 66 miles southeast of Betatakin lies another great home of the "ancient ones"—Canyon de Chelly National Monument. The first residents of the canyon built dozens of dwellings in the cliff faces of the twisting canyon. These stone houses have been well preserved by rock overhangs and by the region's dry climate. This is the only national monument in the country in which its original inhabitants continue to reside and use the land. Throughout the summer, the fertile floor of Canyon de Chelly and its branches are dotted with picturesque Navajo cornfields, peach orchards, and towering cottonwood trees, all irrigated by perennial streams. Visitors can tour the canyon by Jeep or on horseback with a Navajo guide, or travel alone along the two rim roads, gazing down from scenic overlooks.

national historic site is open free of charge year-round. Hubbell's house, which contains a large collection of early Navajo rugs, baskets, and silver jewelry, as well as examples of Southwestern art, is open to the public. At the visitor center, Navajo weavers and other Native craftspeople demonstrate their traditional arts and handicrafts.

Tucked away in the Four Corners, where Arizona, New Mexico, Utah, and Colorado meet, the largest Native American reservation in the United States is a dramatic landscape of mountain peaks, buttes and cliffs, mesas, and plateaus. During the past 600 years that the Navajos have lived here, they have adapted to change and assimilated new skills from the people they came in contact with—the Spanish, the Hopi, and the white settlers. To this day the vibrant culture and majestic beauty of this nation within a nation weave a spell on all those who choose to pass this way.

CLIFF DWELLING
Nestled at the base of a cliff, White House Ruin, opposite page, is perhaps the best-known Anasazi site in Canyon de Chelly National Monument. The structure was named for a wall of white plaster across its upper portion.

RITUAL CHEER
A young Navajo girl, left, wears brightly colored garb to a traditional celebration.

WOVEN LEGACY
The rug room at the Hubbell Trading Post National Historic Site, below, displays 100-year-old Navajo rugs, whose designs still inspire contemporary Navajo weavers.

TRADING POST

South of Chinle, 41 miles from Canyon de Chelly on Highway 264, is the town of Ganado, home of the most celebrated trading post on the Navajo Reservation. John Lawrence Hubbell bought the post in 1876, five years after it was originally constructed.

The post, now a national historic site, was built of stone, timber, and roughly cut planks. Hubbell renamed the settlement of Pueblo, Colorado, for his good friend Ganado Mucho, a tribal leader during the dark Long Walk period. Hubbell was known as Don Lorenzo to white settlers and Old Mexican or Double Glasses to the Navajos. He learned the Navajo language and established a reputation for fair trading. He taught them the ways of the white man, translated letters for them, and explained government policies. During a smallpox epidemic, Hubbell used his home as a hospital and helped care for the sick. He had had the disease as a boy and was therefore immune, but the Navajo believed that his immunity was due to a higher power.

Today the Hubbell Trading Post still serves a large Navajo clientele, which comes to procure supplies and trade excellent rugs and arts. Administered by the National Park Service, the

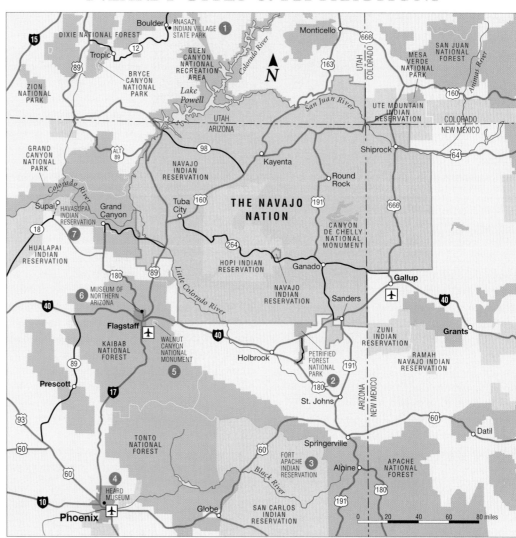

On exhibit at the Heard Museum in Phoenix, elaborately carved kachina dolls, above, have great importance in Hopi ceremonies.

① ANASAZI INDIAN VILLAGE STATE PARK

An Anasazi (Ancestral Pueblo) village flourished in this region between A.D.1050 and A.D.1200. Home to about 200 people, it was the largest such settlement west of the Colorado River. The site was first excavated in 1958–59, when a total of 87 rooms were uncovered. The park includes a museum, the excavation site, and a full-scale, six-room replica dwelling. A self-guided trail allows visitors to tour 20 excavated rooms. The museum displays stone tools and artifacts found at the site. Located in Boulder, Utah.

② PETRIFIED FOREST NATIONAL PARK

With the largest concentration of petrified trees in the world, the park preserves a remarkable slice of geological history. The petrification process began millions of years ago when volcanic ash and mud blanketed the region's forests. Silica-laden groundwater soaked into the wood, which eventually crystallized into the multicolored quartz that is visible today. The park's collection of fossils dates back to the Triassic period, some 225 million years ago, and includes the remains of many different plants, shellfish, sharks, reptiles, dinosaurs, and termites' and bees' nests. More than 600 Ancestral Pueblo archeological sites have been discovered within the park, and the 125-room Puerco Pueblo has been partially excavated and reconstructed. Nearby Newspaper Rock is one of many sites where petroglyphs have been etched onto sandstone. The northern section of the park contains spectacular views of the Painted Desert, a region of multicolored hills. The north entrance is located 26 miles east of Holbrook on Hwy. 40; the south entrance is 20 miles east of Holbrook on Hwy. 180.

③ FORT APACHE INDIAN RESERVATION

Surrounded on three sides by Apache National Forest, the reservation is the homeland of the White Mountain Apache Indians and a paradise for sportsmen. Outdoor activities include camping, hiking, kayaking, rafting, skiing, and fishing in the region's mountain streams and lakes. Kinishba Pueblo Ruins, a national historic landmark, is a partially restored

Mogollon settlement that was inhabited between A.D. 1050 and A.D. 1350. Old Fort Apache, Gen. George Crook's cabin that was built in the 1870's, once served as an army post during the savage struggle between the Apaches and the U.S. Army. The fort now houses the Apache Culture Center Museum, which offers exhibits on Apache history and culture. Located 62 miles west of Springerville on Hwy. 60.

4 HEARD MUSEUM

This internationally acclaimed museum is dedicated to the arts and culture of the Native peoples of the Southwest. The permanent collection exhibits Zuni pottery, baskets, jewelry, textiles, and a unique collection of more than 800 Hopi kachina dolls. Visitors can tour a Navajo hogan, an Apache wickiup, and a Hopi corn-grinding room. The museum also offers many hands-on activities, including weaving on a giant bead loom and building miniature tepees. Native American artists demonstrate the techniques of beadworking, weaving, sculpting, and carving. Located at 22 East Monte Vista Rd. in Phoenix.

5 WALNUT CANYON NATIONAL MONUMENT

The cliff dwellings and rim-top ruins of more than 200 Sinagua pueblos built between A.D. 1125 and A.D. 1250 are located within this 400-foot-deep horseshoe-shaped canyon. Abandoned in the 13th century, the ruins were only discovered in 1883. A visitor center provides information on the history of the pueblos and the people who inhabited them. On display are Sinagua tools, pottery, and textiles. The Island Trail links together 25 of the cliff dwellings. Less physically demanding, the Rim Trail provides visitors with an overview of many of the ruins. Located 10 miles east of Flagstaff on Hwy. 40.

6 MUSEUM OF NORTHERN ARIZONA

Located at the base of the San Francisco Mountains, the Museum of Northern Arizona helps visitors to discover the natural and cultural heritage of the

entire Four Corners region. The museum's four anthropology galleries document 12,000 years of human occupation on the Colorado Plateau with displays on traditional dwellings, settlement patterns, social organization, crafts, and foods. Two of the museum's galleries are devoted to Native American tribes, and include a jewelry gallery and a Hopi kiva. The highlight of the geology exhibit is a life-size skeletal model of *Dilophosaurus*, a dinosaur that once lived in northern Arizona. A mile-long self-guided nature trail allows visitors to view plants and trees indigenous to the Southwest. During the summer, the museum showcases Hopi, Navajo, and Zuni art. Located in Flagstaff on Fort Valley Rd.

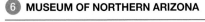

7 HAVASUPAI INDIAN RESERVATION

Havasupai means "people of the blue-green water," and this remote reservation, surrounded by the Grand Canyon, well deserves its name. Tucked within Havasu Canyon—a side canyon of the Grand Canyon—this is a lush landscape of tumbling waterfalls, turquoise pools, and travertine canyons draped with vines and mosses. The reservation is the homeland of the Havasupai Indians, a small tribe of about 660 people who have lived in the canyon and the surrounding plateau since the 14th century. The 518-acre canyon can be accessed only by horse or on foot by means of a rugged 8-mile trail. Supai, the only village, is the site of the Tribal Museum, which displays the baskets and bead-work of the Havasupai. In August, the reservation's Peach Festival features traditional dances and a rodeo. The trail to the reservation begins 125 miles northwest of Flagstaff at the end of Hwy. 18.

The shimmering waters of Havasu Falls in the Havasupai Indian Reservation, above, tumble 100 feet into the blue-green river pool below.

A close-up view of a fossilized log in Petrified Forest National Park, left, reveals the beauty of the quartz formations created as the wood was turned to stone.

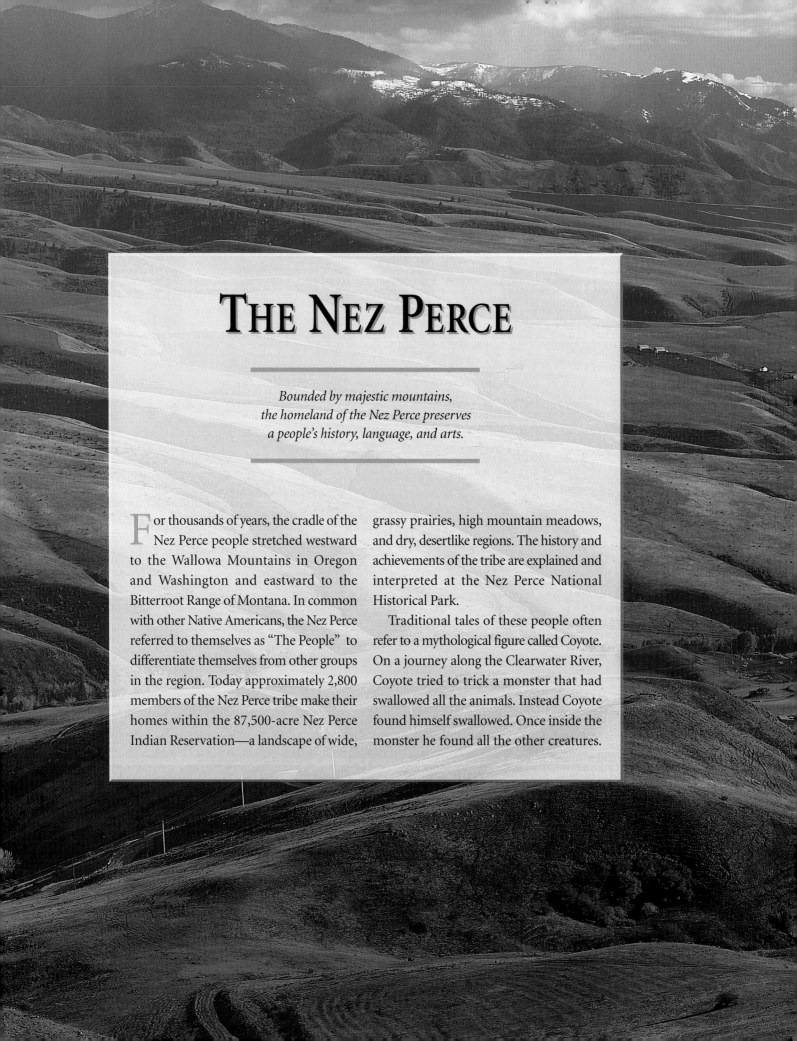

THE NEZ PERCE

*Bounded by majestic mountains,
the homeland of the Nez Perce preserves
a people's history, language, and arts.*

For thousands of years, the cradle of the Nez Perce people stretched westward to the Wallowa Mountains in Oregon and Washington and eastward to the Bitterroot Range of Montana. In common with other Native Americans, the Nez Perce referred to themselves as "The People" to differentiate themselves from other groups in the region. Today approximately 2,800 members of the Nez Perce tribe make their homes within the 87,500-acre Nez Perce Indian Reservation—a landscape of wide,

grassy prairies, high mountain meadows, and dry, desertlike regions. The history and achievements of the tribe are explained and interpreted at the Nez Perce National Historical Park.

Traditional tales of these people often refer to a mythological figure called Coyote. On a journey along the Clearwater River, Coyote tried to trick a monster that had swallowed all the animals. Instead Coyote found himself swallowed. Once inside the monster he found all the other creatures.

The Heart of the Monster, right, is a volcanic rock outcropping carpeted in lush greenery. According to Nez Perce legend, the site was the birthplace of their people.

Originally bred by the Nez Perce, Appaloosa horses, below, can still be seen throughout Nez Perce country.

Overleaf: White Bird Battlefield was the site of the first battle of the Nez Perce War, on June 17, 1877, in which a small band of Nez Perce warriors defeated a much larger force of U.S. Army soldiers.

Brave Coyote pulled out five agate knives and struggled to cut out the monster's heart. When one knife broke, he used another, until only a little part of the monster's heart was attached. Coyote pulled it loose and the monster died.

Then Coyote freed all the creatures and cut up the monster's body. He flung each piece in a different direction, and wherever that part landed, a people sprang up. When he finished, he was left with only the heart of the monster and its blood on his hands. Coyote left the heart of the monster at a place near present-day Kamiah, Idaho, where it can still be seen as a curious rocky knoll rising up from the heather beside the Clearwater River. Then he sprinkled the blood on the ground where he was standing. From the blood of the monster came the Ni-Mii-Poo—The People—whom Coyote declared would be brave and resilient.

The Ni-Mii-Poo became known as the Nez Perce only after contact with French-Canadian fur traders in the early 19th century. The newcomers mistakenly labeled them "pierced noses" because a small group of tribespeople sported nasal ornaments at the time. The renaming of the Ni-Mii-Poo coincided with the beginning of European encroachment on their traditional lands. Within a century the Nez Perce homeland of 17 million acres had diminished to about 86,000 acres.

The lifeways of the Nez Perce were as diverse as the landscape itself. They fished the many rivers that coursed through their land—the Salmon, the Clearwater, the Snake, and the Columbia. They gathered edible camas lily bulbs and other roots in the plateau regions, hunted buffalo and game in the open fields and forests, and traded extensively with other Native peoples. Their crafts included intricate beadwork, leatherwork, and the weaving of cornhusk bags. The contemporary Nez Perce continue to produce some of these traditional crafts.

The advent of the horse in the early 1700's altered the way of life of the Nez Perce. They are most famous for developing and improving the Appaloosa, an Old World breed renowned for its endurance and good nature, and soon they were breeding and trading large herds. Horses allowed the Nez Perce to range far and wide—as far west as the fishing grounds of the Columbia and as far east as the open plains of Montana. Increased contact with Plains tribes led the Nez Perce to adopt aspects of the Plains lifestyle, including tepees for shelter and buffalo-skin robes for clothing.

A TIME OF CONFLICT

Prior to this century, the Nez Perce lived in autonomous bands, with their "headmen" providing leadership. Since the bands coexisted peacefully, the Nez Perce had no need of a centralized form of government. However, this lack of hierarchy complicated their dealings with the U.S. government, which wanted to negotiate with a single leader for the purpose of signing treaties.

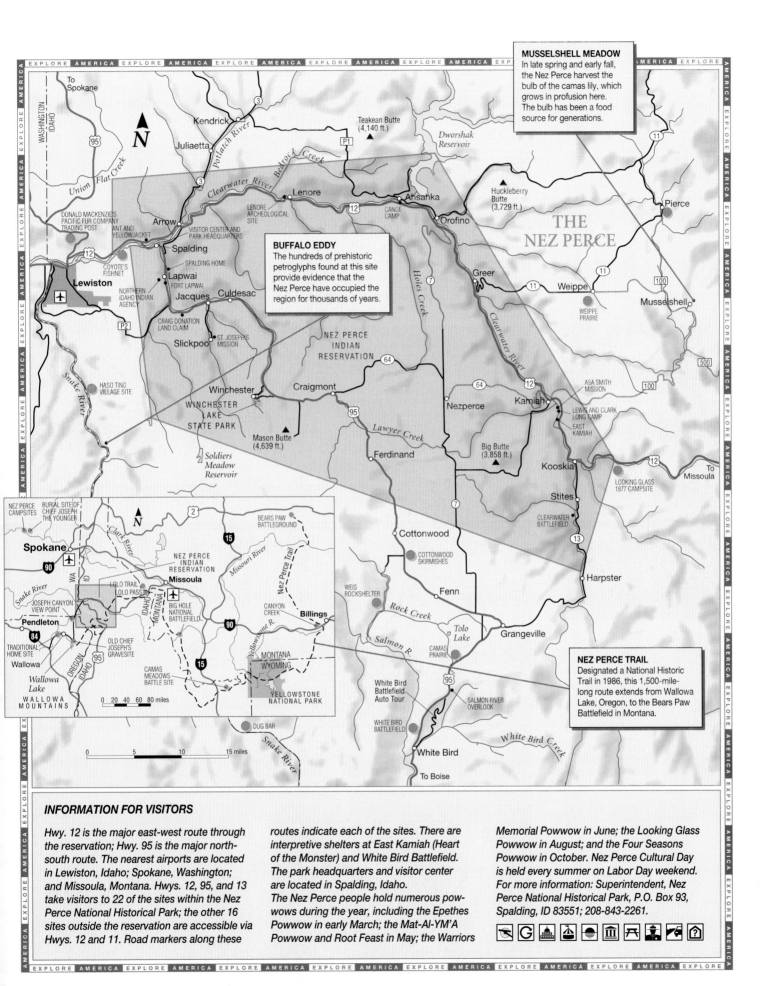

MUSSELSHELL MEADOW
In late spring and early fall, the Nez Perce harvest the bulb of the camas lily, which grows in profusion here. The bulb has been a food source for generations.

BUFFALO EDDY
The hundreds of prehistoric petroglyphs found at this site provide evidence that the Nez Perce have occupied the region for thousands of years.

NEZ PERCE TRAIL
Designated a National Historic Trail in 1986, this 1,500-mile-long route extends from Wallowa Lake, Oregon, to the Bears Paw Battlefield in Montana.

INFORMATION FOR VISITORS

Hwy. 12 is the major east-west route through the reservation; Hwy. 95 is the major north-south route. The nearest airports are located in Lewiston, Idaho; Spokane, Washington; and Missoula, Montana. Hwys. 12, 95, and 13 take visitors to 22 of the sites within the Nez Perce National Historical Park; the other 16 sites outside the reservation are accessible via Hwys. 12 and 11. Road markers along these

routes indicate each of the sites. There are interpretive shelters at East Kamiah (Heart of the Monster) and White Bird Battlefield. The park headquarters and visitor center are located in Spalding, Idaho.

The Nez Perce people hold numerous pow-wows during the year, including the Epethes Powwow in early March; the Mat-Al-YM'A Powwow and Root Feast in May; the Warriors

Memorial Powwow in June; the Looking Glass Powwow in August; and the Four Seasons Powwow in October. Nez Perce Cultural Day is held every summer on Labor Day weekend. For more information: Superintendent, Nez Perce National Historical Park, P.O. Box 93, Spalding, ID 83551; 208-843-2261.

When the Nez Perce encountered the Lewis and Clark expedition at the Bitterroot Range on September 20, 1805, they welcomed and fed the explorers. Trappers, traders, and missionaries soon followed, and by the mid-1800's the Nez Perce were struggling hard to retain their lands. The first treaty with the Nez Perce was signed in 1855, when Washington Territory governor Isaac Stevens met with 56 Nez Perce headmen in Walla Walla to form a reservation that contained much of the traditional Nez Perce land.

Within the space of a few years, however, gold was illegally discovered on the reservation, and trespassing miners and settlers began to clamor for access to the waters and hills that for so many cen-

turies had sustained the Nez Perce. In 1863 the government offered a new reservation to the Nez Perce that contained only one-tenth of the original reservation land. The Nez Perce were divided on whether to accept the treaty, and the government chose to recognize the treaty-friendly faction, led by those who had converted to Christianity.

The Nez Perce opposed to the treaty refused to leave their homes and land and move onto the small reservation. In 1867 the U.S. government threatened to move them to the reservation by force. This began a long, tense decade of resistance, culminating in the Nez Perce War of 1877. Many died during the war and soon after. Among the Nez Perce warriors, the one who came to the fore-

92

front was Hin-mah-too-yah-lat-kekht, whose name means "Thunder Traveling to Loftier Mountain Heights." He is better known as Chief Joseph.

Raised in the Wallowa Mountains of what is now eastern Oregon, Chief Joseph inherited the leadership of the Wallowa band, which was opposed to the treaty. He followed the traditional religion and resisted the illegal treaty of 1863. Widely respected as a man of peace, Chief Joseph met many times with settlers and U.S. government agents, insisting that his people had never signed away or sold their precious homeland.

Compelled by the U.S. military, Chief Joseph and other Nez Perce leaders resigned themselves to relocating their bands to the reservation in June 1877. But before the tribes could move, on June 13, fueled by decades of injustice at the hands of illegal nonnative settlers, three young Nez Perce warriors avenged the murder of one of their fathers by a white man: they killed four settlers who had mistreated Native people. This event set off the Nez Perce War, which lasted until October 1877.

The war's first battle took place on June 17, 1877, in White Bird Canyon, known as Lah Motta in the Nez Perce language. The Nez Perce handed the U.S. forces a crushing defeat: they killed 34 soldiers and lost none.

Under Chief Joseph, the warriors followed an exemplary code of conduct that forbade scalping, mutilation, or attacks on noncombatants. But the Nez Perce and the military were not evenly matched. The U.S. forces included foot soldiers, cavalry, and artillery; the five bands of Nez Perce included wives, children, and the elderly, who were under the protection of the men.

Crossing into Montana, Chief Joseph led the bands through rough terrain, successfully eluding and humiliating their pursuers. The U.S. troops did win a surprise attack at Big Hole, Montana, but were then repulsed by the warriors, who confined the troops to a small area while the Nez Perce families made good their escape from the Big Hole Valley.

Their retreat took them across the newly established Yellowstone National Park, back into Montana, and across the Missouri River. Just 42 miles south of the Canadian border, where the Nez Perce could have found refuge, the five bands were surrounded for several days on Snake Creek, just north of the Bears Paw Mountains. The army even brought up artillery to bombard the encampment of the Nez Perce. After the battle, on October 7, 1877, Chief Joseph addressed his warriors with these famous and heartrending words of surrender: "Hear me, my chiefs, I am tired. My heart is sick and sad. From where the sun now stands, I will fight no more forever."

The Nez Perce were promised that they would be permitted to return to Idaho, but instead were forced into exile in Kansas and Oklahoma, where many died. In 1885, under pressure from public opinion, the U.S. government allowed the Nez Perce to return to the Northwest. Just 118 people came home to Lapwai, Idaho; Chief Joseph and 149 others were exiled to the Colville Reservation in eastern Washington, where their descendants remain to this day. Chief Joseph was never permitted to return to his home in the Wallowas, despite his many requests to do so. He died in Nespelem, Washington, on September 21, 1904, allegedly of a broken heart.

THE HOMELAND

Glimpses of birth, death, war, and tradition can be found within the Nez Perce National Historical Park. The park's sites are scattered throughout southeastern Washington, northeastern Oregon, north-central Idaho, and western Montana. The park was created with 24 sites in 1965 and enlarged in 1992 to a total of 38.

INDIAN MISSION
St. Joseph's Mission, above, was built by Father Joseph Cataldo in an attempt to convert the Nez Perce to the Roman Catholic faith. The mission was one of several that were established on the reservation.

The majority of sites are clustered on the Nez Perce Reservation and include ancient Nez Perce camps, missionary churches, railroads, camas fields, battlefields, fishing grounds, Indian Agency housing, and cemeteries. These historic places are interspersed with grocery stores, schools, farms, basketball courts, community centers, and other hubs of contemporary Nez Perce life.

Natural landmarks that play a role in the traditional tales of Coyote can still be seen as well. Visitors traveling on Highway 12 may stop at Coyote's Fishnet, where the mythical animal turned a mischievous bear into stone; Ant and Yellowjacket, where he froze two feuding insects into a stone arch; and the Heart of the Monster in Kamiah, where he gave birth to the Nez Perce nation.

A one-day auto tour allows visitors to see most of the sites within and near the reservation. The park's headquarters is located in Spalding. This 100-acre site contains a visitor center that displays spectacular Nez Perce beadwork, crafts, and artifacts. A pathway leads to a cluster of historic buildings, including Watson's General Store, built in 1911; a post office and a drugstore; an Indian Agency house; the Spalding Presbyterian Church; and the ruined Spalding Home, where Henry and Eliza Spalding first settled in 1836.

An old railroad line splits the site as a poignant reminder of how the advent of the railroad changed the West. Nez Perce warriors, Indian agents, and missionaries are buried in the adjacent Lapwai Mission Cemetery. The graves of missionaries Henry and Eliza Spalding are there, as well as that of Josiah Red Wolf—the last Native American survivor of the Nez Perce War. Visitors should take extra care when visiting this resting place, as some of the Nez Perce are buried in unmarked graves.

BATTLEFIELD TOUR

The sites along Highway 12 are well marked, and are interspersed with other historic sites. Located near Jacques, St. Joseph's Mission is four miles off the highway but is well worth a detour. This small white church, which was the first Roman Catholic mission among the Nez Perce, stands as a testimony to the impact that the missionaries had on Nez Perce culture. At Camas Prairie, where camas lilies once flourished,

wheat fields now stretch as far as the eye can see. In the distance, visitors can see Tolo Lake, an ancient council site and the place where the nontreaty bands of the Nez Perce camped before they moved onto the reservation.

Perhaps the most dramatic site associated with the 1877 war is White Bird Battlefield, situated in a wide valley whose grasses seem to whisper the names of the men who met their deaths here. A self-guided auto tour winds down the hairpin turns of the old highway into the canyon. At Clearwater Battlefield, Gen. O. O. Howard and his troops hoped to mount a surprise attack; the Nez Perce, however, delivered the troops a humiliating defeat and then escaped across the Clearwater River.

BUCKSKIN BEAUTY

A beaded buckskin dress, above, made by Helen Youngman, adds contemporary design elements to the Nez Perce tradition of fine beadwork. Following the growth of trade contacts with Plains tribes, exquisite beaded robes became a hallmark of the Nez Perce.

Other places of interest include mission outposts, such as St. Joseph's Mission at Slickpoo, and the Asa Smith Mission near East Kamiah. The latter site is located near the Lewis and Clark Long Camp, where the explorers waited for snow in the mountain passes to melt in the spring of 1806.

The story of the Nez Perce War—the last of America's Indian wars—is an epic of bravery that ended tragically. Yet the people have endured, and their culture maintains strong and growing roots. Visitors to this corner of the nation come to understand the reverence the Nez Perce have for their homeland—a feeling that inspired Chief Joseph— and to follow the footprints of Coyote that mark Ni-Mii-Poo country from beginning to end.

ADOPTED ABODE
Tepees like the ones above are among the attractions at the Nez Perce Cultural Day, which is held in Spalding every year. The Nez Perce adopted the tepee after the growth of their contacts with the nomadic buffalo-hunting tribes of the Great Plains.

MONUMENT TO A CHIEF
A stark granite-topped monument, left, was erected at Wallowa, Oregon, in honor of Old Chief Joseph. The chief was the father of the great leader Chief Joseph, who was revered by his people as a warrior and diplomat during the Nez Perce War.

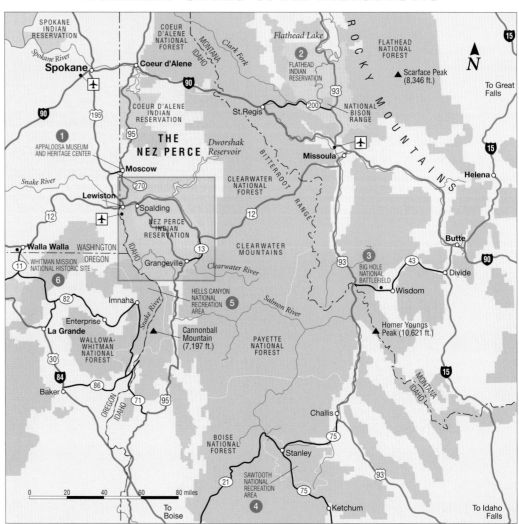

An obelisk, above, set on a hill overlooking the Walla Walla Valley, commemorates missionaries Narcissa and Marcus Whitman. The couple worked among the Cayuse Indians for 11 years before cultural differences and misunderstandings led to an Indian attack on the mission, in which the Whitmans and several others lost their lives.

① APPALOOSA MUSEUM AND HERITAGE CENTER, IDAHO

The story of the famed spotted horse, known for its endurance and good disposition, is the focus of this museum. Appaloosa horses were bred by the Nez Perce from Spanish stock; the name of the breed comes from the Palouse River tribe of the Washington-Idaho border. Photographs document the history of the Appaloosa, which were used exclusively in 19th- and 20th-century circuses. Artwork on display includes sculptures of Appaloosas and their riders, copies of paintings by famed Western artist C. M. Russell, and a James Bama print of Buffalo Bill Cody astride an Appaloosa. The horse's importance to Native Americans is highlighted by displays of a Nez Perce beaded breast collar, as well as a collection of saddles, including a saddle made in 1860 and a woman's saddle that dates to 1877. Also on exhibit are a beaded bridle and apishamore and several rare horse blankets. In the summer months visitors can see Appaloosas in the fenced pasture behind the museum. Located in the Appaloosa Horse Club building, 1 mile west of Moscow on Hwy. 8.

② FLATHEAD INDIAN RESERVATION, MONTANA

Home to the Salish, Kootenai, and Pend d'Oreille peoples, the Flathead Indian Reservation's 1.3 million acres lie between the Mission Range and the 8,000-foot Cabinet Mountains. The reservation also includes several major waterways, such as the Clark Fork and Flathead rivers, and Flathead Lake, which is the largest natural freshwater lake in the West. Within the reservation, the National Bison Range protects a bison herd numbering close to 400 animals, as well as elk, deer, and bighorn sheep. Visitors may join a Native American guide at the People's Center for tours focusing on the arts and cultural heritage of the Native peoples who inhabit the reservation, as well as its wildlife and natural resources. Mineral mud and water baths are open year-round at Camas Hot Springs. St. Ignatius Mission, built in 1891, is the oldest continuously operating mission in Montana. There are five state parks within the reservation. Located 15 miles north of Missoula on Hwy. 93.

③ BIG HOLE NATIONAL BATTLEFIELD, MONTANA

The battle site is dedicated to the Nez Perce women, children, and warriors, as well as to the 7th U.S. Infantry and Bitterroot Volunteers, who fought and died here during the Nez Perce War in August 1877. The site includes a visitor center, the Nez Perce camp, the siege area, and the Howitzer capture site. Using photographs, a video, and relics from the battle, the visitor center recreates the battle. Wooden tepee stands are in place at the Nez Perce camp, and trenches dug by the retreating army are still visible in the siege area. A steep walk leads to a howitzer, a replica of the one captured by the Nez Perce during the battle. Located 10 miles west of Wisdom on Hwy. 43.

④ SAWTOOTH NATIONAL RECREATION AREA, IDAHO

The mountains, lakes, and alpine meadows of south-central Idaho provide a spectacular setting for 750 miles of hiking and horseback-riding trails within this national recreation area. The heavily forested 756,000-acre area embraces three mountain ranges, with some peaks topping 11,000 feet. Rafting and kayaking are popular activities on the mighty Salmon River. Old mining roads are now used for mountain biking, and the history of mining and ranching is told through pictures and artifacts in the Stanley Museum. During the winter, the roads and trails are used for snowmobiling and skiing. Located 7 miles north of Ketchum on Hwy. 75.

⑤ HELLS CANYON NATIONAL RECREATION AREA, IDAHO/OREGON

The deepest canyon in the nation, carved by the turbulent Snake River on its way to join the mighty Columbia, is the centerpiece of this national recreation area. The Snake River flows through Hells Canyon for 67.5 miles, 36 miles of which are classified as scenic and 31.5 miles as wild. Located in Idaho and Oregon, this 652,488-acre recreation area is a premier spot for whitewater rafting, jet boating, fishing, hiking, camping, and wildlife watching. The many species of fish found in the Snake River include salmon, trout, and white sturgeon, which is the largest freshwater fish of all. There are also more than 900 miles of hiking and horseback-riding trails. Located 112 miles south of Lewiston off Hwy. 95, or 35 miles east of Enterprise off Hwy. 82.

⑥ WHITMAN MISSION NATIONAL HISTORIC SITE, WASHINGTON

Built by Marcus and Narcissa Whitman in 1836 to serve the Cayuse Indians, the mission was also a way station for settlers on the Oregon Trail. Eleven years later, the Whitmans were killed by angry Cayuse when their medicine for measles cured white children but not Indian children, who had no resistance to the disease. The site includes the outlines of the mission buildings, the Whitmans' graves, and a visitor center. In the summer months, there are demonstrations of soap- and candle-making, as well as traditional methods of preparing deer hides. Located 7 miles west of Walla Walla off Hwy. 12.

A weathered homestead cabin in the Sawtooth Mountains, above, is a reminder of pioneer days in this rugged corner of south-central Idaho.

A placid stretch of the Snake River in Hells Canyon National Recreation Area, left, belies the river's ferocious reputation. Hells Canyon is renowned as one of the best places in the world for whitewater rafting.

THE PACIFIC NORTHWEST

*Blessed by nature, the people of
the Pacific Northwest reaped the
bounty of land, river, and sea.*

It all begins with the magic of water. From the snowcapped peaks of the Cascade Range and the rain-washed Olympic Mountains, the mighty rivers of the Pacific Northwest plunge and ripple through vale and hollow, building into a single song of praise to nature's abundance. On Puget Sound the song echoes softly through a labyrinth of channels, where forested islands float upon reflections of the shimmering sky. To the west, the moody Pacific Ocean scallops the coastline into haunting coves and lonely strands, rugged headlands, offshore seastacks, and beaches of bone-bleached driftwood.

This is northwestern Washington State, home to Native peoples for thousands of years. Here the Suquamish, Lummi, Makah, and other tribes have lived upon and celebrated the waters of their unique world, building a rich and vibrant civilization supremely gifted in the arts of survival and ceremony. And here the song lives on in a resurgence of Native creativity and a dedication to remembrance.

The sight of salmon baking on wooden stakes over hot coals, right, is a common one at summer powwows in the Pacific Northwest. The salmon is of fundamental importance to the Native peoples of the Northwest coast, and is celebrated in their rituals, art, and myths.

A FINE CATCH

The resolution of disputes over fishing rights has meant that Native fishermen, like the one below, can continue to harvest salmon and other fish from their traditional fishing grounds.

WILD BEACH

Overleaf: Cast ashore by the ceaseless motion of the Pacific Ocean, driftwood jams a beach near La Push, the center of the Quileute Indian Reservation. Just offshore, towering seastacks offer a habitat to colonies of seabirds.

Seattle is a bustling trendsetter in advanced industries such as aerospace and computers. But the great city on Puget Sound also preserves the traces of the peoples who first inhabited the Pacific Northwest. At the Thomas Burke Memorial Museum, situated on the campus of the University of Washington, visitors can catch a first glimpse of the region's indigenous Native heritage. Engaging exhibits and lively displays of artifacts from the museum's permanent collection illustrate many of the lifeways that have bound more than five dozen tribes together in an extended "family" known as the Coast Salish.

Though scattered across hundreds of miles and speaking a multitude of different languages, the Coast Salish peoples were linked by landscape. Waterways connected families, facilitated trade, and ensured that a common stylistic thread ran through the clothes and baskets that each tribe wove from grass.

EXTENDED FAMILIES

The Coast Salish lived in small communities of extended families, like their tribal relatives to the north—the Haida, Kwakiutl, and Tlingit peoples of what is now British Columbia. With these peoples, the Coast Salish shared food, family ties, and ritual customs such as the potlatch. In the Native societies of the Pacific Northwest, a chief's prestige hinged on his ability to demonstrate his wealth by hosting elaborate potlatches. These lavish parties might be prepared for a year and last for weeks, involving endless rounds of storytelling, dancing, and other ceremonies. The chief would give freely of fish, blankets, skins, and woolens to his guests.

The traditional homeland of the Coast Salish peoples originally stretched from southeastern Alaska to northern California. The warm Japan Current that flows just offshore helps to moderate the region's climate, and is responsible for its extremely high levels of rainfall. The damp, temperate climate produces natural wonders such as the lush rain forests of the Olympic Peninsula. Anthropologists estimate that the ancestors of the Coast Salish settled in this bounteous corner of the continent as far back as 10,000 years ago. At the time of first European contact in 1741, most of their settlements were concentrated north of the Columbia River on the riverbanks, islands, and shores of the coast.

The sparkling lakes, gurgling rivers, and placid inlets of the Olympic Peninsula and Puget Sound were not only home to the Coast Salish people, but also their primary source of food. In roughly predictable yearly cycles, hundreds of thousands of salmon launched their desperate surge to upstream

spawning grounds, threading the lacy ribbons of swift-flowing rivers like light itself. All five species of Pacific salmon make this journey from salt to fresh water, swimming upsteam through the river of their birth. The people took their own tribal names—Nooksak, Stillaguamish, Skokomish, Skagit, and Nisqually—from the salmon-laden rivers, just as they partook of the water's bounty. Salmon, trout, eulachon, herring, and other fish made up more than 60 percent of the Salish diet, supplemented with thimbleberries, salmonberries, and an occasional deer.

In such a world, the canoe was the most essential tool of survival. Hand-hewn with stone adzes from a single trunk of cedar or redwood, with a draft shallow for fishing the shoal waters and a bow flattened to dampen splash, the Coast Salish dugout canoe was both functional and graceful.

The power and mystery of the coastal waterways infused the Salish world with spirit. According to traditions shared by many tribes, it was the Transformer who gave the earth its present shape, sculpting the mountains and channeling the rivers, painting the woods with flowers, fruits, and berries. The Transformer also altered much of humanity into the animals of the forest and the sea.

This link to the animal world survives in the masks, motifs, and totems of Coast Salish people. Man and animal are but two manifestations of the same spirit, linked in the web of life. The mask allows the wearer to travel back and forth between these worlds, to dramatize the connections between the two, and to serve as a reminder to man to

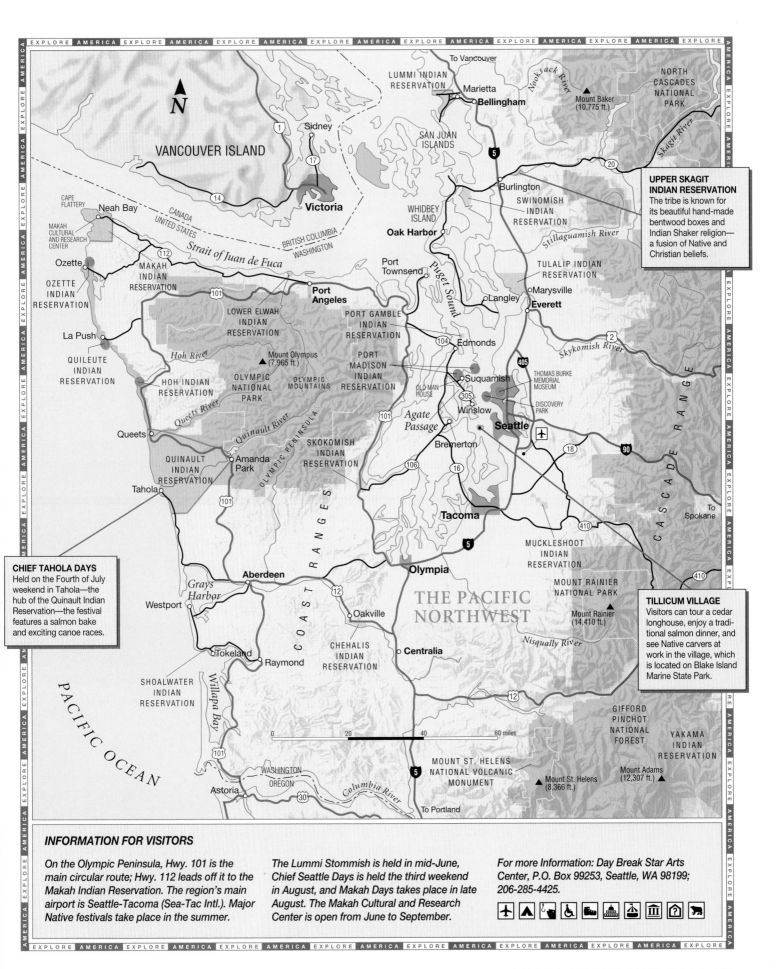

UPPER SKAGIT INDIAN RESERVATION
The tribe is known for its beautiful hand-made bentwood boxes and Indian Shaker religion—a fusion of Native and Christian beliefs.

CHIEF TAHOLA DAYS
Held on the Fourth of July weekend in Tahola—the hub of the Quinault Indian Reservation—the festival features a salmon bake and exciting canoe races.

TILLICUM VILLAGE
Visitors can tour a cedar longhouse, enjoy a traditional salmon dinner, and see Native carvers at work in the village, which is located on Blake Island Marine State Park.

INFORMATION FOR VISITORS

On the Olympic Peninsula, Hwy. 101 is the main circular route; Hwy. 112 leads off it to the Makah Indian Reservation. The region's main airport is Seattle-Tacoma (Sea-Tac Intl.). Major Native festivals take place in the summer.

The Lummi Stommish is held in mid-June, Chief Seattle Days is held the third weekend in August, and Makah Days takes place in late August. The Makah Cultural and Research Center is open from June to September.

For more Information: Day Break Star Arts Center, P.O. Box 99253, Seattle, WA 98199; 206-285-4425.

HAND-HEWN HISTORY
Totem poles fashioned from a single cedar log provide a symbolic record of a family's ancestors. The one above depicts Raven—a traditional trickster figure—below six human figures. A kingfisher is perched on top.

respect and revere the animal beings on whom their survival depends. So, too, the totem pole—"read" from bottom to top—is a chronicle of each clan's ancestry and their powerful animal guardian spirits.

In Seattle's beautiful Discovery Park, an educational center called the Day Break Star displays works by Native American artists living in today's urban America. Although the focus is contemporary, the inspiration for the work on exhibit has its roots in the past, documenting a unique cultural awareness that continues to evolve in a changing world.

A brief ferry ride across Puget Sound to the town of Winslow and a short drive north along Highway 305 brings the visitor to the town of Suquamish, located on the Port Madison Indian Reservation. Parked cars line the road leading into the village, where the tantalizing smell of fry bread and salmon rises from the cook tents. Beadwork, basketry, and other crafts are offered for sale. On the village green, dancers from many tribes dip and swirl, while out on the bay, canoes lance through the water in hotly contested races.

In August the Suquamish host Chief Seattle Days, a powwow named for their illustrious chief Seattle. In order to secure the well-being of his people, Seattle offered friendship to the white settlers who began to flock to the region in the 1800's. He realized that both groups would have to reach an accommodation if the Suquamish were not to be submerged by the swelling tide of newcomers. A memorial service in his honor has been held each year at this time since 1911. In the small cemetery perched on the hillside overlooking the town, visitors and tribal elders alike gather to pay homage to the man whose words of understanding bridged two cultures.

The Suquamish experience was typical for tribes of the Pacific Northwest. By signing the Treaties of Point Elliott in 1855, the Suquamish relinquished claim to most of their territory, receiving in return a reservation and the promise of protection. In the decades that followed, the tribe struggled to survive amid the encroachments of settlers and the ravages of poverty and disease. Children were sent to trade schools and eventually lost contact with their traditional language and lifestyle. Potlatches and other tribal gatherings were forbidden. The Old Man House—a longhouse that served as the symbol of the Suquamish nation—was burned to the ground by federal agents. The destruction of the longhouse symbolically struck at the very heart of Native culture in the Pacific Northwest.

Mist dampens the shoreline forest at dusk as churning waves lap the rocky headlands of Cape Flattery, left, located at the tip of the Makah Indian Reservation.

Learning to hunt, a young bobcat, below, emerges from the cover of a conifer. This wildcat, North America's most widespread, can sometimes be spotted within the forests of the Pacific Northwest.

Masked and costumed dancers perform a welcome dance as paddlers propel cedar-log war canoes to a celebration, below. The Native peoples of the Pacific Northwest traditionally used the cedar canoe for fishing, travel, potlatches, racing, and warfare.

VILLAGE LIFE

The longhouse was the center of village life. Here the Indians smoked surplus salmon for lean months, storing it in bundles suspended from the roof. Here they wove mats and clothing, fashioned fishhooks, twined hats, and beaded jewelry with precious dentalia shells. In winter the house reverberated with sacred songs when important ritual gatherings such as the potlatch were held under the cedar eaves.

The longhouses were immense structures, sometimes reaching lengths of 100 feet and widths of 50 feet. As a rule, they were made of split cedar planks lashed horizontally in overlapping shingles around a frame of huge logs. Grooved cedar planks fused to form a gabled roof. A single longhouse served primarily as a residence for an entire clan of families under the authority of a powerful clan head. Several longhouses made up a village. All the longhouses were oriented toward the water, so that a large village might stretch for up to two miles along the shore.

Families were fluid: a clan leader might have several wives, and intermarriage between members of different villages was common. Longhouses could be enlarged or reduced to accommodate changes in clan size. Although Northwestern peoples no longer occupy such dwellings, they continue to renew important bonds of family and tribe through festivals such as Chief Seattle Days.

Located on the shores of Agate Passage, the Suquamish Museum provides an insightful look

at the Suquamish from the days of Chief Seattle to the present. An oral history project has enabled the tribe to produce award-winning exhibitions for the museum. Slide presentations by tribal elders further complement the museum's excellent collection of artifacts and a reconstruction of a 19th-century longhouse.

Strolling along the quiet beach, visitors will come across the foundation of Old Man House, a long-house erected by Chief Seattle in an attempt to unite the region's tribal groups. If they listen carefully, maybe they will hear his words whispering through the sun-dappled woodlands:

Every part of this country is sacred to my people
Every hillside
Every valley

Every plain and grove
Has been hallowed by some fond memory
Or some sad experience
Of my tribe.

From the shores of the Lummi Reservation, located near Bellingham on the eastern shore of the Puget Sound, a scenic panorama unfolds, stretching across the San Juan Islands and the Strait of Juan de Fuca to the snowy sentinels of the Olympic Peninsula in the southwest. This is hard-won territory. The Lummi fled here to escape smallpox in the 18th century, and spent the next 200 years fending off gold-seekers and other rival claimants.

Today the tribe boasts thriving commercial ventures, including the largest fishing fleet in the sound. Each June, in the spirit of the traditional potlatch, the prosperous Lummi welcome visitors to the Stommish, a week-long celebration featuring salmon bakes, tribal dances, and thrilling races in ornate 50-foot war canoes.

The Stommish hints at the opulence of earlier days, when the potlatch was the dominant social institution on the coast. Generous present-giving confirmed good relations with all invited—especially with neighboring chiefs—and also settled questions of rank. Some theories contend that the potlatch was a way to distribute surplus foodstuffs. Whatever the case, potlatching was more than merely a politically expedient practice, because it persisted even in periods of extreme hardship and often bankrupted the host.

There was also a deeper spiritual meaning. At potlatches, the chiefs sang the sacred songs that belonged to them alone, which conferred special powers. Here secret societies danced the *Klookwalli*, or wolf ritual, their animal masks flashing in the firelight and their figures casting shadows of wolves, bears, and eagles. The celebration confirmed the unity of the human, animal, and spirit worlds.

SEASONS OF LIFE

Today's potlatches are more modest affairs, which last only one evening and mark important events in the life of the extended family, such as marriage, the birth of a child, the receiving of a name—which can take place at birth or adulthood, or to commemorate a special event in a person's life—as well as the remembrance of a person who has died. But the spirit of the potlatch remains unbroken in its confirmation of kinship among all celebrants.

As the road winds west from Port Angeles along the Strait of Juan de Fuca, the towns give way to villages, which in turn give way to rustic board-and-batten fishing camps. At the end of the road lies Neah Bay, located in the extreme northwestern

ALL-WEATHER GEAR
The woven hat worn by the child above recalls the splendid headgear made from the dried and split roots of spruce trees traditionally worn by Native peoples of the Pacific Northwest. The tightly woven fibers afforded excellent protection against winter rains.

corner of the lower 48 states and homeland of the Makah. Across the water, Vancouver Island drifts upon the morning haze, a misty memory for the Makah people, whose ancestors settled here nearly 3,000 years ago.

Many of them lived at Ozette, a windswept cove on the rugged Pacific Coast, south of Cape Flattery's forbidding wooded crags. Three centuries ago, a landslide buried the village. From 1970 to 1981, archeologists excavated the village, revealing a vanished way of life. Today the Makah Cultural and Research Center in Neah Bay immerses the visitor in the life of the Makah, through the seasons and across the centuries, by displays of thousands of artifacts recovered from Ozette.

Like other Northwestern tribes, the Makah were completely adapted to the cycles of the sea. Challenged by an ever-changing environment, they proved themselves to be master seafarers and resourceful fishermen.

The Makah developed many ingenious techniques to catch salmon, from stretching woven weirs across rivers to trolling in the open ocean with baited herring on lines of woven kelp. They caught huge halibut with bentwood hooks and passed among schools of herring with "rakes" of cedar fitted with spikes of sharpened bone.

In a supreme test of skill, strength, and endurance, they also hunted the California gray whale, venturing as far as 50 miles out to sea in

PENINSULAR GROVE
One of the Olympic Peninsula's three temperate rain forests, Quinault Rain Forest, right, is protected within the Quinault Indian Reservation. The largest on the peninsula, the 196,600-acre reservation is home to seven tribes and encompasses extensive stretches of pristine shoreline.

eight-man canoes, navigating only by wind and current. Makah whale hunters used 18-foot-long wooden harpoons with mussel-shell blades to spear the whales. Seal-bladder floats attached to the harpoon kept the carcass afloat until it could be hauled back to the village beachfront and butchered.

To the Makah, the objects excavated at Ozette are much more than stone-age curiosities. For two centuries following the arrival of Spanish explorers in 1792, the Makah nation had steadily declined through disease and assimilation. The discoveries at Ozette rekindled the Makahs' awareness of their proud heritage. This renewed link with the past has inspired a new generation of Makah artists, poets, and teachers.

The reservation is now home to approximately 1,100 members of the tribe. The Makah celebrate their newly revitalized culture with dances, songs, traditional and modern games, canoe races, and a salmon bake during Makah Days in late August.

THE
UNIVERSAL
RESOURCE

From November to June, rains bathe the coastal valleys of the Hoh, Queets, and Quinault rivers in more than 100 inches of water, creating the right conditions for temperate rain forests. Trees such as Sitka spruce, western hemlock, and Douglas fir grow 200 feet tall, and the understory glistens with blue huckleberries, buttercups, and ferns. Woolly sleeves of club moss cling to fallen trees and hang from branches in opulent gauzy swathes. Elk browse among red alders, salmon flash in the shallows, and bobcats prowl in the twilight.

From the coastal rain forests Native peoples derived the essential resource for their way of life— the red cedar. Easy to work and slow to rot, the cedar fulfilled countless practical needs: it was felled and split for house planks, boxes, and cradles; hollowed out with fire and adze for canoes; and carved into masks, rattles, and bowls. Each spring long strips of bark were peeled from standing cedars to make mats and baskets. Interwoven with bird down and then treated with fish oil, cedar bark also supplied warm, water-repellent outerwear for winter. Sturdy rope and twine were made from braided cedar twigs. Of the more than 2,000 different wooden tools a typical Indian household may have contained, most of them were also made of red cedar.

The forest gave not only implements, but also wisdom. It was in the forest that young men found their spirit guides during vision quests. These secret totems provided the supplicant with a sense of identity and the mastery of an individual talent, be it hunting, whaling, or canoe carving.

The legacy of the forest lives on among the Quileute and Quinault tribes. Their reservations

occupy beautiful stretches of forested coast, which visitors enjoy at summer festivals such as Quileute Days and Chief Taholah Days. The tiny Hoh Reservation, at the mouth of the Hoh River, is home to about 100 Native Americans, many of whom are happy to show their cedar-bark basketry work to visitors who inquire at the tribal center. The nearby rain forests of Olympic National Park provide a majestic backdrop to the reservation.

The longhouses are gone, the cedar-bark hats have been replaced by baseball caps, and the potlatch is no longer a political institution. But the salmon still run each year, and the tribes still depend on them for survival, both physical and cultural. Since 1974 federal reaffirmation of Native fishing rights has enabled the tribes of Washington State to grow and prosper. Today Native fish hatcheries stock rivers and bays. Most reservations have tribal centers that offer essential social services, museums in the works, and classes in traditional folkways at tribal community colleges. At summer festivals, cedar canoes once more cut bold wakes through the waters of the shimmering sky.

The children dance—feet tapping, feathers twirling, and spangles glittering in the morning light—as visitors watch and learn. What they are witnessing is not the past, but rather the continuity of an ancient culture, evolving to survive while remaining true to its own heartbeat.

ETCHED IN STONE
Chief Seattle's gravestone, left, is located on a hillside within the Port Madison Reservation. The city of Seattle was named in his honor.

BIRTH PANGS
Unearthed at the buried village of Ozette, this wooden vessel carved in the shape of a woman in childbirth, below, is on display in the renowned Makah Cultural and Research Center, located in Neah Bay.

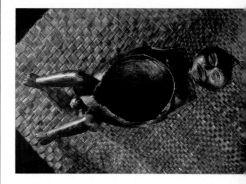

NEARBY SITES & ATTRACTIONS

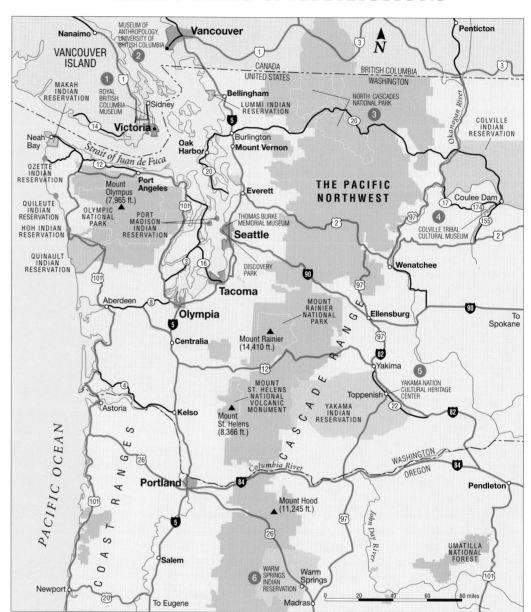

The Pi-Ume-Sha Treaty Days Powwow celebration on the Warm Springs Reservation, above, features traditional dancing by Native Americans in colorful garb.

① ROYAL BRITISH COLUMBIA MUSEUM

Situated in the heart of Victoria, capital of British Columbia, the Royal British Columbia Museum chronicles the human and natural history of the province. On display is a life-size replica of a woolly mammoth, as well as several reconstructed 19th-century buildings, including a railway station, movie theater, pharmacy, printing shop, blacksmith's shop, and saloon. The First Peoples Gallery depicts the lifestyles of nomadic Native peoples who lived in the interior and on the coast. Visitors can tour a genuine cedar longhouse known as the Jonathan Hunt House. The family maintains the right to use the house for traditional ceremonies such as pot-latches. Other items on display include tepees and pit dwellings, deerskin clothing, cedar hats, tools made from animal bones, and quill- and beadwork. Another museum highlight is a simulated trip into the ocean's three life zones. Beside the museum,

Thunderbird Park contains a collection of totem poles carved by the Native peoples of the Pacific Coast. Located at 675 Belleville St. in Victoria.

② MUSEUM OF ANTHROPOLOGY, UNIVERSITY OF BRITISH COLUMBIA

Overlooking the Strait of Georgia, this impressive concrete-and-glass structure is based on the traditional post-and-beam structures of the Native peoples of the Pacific Northwest. The building was designed by renowned Canadian architect Arthur Erickson. Outdoor exhibits include two Haida houses and 10 totem poles. The museum also displays the world's largest collection of works by contemporary Haida artist Bill Reid, much of it sculpted in cedar. The Koerner Ceramics Gallery features 600 rare European ceramic pieces dating

108

from the 15th century to the 19th century. The ethnographic exhibit displays more than 14,000 objects from all over the world. Located at 6393 NW Marine Dr. in Vancouver.

③ NORTH CASCADES NATIONAL PARK, WASHINGTON

Comprising 684,000 acres of the North Cascades Mountains, this is a landscape of towering peaks, mighty glaciers, deep alpine lakes, and swift-moving rivers. Lake Chelan, 55 miles long and 1,500 feet deep, is the third-deepest lake in the nation. Forests of hemlock, Douglas fir, and red cedar cloak the lower elevations; wildflowers thrive in the subalpine meadows; and krummholz ("crooked") trees grow on the high mountain peaks. This rugged terrain is inhabited by black bears, mule deer, and hoary marmots. Home to several varieties of trout, the park's clear waters are an angler's paradise. The park's 350 miles of trails range from 1-mile Thunder Woods Nature Trail to the 35-mile Chilliwack River–Cooper Ridge Loop. The North Cascades Highway, which divides the north and south units of the park, is one of the most scenic drives in the state. Exhibits, slide shows, and interpretive programs in the visitor center give visitors a detailed overview of the park. Located 55 miles east of Mt. Vernon on Hwy. 20.

④ COLVILLE TRIBAL CULTURAL MUSEUM, WASHINGTON

This museum preserves the history and culture of the 11 Native American nations that make up the Colville Confederated Tribes. The clothing collection features moccasins, hats, and a dress made of antelope hide from the 1850's. Cedar baskets—used for gathering, storing, and cooking food—cornhusk and beaded bags, trade beads, coins, and metals

are on display, as well as a re-created fishing village, tepee, and sweat lodge. Located on the Colville Reservation at 512 Mead in Coulee Dam.

⑤ YAKAMA NATION CULTURAL HERITAGE CENTER, WASHINGTON

Dominated by a 76-foot-high lodge modeled after an ancient Yakama design, the museum complex includes a museum, theater, research center, library, and a winter lodge that can be reserved for banquets, dances, and conventions. Artifacts, murals, exhibits, and dioramas showcase the heritage and culture of the Yakama Nation. Displays include traditional clothing, jewelry, and weapons. Located in Toppenish on Hwy. 97.

⑥ WARM SPRINGS INDIAN RESERVATION, OREGON

Flanked on the west by the the towering Cascade Range and on the east by the Deschutes River, the landscape ranges from deep canyons and volcanic formations to high desertlike terrain. The 640,000-acre reservation is the homeland of the Wasco, Paiute, and Warm Springs tribes. A resort owned and operated by the tribes is an excellent starting point for tours of the region. At the museum, visitors can explore a tule mat lodge, plankhouse, and wickiup. Buckskin dresses, baskets, and parfleches are some of the items on display. The interpretive center at the National Fish Hatchery recounts the importance of salmon fishing to the tribes. The Pi-Ume-Sha Treaty Days Powwow takes place in June; other events include the Root Festival in April and the Huckleberry Feast held in August. Located 14 miles northwest of Madras on Hwy. 59.

Titled "After He Has Seen the Spirit," the elegant mask, above, was created by Haida artist Robert Davidson. It is on display at the Museum of Anthropology at the University of British Columbia.

In the city of Victoria, Thunderbird Park features a traditional longhouse, left, surrounded by towering totem poles carved with mythical figures. The totem poles, as well as the longhouse, were created from cedar logs felled in nearby forests.

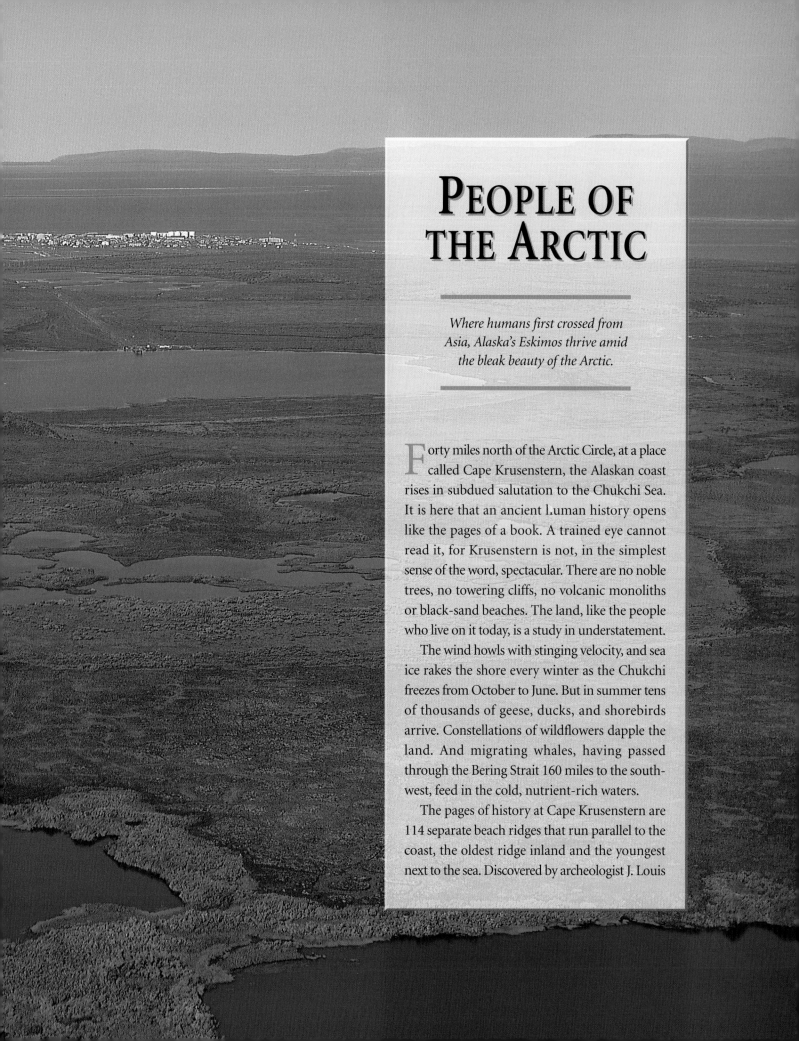

PEOPLE OF THE ARCTIC

*Where humans first crossed from
Asia, Alaska's Eskimos thrive amid
the bleak beauty of the Arctic.*

Forty miles north of the Arctic Circle, at a place called Cape Krusenstern, the Alaskan coast rises in subdued salutation to the Chukchi Sea. It is here that an ancient l.uman history opens like the pages of a book. A trained eye cannot read it, for Krusenstern is not, in the simplest sense of the word, spectacular. There are no noble trees, no towering cliffs, no volcanic monoliths or black-sand beaches. The land, like the people who live on it today, is a study in understatement.

The wind howls with stinging velocity, and sea ice rakes the shore every winter as the Chukchi freezes from October to June. But in summer tens of thousands of geese, ducks, and shorebirds arrive. Constellations of wildflowers dapple the land. And migrating whales, having passed through the Bering Strait 160 miles to the southwest, feed in the cold, nutrient-rich waters.

The pages of history at Cape Krusenstern are 114 separate beach ridges that run parallel to the coast, the oldest ridge inland and the youngest next to the sea. Discovered by archeologist J. Louis

FIRST SETTLEMENT
Windswept Cape Krusenstern, right, presents a lonely vista of low ridges, streams, and lagoons. For centuries this has been a traditional Eskimo hunting ground for marine mammals. In recent years archeologists have explored the remains of camps built on these beach ridges in order to find clues to the early history of the Eskimo people.

ARCTIC ARISTOCRAT
The caribou, above, is well adapted to life in the Arctic. Hollow hairs trap air close to its skin, improving insulation in winter, and wide hooves help to support the animal on both tundra and snow.

VILLAGE ON THE SOUND
Overleaf: The Eskimo community of Kotzebue sits on the shore of Kotzebue Sound—seemingly at the very edge of the continent. Because the subsoil is permanently frozen and blocks drainage, countless small lakes have formed on the surrounding tundra.

Giddings in 1958 and hailed as the Olduvai Gorge of American Arctic archeology, Cape Krusenstern's ridges reveal a chronology of human habitation dating back hundreds of generations. As Giddings unearthed tools, pottery, hearths, artwork, and entire dwellings, he found that each ridge told its own cultural story. As storms pounded the coast through the millennia, new ridges were created. Over time, waves of migrants arrived to occupy these gravel beaches. Here lived travelers of the western Thule people, who would carry the Eskimo language across the Canadian Arctic to Greenland during the 13th century; the Ipiutak Eskimos at the time of Christ; the Choris and Norton people of two millennia earlier; and Alaska's first Eskimos, the Denbigh Flint people of 4,000 years ago.

As he explored the ridges, Giddings speculated about these immigrants from Asia. Faced with Alaska's formidably cold winters and cool summers, these ancient people would have been forced to occupy themselves mainly with the quest for food, as well as to procure adequate shelter and clothing to keep themselves warm. From all of the successive peoples who lived on these beach ridges, sharing similar problems and hardships, there emerged through the centuries the Eskimo of today: a careful, watchful individual, who combines great bravery with tremendous endurance.

Their culture survives today in settlements such as Barrow, Kotzebue, Point Hope, Bethel, and Nome—the end of the historic Iditarod Trail—and in hundreds of smaller villages and camps strewn across the vastness of the tundra, rivers, mountains, and forests of western and northern Alaska. A journey into the Eskimo heartland is a mixture of starkly beautiful scenery and a people who have adapted with ingenuity and fortitude to the unique rigors of this land.

AT THE EDGE OF THE SEA

Cape Krusenstern National Monument lies 36 miles northwest of Kotzebue, which is located at the tip of the Baldwin Peninsula. Accessible by boat or charter plane in summer and by snowmobile or aircraft in winter, the monument has none of the facilities normally found at other National Park Service sites. Visitors can examine the archeological zones, although digging for artifacts is not permitted.

The mainly Eskimo town of Kotzebue is also the headquarters of NANA (Northwest Alaska Native Association)—one of the regional corporations established in the 1970's to manage funds and land turned over to Native peoples under the Alaska Native Claims Settlement Act. The NANA Museum of the Arctic is the first stop for visitors to the region. The museum was designed, according to its directors, so that "generations of Eskimos would know who they were, and why. And so would the rest of America." Visitors are treated to an indoor diorama of wildlife, followed by demonstrations of local crafts and a performance by the Northern Lights Dancers. More dancing occurs each July at Kotzebue's Northwest Native Trade Fair, together with feasting and games for young and old alike.

The ancestors of the Eskimos, like those of every other Native people in the Americas, arrived from Asia. The earliest immigrants crossed to what is now Alaska during the Pleistocene period, when the sea level was as much as 300 feet lower than it is today, and a great land bridge connected Siberia to Alaska. Over time, the ancestors of the Eskimos developed masterful means of adapting to the Arctic coast and hinterland.

Not far from Kotzebue, on the western shore of Kotzebue Sound, lies Bering Land Bridge National Preserve, roughly 2.8 million acres of land that sits

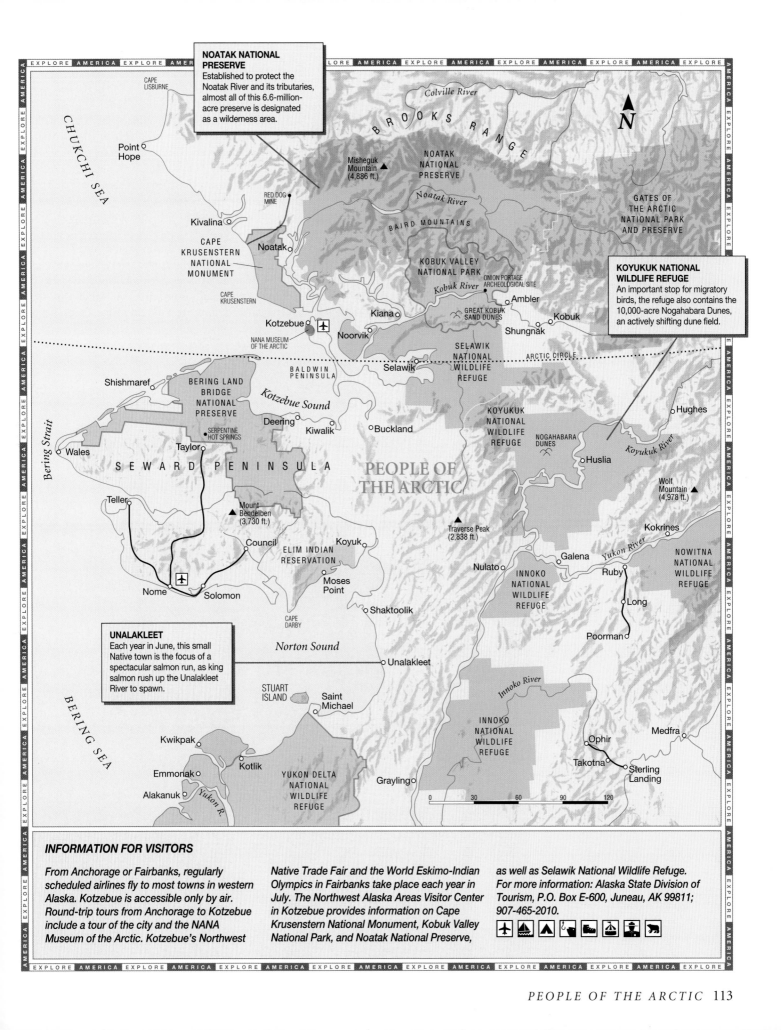

NOATAK NATIONAL PRESERVE
Established to protect the Noatak River and its tributaries, almost all of this 6.6-million-acre preserve is designated as a wilderness area.

CAPE LISBURNE

Colville River

CHUKCHI SEA

BROOKS RANGE

Point Hope

Misheguk Mountain (4,886 ft.) ▲

NOATAK NATIONAL PRESERVE

GATES OF THE ARCTIC NATIONAL PARK AND PRESERVE

RED DOG MINE

Noatak River

Kivalina

BAIRD MOUNTAINS

CAPE KRUSENSTERN NATIONAL MONUMENT

Noatak

KOBUK VALLEY NATIONAL PARK

ONION PORTAGE ARCHEOLOGICAL SITE

Kobuk River

Ambler

KOYUKUK NATIONAL WILDLIFE REFUGE
An important stop for migratory birds, the refuge also contains the 10,000-acre Nogahabara Dunes, an actively shifting dune field.

CAPE KRUSENSTERN

Kiana

GREAT KOBUK SAND DUNES

Kobuk

Shungnak

Kotzebue ✈

Noorvik

SELAWIK NATIONAL WILDLIFE REFUGE

ARCTIC CIRCLE

NANA MUSEUM OF THE ARCTIC

Selawik

Hughes

Shishmaref

BALDWIN PENINSULA

BERING LAND BRIDGE NATIONAL PRESERVE

Kotzebue Sound

KOYUKUK NATIONAL WILDLIFE REFUGE

NOGAHABARA DUNES

Koyukuk River

Deering

Kiwalik

Buckland

SERPENTINE HOT SPRINGS

Huslia

Wales

Bering Strait

Taylor

SEWARD PENINSULA

PEOPLE OF THE ARCTIC

Wolf Mountain (4,978 ft.) ▲

Teller

Mount Bendelben (3,730 ft.) ▲

Kokrines

NOWITNA NATIONAL WILDLIFE REFUGE

Council

Koyuk

ELIM INDIAN RESERVATION

Traverse Peak (2,838 ft.) ▲

Galena

Yukon River

Ruby

Nome ✈

Solomon

Moses Point

Nulato

INNOKO NATIONAL WILDLIFE REFUGE

Long

Shaktoolik

Poorman

CAPE DARBY

UNALAKLEET
Each year in June, this small Native town is the focus of a spectacular salmon run, as king salmon rush up the Unalakleet River to spawn.

Norton Sound

Unalakleet

Innoko River

BERING SEA

STUART ISLAND

Saint Michael

INNOKO NATIONAL WILDLIFE REFUGE

Medfra

Kwikpak

Ophir

Kotlik

Takotna

Sterling Landing

Emmonak

YUKON DELTA NATIONAL WILDLIFE REFUGE

Grayling

Alakanuk

Yukon R.

0   30   60   90   120

INFORMATION FOR VISITORS

From Anchorage or Fairbanks, regularly scheduled airlines fly to most towns in western Alaska. Kotzebue is accessible only by air. Round-trip tours from Anchorage to Kotzebue include a tour of the city and the NANA Museum of the Arctic. Kotzebue's Northwest

Native Trade Fair and the World Eskimo-Indian Olympics in Fairbanks take place each year in July. The Northwest Alaska Areas Visitor Center in Kotzebue provides information on Cape Krusenstern National Monument, Kobuk Valley National Park, and Noatak National Preserve,

as well as Selawik National Wildlife Refuge. For more information: Alaska State Division of Tourism, P.O. Box E-600, Juneau, AK 99811; 907-465-2010.

on the site of the land bridge that connected Asia with North America. At the end of the last ice age, melting glaciers caused the sea level to rise, completely covering the route. Modern visitors have come to appreciate the allure of this isolated part of the Seward Peninsula, where lakes, lagoons, and streams support populations of birds. At Serpentine Hot Springs, a covered pool allows visitors to luxuriate in water heated to 140°F by underground volcanic activity. Within Bering Land Bridge National Preserve, local Eskimos still pursue a lifestyle based on hunting and fishing.

From the migrants that crossed the Bering land bridge, two distinct Eskimo groups evolved: the Inupiat Eskimos of northern Alaska, who speak Inupiaq, and the Yuit Eskimos of western and

TOOTHY TORPOR

Prized by some Eskimo communities as food, the meat of the ungainly Pacific walrus, above, was often fed by hunters to their dogs. Walrus bones were turned into harpoon parts, its teeth became fish hooks, and its long tusks were used for carvings.

POINT OF ORIGIN

A whalebone fence around Point Hope's burial ground, right, proclaims this Eskimo community's ties with the sea. According to local legend, the world began at Point Hope, when the flow from a seal oil lamp and the skin of an eider duck mixed together to form Man.

south-central Alaska, who speak Yup'ik. The huge delta of the Yukon River, encompassed today by the Yukon Delta Wildlife Refuge, is a major center of Yupik culture. According to anthropologists, the difference between the Inupiat and Yup'ik languages is roughly the same as that between English and German. Alaskan Eskimos are closely related to Siberian peoples such as the Chukchi, and are generally heavy-boned, muscular, and lean. Recent studies indicate that Eskimos have genetically adapted to the Arctic cold by retaining certain fat tissues into adulthood that are present only in childhood in other human populations. This tissue helps to sustain core body temperatures under extreme cold, for example, by maintaining higher temperatures in the hands and feet.

The Yuit Eskimos numbered as many as 30,000 at the time of first white contact, from 1780 to 1840. Based on technological and language differences, the Yuit are generally separated into two groups: the Bering Sea Yuit (from St. Lawrence Island to Bristol Bay) and the Pacific Yuit (from the Alaska peninsula to Prince William Sound). Given this vast geographical range, the Yuit are considered the most diverse group of Alaskan Native peoples. Whereas those on St. Lawrence Island, in the Bering Sea, made their homes in partially dugout structures, those in Prince William Sound lived in planked wooden houses built with material from their deep forest surroundings. During the summer months the Bering Sea Yuit of Bristol Bay reaped the bounty of one of the world's richest salmon fisheries, picked berries, collected birds' eggs, and hunted caribou, Dall sheep, snowshoe hares, parka squirrels, and ptarmigan.

THE BOUNTY
OF THE SEA

For thousands of years Inupiat Eskimos built dome-shaped, partially underground homes, made of sod blocks on a wood framework. The entrance passage ran underground so that cold air was trapped under the house and warm air was retained in the living areas above. Driftwood, whale bones, and sod made suitable building materials, and seal oil lamps provided light and warmth. The Inupiat of northern Alaska

FROZEN WINTER
With the coming of spring, the ice that chokes the coastal waters of western Alaska during the winter begins to break up, above. The sun barely rises above the horizon during the long winter months, and the land slumbers in alternating twilight and darkness.

*Tattoos have long been used
by Eskimos as facial adornment.
Tattoos are commonly positioned between the lower lip and
the chin, as in the face of the St.
Lawrence Island woman, right.
For young girls, facial tattoos
indicate eligibility for marriage.
Tattoos are made by an older
woman who first passes a needle
and thread through the soot of
an oil lamp and then through
the girl's skin.*

and the Bering Strait hunted bowhead and beluga whales, walruses, and seals—a tradition that some still follow to this day.

From their *umiaks*—open sealskin boats that could carry up to 15 men and a ton of cargo—and kayaks, which carried one man, they patrolled the seas with careful resolve. To kill a bowhead whale, a skilled hunter threw a toggle-headed harpoon. Sealskin floats tied to the harpoon slowed the whale as it attempted to escape, until the animal could be finished off with another well-aimed stroke by the harpooner. Following the hunt, the villagers harvested virtually every piece of the whale, and celebrated by tossing one another high into the air in a large sealskin blanket to the beat of a drum.

Because of the great amount of valuable oil rendered by a single bowhead, commercial whaling almost wiped out the whale during the 1800's. Since 1935 these great mammals have been protected by

the caribou funnel down from the Baird Mountains to the rushing river, archeologists have discovered a trove of artifacts that represent more than 9,500 years of continuous human occupation. The site is named for a small, edible wild onion. Now, like then, Eskimos gather here to hunt, pick berries, and fish the rivers.

TRACKING
THE CARIBOU

Caribou have for centuries sustained the Native peoples of Alaska's interior. The animals yield meat and fat for food; hides and sinews for clothing, boots, and tents; and antlers and bones for tools and implements. The surefooted caribou roam the tundra in search of grasses, sedges, berries, twigs, bark, and reindeer moss. Their spring migration northward begins in March. In September the northwestern herd—numbering about 500,000 animals—crosses the Kobuk River on its way south.

Onion Portage lies within the 1.7-million-acre Kobuk Valley National Park, which protects the central part of the Kobuk River as well as the 25-square-mile Great Kobuk Sand Dunes—North America's largest actively shifting dune area. This unique natural feature was formed from sand deposited by wind and water.

Life in Alaska is not easy. Through generations of experience, hunters have learned the patterns of ice and wind, the migrations of caribou, the tracks of foxes, and the antics of ravens. Yet the old ways are changing. "Nowadays, young men might find it hard to hunt this way," Eskimo author Lawrence Akisaqpak Gray has written. "Today you can just reach out and get it off a shelf."

Today a rough gravel road cuts across the north end of Cape Krusenstern National Monument,

INTRICATE SCRIMSHAW
*The skill and sophisticated visual
sense for which Eskimo artisans
are renowned is evident in the
scrimshawed walrus tusk, above,
crafted by an Inupiat artist.*

law. Only Alaska's Eskimos are permitted to hunt the bowhead, which can reach a length of 60 feet and weigh up to 80 tons.

In lieu of a whale, the hunter might stalk a seal—the Eskimos' main means of sustenance after the caribou—by waiting patiently next to a breathing hole in the ice, scratching a board to attract the animal, and striking suddenly when it appeared.

Inupiat Eskimos lived in large communities and numbered perhaps as many as 10,000 at the time of their first contact with whites, between 1850 and 1870. Time after time, when Yankee whalers underestimated the power and danger of the shifting Arctic sea ice, generous and resourceful Eskimos came to their rescue.

Inland, such as up the Kobuk River on the southern side of the Brooks Range, Inupiat Eskimos still continue to hunt caribou, which migrate every year between their winter feeding grounds south of the Kobuk River and summer calving grounds on Alaska's North Slope. At Onion Portage, located between the villages of Ambler and Kiana, where joining the stormy, historic coast with the Red Dog Mine, one of the richest lead and zinc deposits in the world. Bulldozers and trucks track across the fragile tundra. Eskimos, whose ancestors hunted and fished to survive, now make their living as miners and equipment operators.

Satellite dishes, televisions, microwaves, computers, and other modern conveniences have arrived in the remote villages of Alaska, altering the pattern of life of today's Eskimos. Some hold on to the old ways as best they can, while others move to Fairbanks and Anchorage to test the waters of mainstream America. The more than 200 Native regional and village corporations that have been created in Alaska give Eskimos and other Native Americans an opportunity to play a stronger role in the state's economic development.

If the past is a prologue, then the Eskimos, whose forefathers occupied Cape Krusenstern, will themselves face an uncertain future—one dictated more by contemporary Western culture than by the elements of nature. Poised between the jet age and the ice age, alcoholism, diabetes, poverty, stress, unemployment, and suicide now imperil the lives of many Eskimos.

Yet a pride endures. Every July Native athletes from Alaska and the lower 48 states, Canada, Greenland, and Russia converge on the city of Fairbanks to take part in the Eskimo-Indian Olympics. They test their mettle in the exciting one-foot- and two-foot-high kicks, the men's and women's blanket toss, the tug-of-war, the stick pull, and fish cutting. Authentic costumes are also judged, and the days are filled with laughter and storytelling. The games prove that tradition is its own form of wealth, more valuable than lead or zinc or oil; that the ridges of Cape Krusenstern, like the pages in a book, cannot be rewritten.

HUNTING SHELTER
Caribou antlers crown the entrance to a shelter at Onion Portage in Kobuk Valley National Park, left, signifying the importance of this hunting ground for the Eskimo.

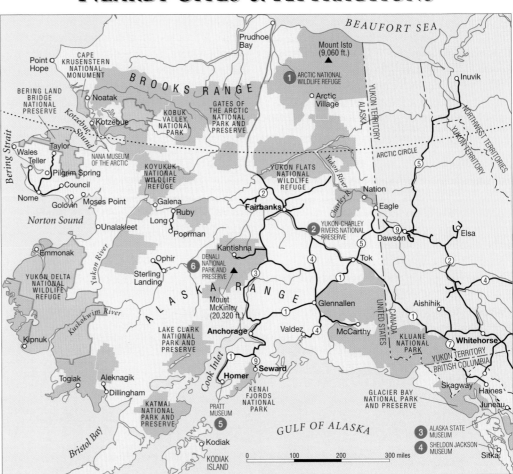

The Pratt Museum in Homer, above, offers exhibits on the natural and cultural history of the Kenai Peninsula. The museum also displays a collection of objects excavated at Kachemak Bay that documents the lifestyle of the region's prehistoric inhabitants.

① ARCTIC NATIONAL WILDLIFE REFUGE

Stretching from the Dalton Highway to the Canadian border and from Yukon Flats National Wildlife Refuge to the Beaufort Sea, Arctic National Wildlife Refuge is the northernmost and second-largest wildlife refuge in the nation. This landscape of rugged mountains, shallow lakes, twisting rivers, boreal forest, and tundra-covered plains offers opportunities for hiking, camping, wildlife watching, rafting, fishing, and hunting. The refuge's northern coastal plain is the summer calving ground for the massive Porcupine caribou herd. Also within the refuge's 19.8 million acres live musk ox, grizzly bears, wolves, wolverines, and Dall sheep. More than 160 species of birds rest, feed, and nest here. During the short summer, wildflowers such as purple mountain saxifrage, yellow arnica, and pink phlox abound. Most visitors fly from Fairbanks to Arctic Village, Fort Yukon, Deadhorse, or Barter Island, and then charter a bush plane into the refuge.

② YUKON-CHARLEY RIVERS NATIONAL PRESERVE

Encompassing 2.5 million acres of wilderness in eastern Alaska, the preserve protects a 130-mile section of the great Yukon River, as well as the entire length of one of its largest tributaries—the 106-mile-

long Charley River. The Yukon River flows 1,979 miles from its headwaters in Canada's Northwest Territories west to the Bering Sea. A float trip down the river from the town of Eagle is one of the best ways to see the preserve; sidetrips up its many tributaries reveal abandoned cabins, wildlife, and granite mountains. Untouched by glaciers during the Ice Age, the region has been shaped by the many rivers that course through it. The varied topography, cloaked with mixed forest, provides spectacular vistas for river rafters. The riverbanks and mountainsides are covered in tundra, muskeg, cottonwood, spruce, and birch. Among the wildlife in the preserve are brown and black bears, wolves, wolverines, Dall sheep, lynx, and beavers, but the most famous inhabitant is the peregrine falcon. Using river bluffs to spot its prey, the peregrine reaches speeds in excess of 200 miles an hour in a dive. Headquarters of the preserve is in Fairbanks; a contact center is located at Eagle on Hwy. 5.

③ ALASKA STATE MUSEUM

Located in the state capital, the museum was established in 1900 to showcase Alaska's natural wonders, diverse cultures, and colorful history. The state's Native heritage is given prominent focus in the museum. On display are gut parkas, hats, and grass baskets from the Aleutian Islands, and ivory

6 DENALI NATIONAL PARK AND PRESERVE

One of the few remaining areas on earth that has been left virtually untouched by humans, Denali covers a total of 6 million acres, making it larger than the state of Massachusetts. The centerpiece of the park is 20,320-foot Mount McKinley, which dominates the 600-mile-long Alaska Range and is North America's highest mountain. The name of the park comes from an Athabascan word meaning "The High One," in reference to the mighty mountain. Originating just below the summit of the mountain, Muldrow Glacier—one of many glaciers within the park—extends 35 miles from Mount McKinley. Most of the park consists of taiga, characterized by forests of white spruce and black spruce, and tundra, an often-waterlogged landscape of willow and dwarf birch, brightened in summer by spectacular displays of wildflowers. Denali is home to more than 430 species of flowering plants, among them white mountain avens, moss campions, alpine azalea, saxifrage, and geraniums. Some 37 species of mammals, including caribou, wolves, beavers, foxes, grizzly bears, and Dall sheep, live in the park, and snow buntings, plovers, and hawk owls are among the 157 species of birds that can be spotted. Shuttle buses travel along the 85-mile road that leads from the main entrance to Wonder Lake. Located 120 miles southwest of Fairbanks on Hwy. 3.

Wildflowers such as the delicate ice-coated ranunculus, left, are one of nature's works of art in Arctic National Wildlife Refuge. Alaska's short arctic summer means that flowers bloom only briefly.

With the Toklat River and 5,790-foot Mount Polychrome in the background, these dwarf birch and willow trees in Denali National Park, below, create a palette of autumn colors.

figurines, mittens, drums, masks, and parkas of the Eskimos of the north and west. Other exhibits include hunting tools and beadwork of the interior Athabascan Indians, along with Chilkat robes, carved helmets, spruce root baskets, and bentwood boxes made by southeastern Alaska's Tlingit and Haida peoples. The highlight of the natural history section is a diorama depicting a 30-foot eagle nesting tree, complete with a nest and a family of bald eagles. The museum also traces Russia's contribution to Alaskan history. Located at 395 Whittier St. in Juneau.

4 SHELDON JACKSON MUSEUM

Alaska's oldest museum houses Native artifacts amassed between 1888 and 1898 by missionary Rev. Sheldon Jackson, who recognized the need to preserve the heritage of the "Great Land." The collection focuses on the state's four main Native groups: the Eskimo, Aleut, Athabascan, and Northwest Coast Indians. Masks, ivory carvings, baskets, kayaks, and gut and skin clothing are part of the Eskimo collection. The Athabascan section displays a birchbark canoe, baskets, and clothing. The highlight of the Aleut collection is a *baidarka*, a traditional hide-covered boat. The Northwest Coast exhibit features items from the Tlingit, Haida, and Tsimshian cultures, including Haida carvings and a Tlingit dugout canoe. Also on display are fishing and hunting implements, ivory carvings, beads, and basketwork. In 1897 the artifacts were moved into the first concrete structure to be built in Alaska. Located at 104 College Dr. in Sitka.

5 PRATT MUSEUM

Focusing on the culture and natural history of the lower Cook Inlet, Kachemak Bay, and the Kenai Peninsula, the varied collection of this fine regional museum includes some 7,000 artifacts related to Alaska's Eskimo, Aleut, and Athabascan cultures. On display are clothing, tools, dolls, baskets, fishing and hunting implements, and household items. Other exhibits feature Alaskan art, marine mammals, and seabirds. There is also a botanical garden that showcases native Alaskan plants. Located at 3779 Bartlett St. in Homer.

Pueblo del Arroyo, Chaco Culture National Historical Park.

MOUNDVILLE ARCHAEOLOGICAL PARK

When the mist rises off the Black Warrior River, deep in the heart of Alabama, more than 20 mysterious, flat-topped mounds emerge on the horizon. Set on a high bluff, these ceremonial mounds are easily discernible in the distance. Their builders, the Mississippian Indians, intended that they dominate the neighboring landscape of quiet woods and grass-clad plains.

Although countless mounds nationwide have been razed by plows, a number of survivors can be found at the Moundville site. Occupied from about A.D. 1000 until A.D. 1550, Moundville was an ancient metropolis protected on three sides by a wooden palisade. Located just 15 miles south of the present-day city of Tuscaloosa, the ceremonial center at Moundville was one of the most powerful communities of the prehistoric Southeast, with trade routes that spanned the lower Mississippi Valley. More than 3,000 people lived in this ancient city, which was supported by farms along a 50-mile stretch of the valley. Here they

fashioned more than 26 earthen mounds—including one almost 60 feet high—laid out in a rectangle around a central plaza. These mounds resembled pyramids shorn of their tops. Some of the larger ones may have had buildings that were used for ceremonies, residences, or mortuaries.

Travelers can explore the reconstructed temple and village at the park. A stroll through the forest along a boardwalk nature trail leads to the panoramic Black Warrior River, once the main water source for the Indians' crops of corn, beans, and squash. The park museum displays engraved pots, copper jewelry, and stone vessels that recall Moundville's apex as an artistic and cultural center. Among the museum's finds are beautiful ornaments made of mica, galena, and marine shells, which adorned the nobles of the town. The abrupt decline of the Mississippian culture in the 16th century remains shrouded in mystery, and the abandoned mounds offer few clues to the reasons for the disappearance of the people.

Each fall members of the Southeastern tribes display arts and crafts and reenact traditional tales in the Moundville Native American Festival.

FOR MORE INFORMATION:
Moundville Archaeological Park, University of Alabama Museums, P.O. Box 66, Moundville, AL 35474; 205-371-2572.

RUSSELL CAVE NATIONAL MONUMENT
Almost 9,000 years ago, a nomadic band of forest-dwelling Indians discovered Russell Cave, which was embedded in a ridge of limestone bluffs. Within its safe shelter, these hunters and gatherers made campfires to keep themselves warm during the

autumn and winter. When not hunting deer or turkey, they subsisted on nuts, seeds, and wild plants, and fashioned spear and arrow points from chert, which formed as hardened nodules in the limestone. From 6550 B.C. to A.D. 500, generations of cave dwellers left behind their pottery, arrow points, and tools made of bone, including awls and fishhooks. These relics were found in the mid-1950's and are now preserved as a national archeological treasure in this 310-acre park, established in 1961.

Items unearthed from the site are displayed on the museum grounds. Visitors may also take a self-guided tour into the cavern depths and view an actual archeological dig, where each successive layer of soil represents a different period of Native American occupation. In one layer—the oldest burial site ever discovered in Alabama—archeologists dug up the partial remains of a two-year-old male child. Another excavation revealed the bodies of a woman and a man who once lived in Russell Cave. Museum staff demonstrate how these Native American peoples made tools from flint, hunted game with their throwing sticks, ground corn, cracked walnuts, and fashioned leather thongs.

FOR MORE INFORMATION:
Russell Cave National Monument, Rte. 1, P.O. Box 175, Bridgeport, AL 35740; 205-495-2672.

The Rattlesnake Disk, above, was probably used by the Mississippian Indians to mix pigments during ceremonial events.

A reconstructed Indian village at Moundville Archaeological Park, left, shows how the Mississippian Indians once lived.

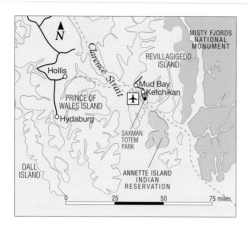

With its eyes set in a watchful gaze over the southeastern Alaska town of Ketchikan, an eagle carved out of red cedar sits atop a pole in Eagle Park. The creature's curved beak and thundering wings are one of the first sights to greet visitors as they descend from cruise ships at Ketchikan's dock. The striking carving embodies the spirit of the town: the name Ketchikan is derived from a Tlingit Indian word that means "the spread wings of an eagle."

Ketchikan's totem poles tell the story of the Tlingit and Haida peoples, who were the first inhabitants of coastal Alaska and British Columbia. Lacking a written language, the coastal Indians carved cedar poles to record great events from their past, to mark the graves of prominent individuals, and to identify clans. The majority of

Following Prohibition in 1920, many of the houses on Creek Street, above, became speakeasies. Bootlegged liquor was passed through trapdoors in the floors from small boats at high tide.

these striking carvings were inspired by the wild creatures that inhabit Alaska's rugged coastal wilderness, such as beavers, orca whales, bears, and ravens.

WEATHERED TREASURES

Ketchikan today is one of the best places in the world to view totems in their majestic natural setting. The Totem Heritage Center, a national historic landmark located beside the salmon-spawning waters of Ketchikan Creek, contains contemporary totem poles, as well as the nation's largest authentic collection of 19th-century totems. Included among them are 33 poles retrieved from deserted Tlingit villages on Tongass and Village islands and the Haida community of Old Kasaan. Visitors can also see modern-day artists at work creating bentwood boxes, wooden dance masks, beadings, and argillite carvings.

A walking tour of Ketchikan's historic district reveals its rich Native heritage. The interior of St. John's Episcopal Church, built in 1903, is adorned with intricate cedar panels carved by turn-of-the-century Tlingit artists. At the nearby Tongass Historical Museum, carving tools are on display, along with ceremonial potlatch hats, Haida dance blankets, and cedar bark and spruce root baskets. Some of the finely woven baskets are watertight. On Stedman Street, the imposing Return of the Eagle mural was painted by Don Barrie and 25 Native youths in 1978. This work of art

illustrates various ancient stories and symbolizes the renewal of the earth.

Tlingit, Haida, and Tsimshian people offer visitors a two-hour cultural tour that includes a visit to the Deer Mountain Hatchery, a facility that raises some 350,000 king, coho, and steelhead salmon smolts each year. Salmon was, and still remains, a staple of the coastal Indian diet. About three miles south of Ketchikan, Saxman Totem Park stands in the Tlingit village of the same name. Founded in 1886, the town contains the largest cedar clan house in Alaska and the only traditional clan house to be built in the state in the past half century. At the Saxman Carving Center, visitors can watch master carvers and apprentices creating poles and large cedar canoes using traditional techniques.

Totem Bight State Historical Park was once a summer fishing camp for Tlingit Indians. A short trail winds through a dense rain forest of red cedars and hemlocks. When visitors emerge from the woods, they are greeted by a clan house that overlooks the Tongass Narrows. Towering totem poles face the sea, welcoming signposts for canoes returning home with the day's catch.

FOR MORE INFORMATION:

Ketchikan Visitors Bureau, 131 Front St., Ketchikan, AK 99901; 907-225-6166.

Raven House totem pole, above, is located in Saxman Totem Park. The park contains the world's largest collection of totem poles.

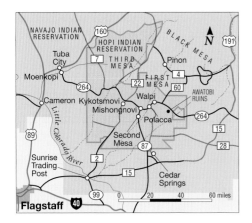

According to the legends of the Hopi, when their ancestors came forth from the Sipapu—the "place of emergence"—they traveled the four corners of the globe searching for a land to call home. The Mootiyungqam, or "Ones Who Came First," finally chose a sacred place on an arid plateau between the Rio Grande and the Colorado River, which they believed to be the spiritual center of the earth, and the spot where the Hopi people had been prophesied to live.

Reaching out from the giant Black Mesa to the north, three steep, flat-topped mesas rise from the sun-baked desert floor like stone altars. The land in this corner of northeastern Arizona is dry and barren. Even in a good year, the parched soil receives just 10 inches of rain and snow. There are tiny springs that skirt the mesas, but they are meager sustenance for some 10,000 Hopi Indians who live here. Created in 1882, the 1.5-million-acre Hopi Indian Reservation lies completely surrounded by Navajo lands.

A deeply spiritual people, the Hopi see in their homeland's stark landscape a reminder to pray for rain and food, and to be thankful to the Creator. Their beliefs, which they call *Hopivötskwani*—the "Hopi path of life"—are expressed in elaborate ceremonial dances that are staged throughout the year. Among the most dramatic rituals is the summer buffalo dance, in which dancers with buffalo-style headdresses emerge from kivas to appeal to the spirits for rain. During the Niman ceremony, which takes place at the summer solstice, Katsinam—the Hopis' spiritual helpmates, who are also called katsinas—are said to return home to the San Francisco Peaks, where they manifest themselves as clouds. During the snake dances held in August, dancers perform with poisonous serpents in their mouths. This ceremony honors the snake people, with the hope that they may answer the Hopis' prayers for rain.

Although Hwy. 264 runs straight through the heart of the reservation, the Hopi have steadfastly resisted the encroachment of the outside world. Many of the sacred dances are closed to outsiders, and commercial tourism is frowned upon. Visitors are advised to stop at the Hopi Cultural Center, on Second Mesa just beyond the village of Mishongnovi, to confirm the dates and locations of public dances. This pueblo-style complex houses a museum and shop filled with Hopi crafts. Accommodations are available at the center, where visitors may also dine on various traditional Hopi staples, including hominy stew, blue pancakes, and piki—a parchment-thin bread made of blue cornmeal, water, and a pinch of ashes.

EXPLORING THE MESAS

When exploring the mesas, some visitors may drive right past an old Hopi pueblo, mistakenly assuming it to be a pile of sandstone rubble. Many of the 17th-century stone villages were built low and flat-roofed on the edge of the mesas in order to camouflage them from the Navajo and Apache. Today many Hopi live in 12 villages, which are clustered around the old sites, some with tongue-tying names such as Bacavi, Shungopovi, and Moenkopi. On First Mesa, at Walpi and Polacca, local artisans are noted for their traditional hand-shaped pottery, which is made without a potter's wheel and decorated with paint derived from wild spinach.

The most important village on Second Mesa is Shungopovi, or "place by the spring where the tall reeds grow." Once situated below the mesa at Gray Spring, the pueblo was relocated to the mesa following the violent 1680 revolt against Spanish rule. Visitors to Second Mesa may also purchase the fine silver objects, and other Hopi arts and crafts, which are on display at the Hopi Silvercraft Cooperative Guild. History buffs should visit the ancient pueblo of Old Oraibi on Third Mesa, which was founded in 1150 and is reputed to be one of the oldest continuously inhabited settlements in the nation.

Those who still remain untouched by the spirit of the Hopi land should take a moment to scan the dusty, rock-strewn fields. Everywhere the sandstone hills show signs of dry farming, a method of cultivation that the Hopi learned from their Ancestral Pueblo forebears, which allows them to coax corn, beans, and melons from the desert floor. These hard-earned crops are a testament to the faith and resourcefulness of the Hopi people, who have endured through the centuries by reaping a miraculous harvest from this rocky soil.

FOR MORE INFORMATION:
The Hopi Tribe, Cultural Preservation Office, P.O. Box 123, Kykotsmovi, AZ 86039; 520-734-2244.

These colorful Hopi plaques, above, are on display at the Heard Museum in Phoenix.

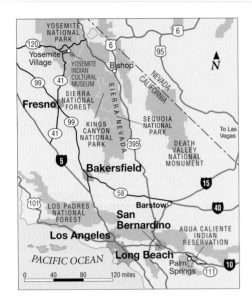

Slabs of granite pitted with mortar holes, above, are found in Yosemite National Park.

AGUA CALIENTE RESERVATION

Undaunted by the searing desert and rocky gorges of present-day Southern California, the Cahuilla Indians were quick to fathom the physical and spiritual powers of their homeland. For more than 2,000 years, they hunted game in the outlying canyons, grew crops, and gathered plants and seeds for food, medicine, and basket weaving. The only North American Indians known to dig wells, the Cahuilla tapped into the desert's underground springs when surface water was in short supply.

The desert also bubbled with natural wonder. The hot mineral springs lent the name Agua Caliente—or "hot water"—to the band of Cahuilla Indians that made this area their home. The springs soon became the focal point for healing and ceremonial rituals of the Palm Springs settlement. The Indians believed that the waters had

a therapeutic effect. The rough-planked bathhouse they erected centuries ago has been today transformed into the Palm Springs resort, situated on the Agua Caliente Reservation.

The Cahuilla, who struggled to make ends meet early in this century, now control about 42 percent of the Coachella Valley, making them one of the richest tribes in North America.

Like the ancient Cahuilla before them, present-day visitors are struck by the region's breathtaking beauty. The Palm, Andreas, and Murray canyons are the first-, second-, and fourth-largest natural palm oases in the world and are home to a surprising array of wildlife, including bighorn sheep and wild ponies. Andreas Canyon, a populous bird habitat, also contains more than 150 species of plants, examples of unique Cahuilla rock art, and the remains of mortars and metates used centuries ago to prepare food. Tahquitz Canyon, just west of the city of Palm Springs, features a spectacular waterfall and is the future site of the Agua Caliente Cultural Museum.

FOR MORE INFORMATION:

The Agua Caliente Tribe, 960 East Tahquitz Canyon Way, Ste. 106, Palm Springs, CA 92262; 619-325-5673.

YOSEMITE INDIAN CULTURAL MUSEUM

Yosemite is a national park bestowed with towering waterfalls, shimmering lakes, alpine meadows, forests, and a stretch of the Sierra Nevada. For more than 2,000

years, its lush, sheltered valley was the homeland of the Miwok and Paiute peoples, who came to be called Ahwahnichi— the "Ones Who Live in the Valley Shaped Like a Big Mouth"—and whose descendants still inhabit areas of Yosemite today.

The Indian Cultural Museum was opened in 1976 to exhibit Yosemite's native history. Among the artifacts on display are those collected by early park residents such as artist Chris Jorgensen and photographer J. T. Boysen. The Atkinson family, who lived in Yosemite at the turn of the century, amassed one of the finest collections of woven baskets from that period. Women wove them from shoots and roots of native grasses. Their baskets were created essentially as tools to gather and store food, sift flour, and cook acorn mush. In later years, some baskets were decorated with glass beads. One of the museum's finest baskets, patterned in redbud and black bracken fern root, took almost four years to complete.

The men hunted with bows and arrows made from cedar branches, which they covered in deer sinew, and fished with deer-bone hooks attached to long lines made of hemp. Examples of these hunting tools are on display at the museum. A reconstructed Indian village of bark houses, a round-house, and sweat lodge provides visitors with a further glimpse of their lifestyle.

FOR MORE INFORMATION:

Yosemite Indian Cultural Museum, National Park Service, P.O. Box 577, Yosemite National Park, CA 95389; 209-372-0282.

Named for its abundance of palm trees, Palm Canyon, below, contrasts with the surrounding desertlike landscape within the Cahuilla lands.

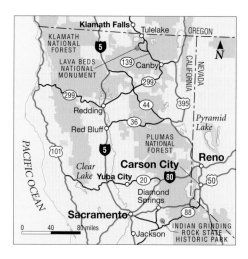

Schonchin Butte Trail in Lava Beds National Monument provides visitors with a sweeping view of the surrounding landscape, above, including Tule Lake, seen in the distance.

INDIAN GRINDING ROCK

In spring an alpine meadow in the Sierra Nevada foothills blossoms with mountain violets, phlox, buttercups, and wild roses, its carpet of wildflowers laid out in welcome at the entrance to Indian Grinding Rock State Historic Park. Here, in a tiny valley nestled 10 miles east of the town of Jackson, gnarled oaks and a grove of pines frame the meadow and a cluster of ancient limestone grinding rocks, which jut from the land. Weathered and gray, their surface is pock-marked with holes, which are shaped like miniature craters.

For the Miwok people, this place was Chaw'se, the "grinding rock" where they came to pound acorns and other seeds into meal using a mortar against the bed-rock. Over time, the friction of stone on stone caused the fragile, marbleized lime-stone to chip away, creating the largest concentration of mortar pits ever found in North America: exactly 1,185 holes in all. Petroglyphs that decorate the rocks include spoked wheels, pawprints, animals, and wavy lines that date back at least 3,000 years, and which are slowly eroding.

North Trail offers a good view of the bedrock mortar and leads to the Chaw'se Museum, which displays Northern Sierra Indian baskets, bird traps, and portable mortars. Visitors can see evidence of the acorn's importance in the Miwok diet at an acorn granary ingeniously lined with rodent-repelling cedar needles and worm-wood leaves, as well as a 60-foot-wide roundhouse still used several times a year to celebrate the harvest.

Farther west along this picturesque trail is a reconstructed traditional Miwok village of bark houses built of cedar, willow, and grape vines. Adventurous groups looking for a unique experience can spend the night sleeping in one of seven bark houses at the U'macha'tam'ma campsite.

FOR MORE INFORMATION:

Indian Grinding Rock State Historic Park, 14881 Pine Grove–Volcano Rd., Pine Grove, CA 95665; 209-296-7488.

LAVA BEDS NATIONAL MONUMENT

Thousands of years before white settlers stumbled upon this volcanic territory, Lava Beds National Monument was the home-land of the Modoc Indians. Living on both sides of what is now the California–Oregon border, the Modocs hunted the valleys and mountains, fished the lakes and rivers, and learned to survive in this rugged land, which was millions of years in the making. Seemingly barren and inhospitable, the region covers 75 square miles of natural beauty. The scruffy grasslands in the north-ern region gradually become lush fields dotted with junipers, before giving way to a wilderness of pine forests.

The most striking legacy of the volcanic activity is the vast array of approximately 200 lava tube caves. The tubes are created when hot lava pours from a volcano and its outer layer cools, serving as an insulator, which allows a river of fire to flow beneath its crust. After the eruption ceases, a tunnel or tube is left behind.

Geological turbulence has not prevented plant and animal life from thriving at Lava Beds. Many predatory animals and a large concentration of raptors—including 24 species of hawks, falcons, owls, and other birds of prey—feed on the monument's resident population of squirrels, kangaroo rats, and yellow-bellied marmots. Nesting in the cliffs overlooking Tule Lake, the bald eagle winters here in greater numbers than at any other place except Alaska. This area is situated along the Pacific Flyway and the sky above it is often darkened by birds during the semi-annual migration.

Lava Beds National Monument also contains a treasure trove of rock art. Pictographs are found at the entrances to the larger lava tubes at Symbol Bridge and Big Painted Cave. Archeologists estimate that the pictographs date from about A.D. 500 to A.D. 1600. Petroglyphs, includ-ing wavy lines, dots, human figures, and rakes, adorn the cliff faces and boulders along the entrance to the monument.

Today the Modoc no longer roam the region along the banks of Tule, Lower Klamath, and Clear lakes. All that remains is the wildlife, the rugged and wondrous terrain, and the faint echoes of a people who once called this place home.

FOR MORE INFORMATION:

Superintendent, Lava Beds National Monument, P.O. Box 867, Tulelake, CA 96134; 916-667-2282.

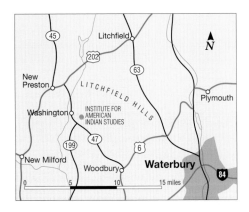

S et in one of the most scenic corners of Connecticut—a picturesque blend of clapboard homes, white-steepled churches, and covered bridges in the Litchfield Hills—is an acclaimed research and educational center dedicated to the people who lived here long before the arrival of European settlers. The Institute for American Indian Studies (formerly known as the American Indian Archeological Institute) keeps alive the history, culture, and living traditions of the Indian peoples of the Northeast. Among the first Native Americans to come into contact with Europeans, these Algonquian tribes lived through revolutionary changes brought about by white settlement, industry, and commerce. They remain part of New England's cultural fabric.

Archeologists have determined that these forests have been inhabited for thousands of years. In the days when great hardwood forests stretched almost unbroken over the eastern part of North America, western

Connecticut was home to the Golden Hill Paugussett, the Pootatuck, the Pequot, the Weantinock, and the Schaghticoke. These clans belonged to the same Algonquian-speaking group as the Micmac Indians of eastern Canada, and the Niantic, who inhabited the region south of Cape Cod. Today the rich and quiet beauty of their ancestral lands is easily accessible to hikers, canoeists, and motorists.

The burning colors of autumn wash over the slopes and valleys of this wooded landscape. Familiar from countless post-cards and paintings, the leafy glens of the Litchfield Hills were once home and hunting grounds to the Eastern Woodland Indians. Nuts, berries, wildfowl, deer, beaver, fish, and crustaceans provided a rich and varied diet, and glades were cleared to grow crops such as corn, beans, squash, and tobacco. Branches and bark were skill-fully used to fashion bows and arrows; wood and stone were carved and pounded into tools, household implements, and housing. Even the Woodlanders' trans-portation needs were met by the forest, whose timber yielded snowshoes, birch-bark canoes, and frames used to carry infants along woodland trails.

A LIVING PRESENCE

Although the Woodlanders' numbers have been reduced through disease, disruption, and assimilation, their presence is still felt in this section of the country. In western Connecticut, Golden Hill holds a quarter-acre remnant of a 1659 reserve granted to the Paugussett, Pootatuck, Weantinock, and Schaghticoke peoples. Stone cairns can be

found in the forests, commemorating sites where remarkable events occurred. Rocks and caves sometimes reveal petroglyphs. The remains of Waramaug, a clan leader of the Weantinock, are located on the Housatonic River near New Milford, at a traditional fishing spot known as Lover's Leap. This was the location of an important village and sacred site up until the early colonial period.

The exhibits, reconstructions, and living-history demonstrations presented by the institute serve as reminders of the vital presence that links the present and the past. Among the highlights of the institute is the reconstructed Algonquian Village—an authentic settlement with wigwams, a longhouse, rock shelter, simulated archeo-logical site, and garden filled with Native American crops. There are exhibitions that detail excavations of prehistoric villages, some which are believed to be 10,000 years old, and Native tools, baskets, pottery, and art objects are displayed. The institute also runs education programs in Native life-ways, history, and storytelling, as well as summer camps for children. Throughout the year, workshops bring traditional knowledge into the present: participants can try their hand at making a talking stick or a dream catcher, or tracking animals through the surrounding woods.

A permanent exhibit titled "As We Tell Our Stories" features the voices of many Native Americans, who recount their life experiences. Native storytelling, dancing, and other performances are held in the Algonquian Village. Accompanied by a guide on nature trails, visitors can learn to identify varieties of mushrooms, medicinal plants, and herbs traditionally used by Native peoples. The institute is also a center for the arts, featuring major exhibitions of contemporary Native artists in its museum gallery and exhibit hall. Although the main focus of the Institute for American Indian Studies is the Native peoples of Connecticut and New England, it is also a place to learn about the histories and cultural traditions of Indians throughout the Americas.

FOR MORE INFORMATION:
Institute for American Indian Studies, P.O. Box 1260, 38 Curtis Rd., Washington, CT 06793-0260; 203-868-0518.

The Algonquian Village at the Institute for American Indian Studies, left, re-creates Eastern Woodland Indian life in about A.D. 1600.

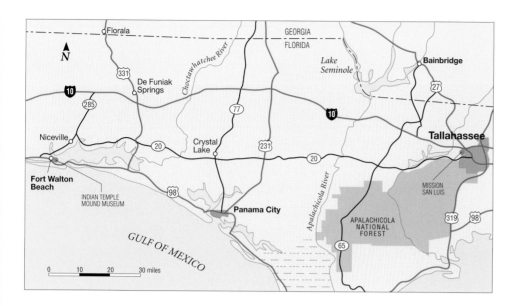

Today the 50-acre site is an archeological research station, where scholars attempt to determine the ways in which Spanish and Apalachee cultures influenced each other in the areas of technology, diet, settlement layout, social organization, and religious life. Excavations begun in 1985 have uncovered a religious complex that includes a church, friary, cemetery, and kitchen; two Apalachee villages, a central plaza, an Apalachee council house, and a Spanish fort. Visitors can watch archeological excavations in progress from April through September or visit the research lab's vestibule. On display are drawings depicting the reconstruction of the mission, the Indian council house, and the fort. The annual Rediscover San Luis festival re-creates daily life at the site.

INDIAN TEMPLE MOUND MUSEUM

The largest prehistoric earthwork on salt water rises 12 feet high in the town of Fort Walton Beach, Florida. The truncated pyramid was built about A.D. 1400 by the Mississippian people, a fishing and farming culture with a complex government system and a trade network that extended as far north and south as Maine and Texas.

Measuring 223 feet long and 178 feet wide at its base, the mound is made of some 100,000 cubic feet of sand, dirt, clay and shells that the Indians hauled to the site by the basketful. The pyramid, positioned in the middle of a village, was surrounded by numerous houses made of wood and clay, whose roofs were thatched with grass. Serving as the foundation for a temple or the residence of a chief, the mound was the religious and political center of the community. Ceremonies, games, and public events were held in a central plaza on the mound's southern side.

Designated a national historic landmark, the earthwork is crowned with a replica of a temple. The Indian Temple Mound Museum's collection reflects the technological, spiritual, and artistic achievements of the prehistoric peoples of the Paleo, Archaic, Woodland, and Mississippian cultural traditions. More than 4,000 artifacts were collected from a radius of 40 miles around the site. Made of stone, bone, shell, and clay, these objects include 10,000-year-old projectile points and unusual effigy containers. Most notable are a burial urn depicting a man with pierced ears sitting in a chair with a cloak around his shoulders, and a number of animal-shaped vessels. The museum's extensive collection of prehistoric Southeastern pottery is considered one of the nation's finest.

FOR MORE INFORMATION:

Indian Temple Mound Museum, 139 Miracle Strip Pkwy., Fort Walton Beach, FL 32548; 904-243-6521.

MISSION SAN LUIS

After the Spanish founded St. Augustine in 1565, they began to establish a network of missions and town sites in the new colony of La Florida, hoping to advance Spanish religious and commercial interests in the area and prevent Native uprisings. The Apalachee Indians were the wealthiest tribe in the region during this time.

Considered the most populous tribe in northeastern Florida, the Apalachee tribe numbered more than 6,000 in the mid-16th century. After Hernando de Soto passed through this part of Florida in 1539 in search of gold, the Spanish realized the Apalachee would make formidable opponents unless they became allied through religious conversion. Their fertile homeland became a key destination for Franciscan friars in the early 17th century.

San Luis de Talimali, located just outside Tallahassee, was one of eight major Apalachee towns. It served as the capital of the Spanish mission system from 1656 to 1704. The town included a circular thatched council house that archeologists consider to have been the largest Native building in the Southeast. The Spanish mission and Apalachee Indian town site was abandoned by residents in 1704. The people of San Luis burned their homes to the ground to keep them from falling into the hands of British forces and their Creek Indian allies invading from the north.

A reconstructed tannery at Mission San Luis, above, is one of many displays that re-create life in this 17th-century Apalachee town.

Interpreters in period costume demonstrate 17th-century Spanish crafts.

Outdoor exhibits are linked by a path with markers detailing history. On the site's northeastern corner, a nature trail rambles through a ravine of hardwoods and a pine hammock. Bluestem palmetto, yaupon holly, and southern lady fern now grow along springs that supplied water to the Apalachee people for thousands of years.

FOR MORE INFORMATION:

Mission San Luis, Florida Dept. of State, 2020 West Mission Rd., Tallahassee, FL 32304-1624; 904-487-3711.

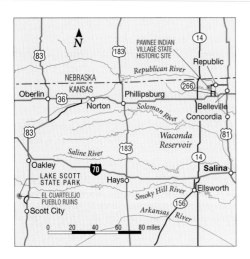

A wooden fence, complete with interpretive plaques, above, safeguards the excavated foundation walls of El Cuartelejo, located within Lake Scott State Park.

EL CUARTELEJO PUEBLO RUINS

In 19th-century Kansas, a slight mound on the western plains was the only sign that an abandoned 17th-century Indian abode lay underground near Scott City. Archeologists began excavations in 1898 and unearthed the northernmost pueblo settlement in the nation. The settlement, uncharacteristic of the Plains tribes, was built by Pueblo Indians who fled to the Plains from what is now New Mexico. Having escaped the noose of Spanish rule that was tightening around their native land, the Taos Indians established El Cuartelejo in 1650 with a tribe of Plains Apache, who became known as the Cuartelejo band.

The Taos built the pueblos with willow poles and stone from the surrounding hills, plastering the insides with adobe. Having neither doors nor windows, the houses were entered by ladder through an opening in the roof. The tribe cultivated corn and other crops using a system of irrigation ditches fed by a nearby spring.

Persuaded by the Spanish to return to New Mexico, the tribe left El Cuartelejo after 20 years, but the settlement was revived in 1701 by the Picuris Indians. The second Pueblo tribe stayed for two years before returning south.

Indians reported various occupations by the Spanish military and French traders at the settlement, but El Cuartelejo was abandoned for good around 1730, when attacks by bands of Comanche, Ute, and Pawnee forced the Cuartelejo Apache southward out of the Plains.

When first excavated, the ruins were strewn with charcoal, burned tools, and bits of charred corn, suggesting that the settlement was razed. Archeologists also found stone and bone tools, ornaments, and pottery shards.

By 1970 portions of the stone hearths and two lower sections of the outer wall were all that remained at the site; restoration work began in earnest in 1971. Visitors can view the reconstructed foundation, and interpretive panels describe the Indians' way of life in the pueblo.

FOR MORE INFORMATION:
El Cuartelejo Pueblo Ruins, Lake Scott State Park, Rte. 1, P.O. Box 50, Scott City, KS 67871; 316-872-2061.

PAWNEE INDIAN VILLAGE

The fertile banks of the Republican River were the seasonal home of the Pawnee Nation, which grew corn, beans, and squash and hunted buffalo. The tribe inhabited the Platte and Loup valleys of present-day Nebraska and northern Kansas, far from the trade routes of white settlers. Because of their relatively remote geographical location, they were among the last of the Plains Indian tribes to come into contact with European settlers.

Pawnee warriors greased their hair into thick locks that stood up from the scalp in shapes resembling horns. In fact, their tribal name means "horn." Other Plains tribes, including the Sioux, Cheyenne, Arapaho, and Osage, considered the Pawnee to be among their fiercest adversaries.

The Pawnee Nation, composed of the Chaui, Pitahaurat, Kitkehahki, and Skidi subtribes, once numbered as many as 20,000. Ravaged by war and disease, the tribe was already in decline by the time the settlement was built.

Located west of Belleville, Kansas, the Pawnee Indian Village Museum was built on the excavated floor of an earthlodge that was constructed by a band of Republican River Pawnee in the 1820's. A path leads through some of the grounds surrounding the museum, and interpretive signs describe remnants of the village.

Inside the circular museum, wall dioramas depict the Pawnee village as it looked before it was abandoned. Stone, bone, and metal tools are spread out on the hardened clay floor of the museum in the exact position in which they were found, along with hoe blades made from the scapula of a bison, arrow shaft smoothers made of sandstone, and parts of a typical trade gun. Sections of mussel shell and bits of corn are scattered on the floor, where the hearth contains ashes from the last cooking fires.

A model of a Pawnee earthlodge explains how the round structures were built. Sod blocks supported the domed roof, framed with willow saplings and thatched with grass. Each lodge had a smoke hole at the top and storage pits for corn, squash, and dried meat. The original village would have had up to 40 lodges and more than 1,000 inhabitants; today the remains of 22 lodge sites, storage pits, plazas, and a fortification wall are visible at the 12-acre site.

FOR MORE INFORMATION:
Pawnee Indian Village State Historic Site, R.R. 1, P.O. Box 475, Republic, KS 66964-9618; 913-361-2255.

I t took a bird's-eye view for archeologists to recognize a pattern in the odd structures and mysterious earthen mounds left by an ancient bird-worshiping culture at Poverty Point, poised on Macon Ridge above the Mississippi River floodplain in northeastern Louisiana. First studied in 1872, the group of mounds was considered insignificant until 1953, when aerial photographs taken by the U.S. Army Corps of Engineers revealed an intriguing configuration of six concentric, horseshoe-shaped ridges bordering a 37-acre plaza.

Archeologists found evidence here of a major prehistoric city, built eight centuries after the Egyptians had constructed the Great Pyramids. A highly civilized community of 4,000 inhabitants flourished at Poverty Point from 1800 B.C. to 500 B.C.

Neatly spaced in rows, the ridges may have been the foundations for primitive dwellings. Originally 5 to 10 feet high, the hillocks now stand 2 to 4 feet in height and measure three-quarters of a mile in diameter from the outermost edges. No one knows why the six ridges were arranged in concentric formation. Outside the ridge formation, the huge, bird-shaped Poverty Point Mound stretches 710 feet in length, its outstretched wings spanning some 640 feet. The siting of this large mound may be connected to astronomical observations.

Seasonal guided tram tours bring visitors to Poverty Point Mound, allowing time for the 70-foot climb to the top. The tram then travels to Mound B, a 20-foot conical-shaped mound, which covered a human crematorium. From the top of the site's observation tower, a view of the prehistoric earthworks reveals the huge scale of this

From the air, the enormous expanse of Poverty Point, right, is apparent. The pattern of rings reveals an engineering feat on a grand scale.

amazing engineering feat. It is estimated that the construction of the mounds took approximately 5 million hours of labor. Impressions found at the site indicate that the baskets used at Poverty Point could hold 50 pounds of earth, and were probably used by laborers to haul the dirt required for the construction of the earthworks.

A STARTLING DISCOVERY

The discovery of the massive structures toppled the long-cherished idea that all prehistoric Native Americans led a primitive and nomadic existence. Objects excavated at the site revealed that the Poverty Point culture formed part of an extensive trade network. The inhabitants imported copper from the Great Lakes area, soapstone from the Appalachian regions of Alabama and Georgia, lead ore from Missouri, and stone from Arkansas, Tennessee, Mississippi, Alabama, Kentucky, Indiana, and Ohio. Since little seems to have been exported, some archeologists believe that the settlement was the hub of highly structured religious activity, where citizens came to barter spiritual services for the basic necessities of life. Echoed in archeological sites sprinkled across Louisiana, Arkansas, and Mississippi, the influence of the Poverty Point culture extended over a vast area.

The people who lived at Poverty Point enjoyed access to upland hunting grounds and harvested a bounty of wild food from their riverside environment. They gathered plants, fished in nearby oxbow lakes, and cultivated bottle gourds and squashes.

Their ingenuity extended to cooking methods: lacking stones, they molded earth balls by hand, dried them in the sun, and heated the balls in earthen pits, which served as ovens for cooking food. Today visitors to the site can sample earth-oven cooking in September during Poverty Point's Louisiana Archeology Week. They can also watch traditional activities including flint-knapping demonstrations and atlatl, or spear-throwing, competitions.

Poverty Point was acquired by the state of Louisiana in 1972, and it has since been designated a national historic landmark. A museum displays some of the 3,000-year-old artifacts found at the site, including darts, spear points, knives, beads, and stone figures sculptured into effigies of birds and pregnant women. Serrated-edge stone blades, or microliths, were probably used to make bone tools. A video presentation provides information about the early Indian inhabitants.

Summer visitors to the 400-acre park may come across excavation sites where archeologists search for clues to help them understand how this ancient culture lived, and the significance of the configuration of this archeological treasure.

FOR MORE INFORMATION:

Poverty Point State Commemorative Area, P.O. Box 276, Epps, LA 71237; 318-926-5492.

When the Pilgrims stepped ashore, more than 350 years ago, at what is now Plymouth, Massachusetts, they met the Wampanoag, or Eastern People, who were one of the principal Native peoples of New England. The Wampanoag ruled over territory that extended from Narragansett Bay and the Pawtucket River east to the Atlantic coast, including Cape Cod and the islands of Martha's Vineyard and Nantucket. Without the friendship extended by these Native Americans, the Pilgrims would have faced a bleak future. At the renowned Plimoth Plantation reconstruction, this meeting of cultures vividly comes to life.

Visitors to Plimoth Plantation can glimpse 17th-century life in the village built by the Pilgrims after their voyage across the Atlantic Ocean in the *Mayflower*. They can watch Mistress Alice Bradford tend her garden behind her clapboard house, hear Elder William Brewster preach the Puritan dogma of the times, or sit beside a family preparing and eating their midday meal.

Re-created with painstaking authenticity, Plimoth Plantation occupies 150 acres of a rolling hilltop overlooking Cape Cod Bay, three miles south of the modern town of Plymouth. The site includes three open-air exhibits: the 1627 Pilgrim Village, the Wampanoag Indian Homesite, and *Mayflower II*, moored at the State Pier in Plymouth Harbor.

At Plimoth Plantation, costumed interpreters assume the identities of individuals from some 50 families, all of whom speak in period dialect. Visitors are free to discuss any topic with the interpreters—from politics to religion to the harsh winter. Unfazed by the throng of onlookers who usually outnumber them, the Pilgrims go about their daily chores with equanimity. Women bake bread, mend coarse wool dresses, and tend their gardens. Men can be seen shearing sheep, conducting musket drills, and chopping wood. Even the breeds of livestock are bred to resemble animals brought to the New World by the Pilgrims.

Enclosed by an oak palisade, the village comprises 20 thatched-roof dwellings, all cramped and dank and built using the tools and materials available in 1627. The air smells of wood smoke, salted fish, and manure; the Pilgrims' clothes are often soiled and worn. A larger structure, serving both as a fort and religious meeting house, sits on high ground, indicating the importance of spirituality to these devout people.

PILGRIM THANKSGIVING

Special events are conducted according to the seasons. Court days, funerals, weddings, and arms demonstrations take place during the warmer months; in autumn visitors are treated to a variety of harvest festivals, sporting contests, and militia drills. On Thanksgiving Day, there's a lavish 19th-century–style feast that debunks one of America's most enduring myths: although the settlers did feast in 1621, dining alongside Wampanoag chief Massasoit and his tribesmen, the menu featured venison, wildfowl, corn meal, and fish. The secular holiday observed today, replete with turkey, cranberry sauce, and pumpkin pie, dates from 1863.

Outside the village, the Eel River Nature Walk leads to the Wampanoag Homesite, where a completely different culture is brought to life through craft activities and storytelling. A Pokanoket Wampanoag tribesman named Hobbamock and his family lived next to the colony and helped the Europeans adapt to the land and its Native peoples. The site features examples of the traditional Wampanoag dwelling, or *wetu*, which are re-created with bent saplings covered with bark or woven cattail mats. Native American interpreters dress in loincloths, deerskins, and jewelry, and recount the often tumultuous relations between Native Americans and the colonists.

It was Massasoit who made a long-lasting peace treaty with the colonists and taught them to cultivate Indian corn, which grew much better in the New World than English grains such as wheat, rye, and barley. The change of diet greatly contributed to the newcomers' economic success: plentiful harvests were traded for skins, which were sent to England to pay off the colony's debt.

Mayflower II is located near Plymouth Rock. Aboard the full-scale reproduction ship, which was built in England in 1955 and sailed to America two years later, interpreters portray the crew and passengers who made the first Pilgrim voyage in 1620. Of the 102 passengers, nearly half succumbed to disease or the harsh climate. Some of the role-players are preparing to return to England, while others are about to disembark for their New World adventure.

FOR MORE INFORMATION:
Plimoth Plantation, P.O. Box 1620, Plymouth, MA 02362; 508-746-1622.

The bulrush mats covering the interior walls of this Wampanoag wetu *at Plimoth Plantation, above, insulated the dwelling in winter. The only items of furniture were skin-covered sleeping platforms.*

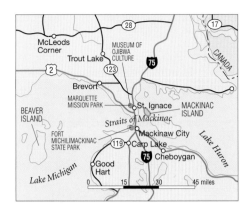

The reconstructed log palisade at Fort Michilimackinac, above, encloses barracks, traders' houses, and the Church of Ste. Anne.

Described by a missionary in 1670 as "the door and the key," Mackinac Island is strategically placed in the narrow straits at the junction of Lake Huron and Lake Michigan. The steep-sided island has a turbulent past: the French, British, and Americans have all fought to dominate it. Today the island and the straits are a rich repository of upper Great Lakes history, replete with tales of the Native Americans, explorers, missionaries, voyageurs, and soldiers who have landed on its rocky shores.

The straits' original inhabitants were the Ojibwa, whose original name was Anish-naw-beeg, or "The True People." One of the largest tribes north of Mexico, the Ojibwa were skilled hunters, fishermen, and farmers who migrated with the seasons. Although they did not live on Mackinac, they came to fish and to bury their dead in its limestone caves. Their pottery, copper arrow tips, and stone fragments still turn up on island soil. The Ojibwa also gave the island its original name of Michilimackinac, or "Great Turtle."

The late 1600's brought change to the straits area. French explorers and Jesuit missionaries were pushing west through the Great Lakes at the same time as Huron and Ottawa refugees from the Iroquois' beaver wars in lower Ontario. In 1671 the Jesuit explorer Father Jacques Marquette established a mission at St. Ignace, on the northern shore of the Straits of Mackinac. Thriving Huron and Ottawa settlements were located next to the mission. Today these reconstructed settlements make up Marquette Mission Park. The park, which has been declared a national historic landmark, contains a memorial to Father Marquette, who died aged 38 on a journey down the Mississippi River.

Excavations carried out at the site of the Huron village at St. Ignace have yielded a wealth of artifacts and revealed the outlines of longhouses, storage pits, living quarters, and fireplaces. A 150-year-old Catholic church was moved here from its original site and now houses the Museum of Ojibwa Culture. The museum mounts exhibitions and demonstrations that re-create the arts, crafts, cooking, and history of the Ojibwa Nation. Each Labor Day weekend a pow-wow is held in a nearby arbor.

FORTS AND FUR TRADERS

In the closing years of the 17th century, the French built a fort at St. Ignace, and the French and Indian populations flourished. By 1705, however, the mission and the fort were abandoned, to be replaced by Fort Michilimackinac on the southern shore. For 50 years the fort was a center of the fur trade, until the straits came under British rule in 1761. Mackinac Island rose to prominence once again when the British moved Fort Michilimackinac across the ice as a defense against Revolutionary forces.

The British remained at the fort until the summer of 1796, and occupied it again briefly during the War of 1812. A thriving community developed on the island, mostly centered on the booming fur trade. Active participants in this industry, the Indians soon became economically dependent on it. Many buildings from this era are preserved on the island, including the Agency House and the Astor Warehouse, formerly occupied by John Jacob Astor's American Fur Trading Company. Accessible by a long ramp, Fort Mackinac still dominates the island and contains many original structures, including the officers' quarters, a

Built as lodgings for Native American visitors to the Indian Agency on Mackinac Island, Indian Dormitory, right, is now a museum.

blockhouse, and the fort's original protective stone ramparts. Interpretive displays outline the fort's history, and the soldiers' barracks serve as a museum.

By the 1830's the fur trade had slowed, tourists were summering on the island, and the Indians were forced to accept a land-rights treaty containing a provision for lodging "to receive Indians, as are called here for the transactions of public business with the Agent." The three-story Indian Dormitory now houses a museum of Great Lakes Indian artifacts. The agent at that time was linguist and writer Henry Schoolcraft, who recorded the Ojibwa legends that inspired Longfellow to write his famous poem, *Hiawatha.*

The island is accessible only by ferry or aircraft and must be explored by foot, bicycle, or horse-drawn carriage. Walking and bicycling paths meander through woods of spruce, larch, and laurel that are filled with scampering rabbits and stalking pheasants. Running around the perimeter of the island is Hwy. 185, the only highway in Michigan that is not open to automobiles. The road provides access to sites such as Arch Rock, a 140-foot limestone rock, and Skull Cave, an ancient Indian burial site.

FOR MORE INFORMATION:
Michigan Travel Center, P.O. Box 3393, Livonia, MI 48151; 800-543-2937.

GRAND PORTAGE

Built on the western shore of Lake Superior in 1778, Grand Portage was once the headquarters of the North West Company and a meeting place for Native Americans and French Canadian voyageurs during the peak years of the fur trade. Each year in July, voyageurs coming from Montreal with trade items met those coming from the interior with furs. After they swapped cargo, they headed back for Montreal or the interior. The Ojibwa (or Chippewa) people were vital participants in this empire. Native Americans shared their knowledge of the land and showed the voyageurs how to build lightweight birchbark canoes.

Birchbark canoes similar to this reproduction of a Montreal canoe, left, were used to carry loads weighing up to 5,000 pounds.

The reconstructed palisade wall and buildings at Grand Portage bring to life the eastern terminus of the Grand Portage, an overland route where watercraft and supplies were carried around the rapids on the Pigeon River. (Grand Portage is French for "great carrying place.") Designated a national monument in 1958, the site lies within the Grand Portage Reservation of the Minnesota Ojibwa.

Grand Portage was run by the North West Company—a group of Scottish fur traders based in Montreal. At the peak of the fur trade in 1792, some 200,000 beaver pelts passed through the post. Hikers can follow the 8.5-mile portage to the former location of outlying Fort Charlotte. Portaging through pine and birch forests, past jagged cliffs and the roaring Pigeon River, a voyageur would carry 180 pounds over the route in about 2.5 hours.

Built from cedar pickets, the stockade originally contained 17 wooden buildings. Of these, the kitchen and the Great Hall have been reconstructed. The latter building was where the fur traders would gather to drink and strike deals. Outside, a warehouse shelters four birchbark canoes.

Every August Rendezvous Day re-creates the rowdy gatherings of the fur-trade days, with fiddling, dancing, singing, and canoe races on Lake Superior. The event coincides with the Ojibwa Powwow.

FOR MORE INFORMATION:
Grand Portage National Monument, P.O. Box 668, Grand Marais MN 55604; 218-387-2788.

PIPESTONE

Author and painter George Catlin visited these small, ancient Indian quarries in the early 1800's. He recorded Native American activities at the site and collected samples of the red stone, which was given the geological name of catlinite.

Native American ceremonial and casual smoking pipes were made from the soft red stone found at the quarry. According to Indian legend, the red stone and Native American people were made of the same substance, so smoking a blessed sacred ceremonial pipe was believed to create a vital link to the Great Spirit. Thus the pipe could procure spiritual guidance on matters such

These pipe bowls, above, were fashioned from reddish stone that was quarried at Pipestone National Monument.

as proclaiming war or peace, assisting in trading goods, and enacting ceremonies.

Once the clay of a prehistoric seabed, the formations exposed at Pipestone National Monument are among the oldest rocks in Minnesota. Pipestone was first quarried in the early 17th century. The Yankton Sioux were stewards of the mineral, which was prized by the Lakota, Arapaho, Omaha, Iowa, and virtually every other group of Northern Plains Indians. The land around the quarry belonged to all tribes, who followed a strict code of peace whenever they were in the vicinity.

Pipes were sometimes carved into human and animal effigies, or inlaid with bands of metal. The calumet—a T-shaped pipe— was traditionally smoked during the signing of treaties. This is the instrument that became known as the peace pipe.

A walking trail winds through stands of tall prairie grass to the quarries. The trail passes a group of boulders called the Three Maidens, where the Sioux leave offerings of food and tobacco. Following the tradition of their ancestors, quarriers use hand tools to pry the soft stone from the layers of quartzite. Native Americans give demonstrations of the art of pipe making at the Upper Midwest Indian Cultural Center. The center also displays quillwork, beadwork, and pottery.

FOR MORE INFORMATION:
Pipestone National Monument, P.O. Box 727, Pipestone, MN 56164; 507-825-5463.

Montana ▪ BLACKFEET INDIAN RESERVATION

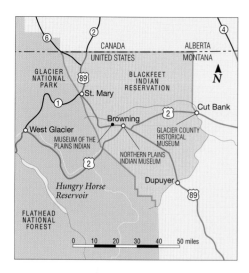

The point where high rolling plains rise suddenly to crystalline peaks signals the border of the Blackfeet Indian Reservation. The land is covered with waving sage and painted with great swaths of deep blue monkshood and golden yarrow. This is the homeland of the Plains Indians, including the Siksika, Piegan, Blood, and Blackfeet. These tribes drifted south in search of the buffalo, an animal that provided them with food, tools, and clothing. The paintings of renowned Western artist Charles M. Russell captured these hunters of the buffalo, poised astride their nimble ponies against a background of shrouded peaks and the endless grassy plains of the prairies.

Today the vast herds of buffalo no longer roam this land. In the 19th century, after Lewis and Clark first described the riches of this Western territory, settlers, fur traders, and missionaries made the long trek to Montana and quickly established a new era on the plains. By the 1880's the buffalo were virtually wiped out. The Blackfeet—who took their name from their moccasins, which were stained with dust and soot—were beset by smallpox and starvation, unable to cope with the loss of the staple of their economy and way of life. By the early 1900's, after decades of treaty-making, the shrinking boundary of the Blackfeet Reservation was made painfully obvious by a fence that encircled it. The Blackfeet were left with little but the legends that recalled the days when their lands stretched from west of the Rockies to present-day Yellowstone National Park.

Amid the magnificent emptiness of the Northern Rockies, an isolated ranch, right, stands near Browning, on the thinly settled Blackfeet Reservation.

WILD COUNTRY

But in many ways, their homeland remains unchanged. Moose are often spotted at glacier-fed Hidden Lake, and trout, whitefish, and kokanee salmon are plentiful in the network of rivers that runs through the reservation. Bighorn sheep and elk still scramble along the mountain slopes that lead up into the vast wilderness of Glacier National Park, which adjoins the reservation to the west. Browning, the tribal capital and major center of the reservation, lies nestled below the 10,000-foot peaks of the Rocky Mountains.

The Museum of the Plains Indian, located a few miles west of Browning, is a living repository for the creative work of the Plains Indians. Its numerous exhibits showcase traditional and contemporary arts and crafts, including children's toys and the magnificent finery worn by tribal leaders. At the Northern Plains Indian Museum in Browning, a series of murals portrays the Blackfeet way of life as it was 200 years ago.

In early July the Blackfeet Tribal Campgrounds is the site of North American Indian Days—one of the largest powwows in the nation. Distant tribes from Canada and the United States gather here for competitive dancing, music, parades, sporting events, and social gatherings. They pitch their tepees and don their traditional buckskin costumes decorated with feathers, intricate beadwork, and bells. The sound of the drums reverberates into the dusk as dancers whirl and sing, as their ancestors have done for generations before them.

Historical tours offered by Blackfeet guides reveal treasures off the beaten track. More than 30 buffalo jumps exist on the reservation—some of them more than five centuries old. Buffalo bones can still be found at these sites, where herds of buffalo were driven over the cliffs to their deaths by Native American hunters and their dogs. Other memorial sites include the place where Lewis and Clark encountered the Blackfeet, which resulted in the only Indian deaths on their expedition; the reservation's first school, built by the Jesuits in 1898; and Sundance, an area where the Blackfeet honor the sun.

Elsewhere on Blackfeet land, cattle drives fill the broad valleys. Oil and gas fields dot the land as it flattens out toward Cut Bank, home of the Glacier County Historical Museum, with its restored 1914 schoolhouse, dinosaur bones, and oil and cattle ranching memorabilia. Rodeos and Western festivals enliven the summer months here. The crystal waters of Four Horns, Two Medicine, and Dog Gun lakes offer avid anglers world-class fishing.

FOR MORE INFORMATION:
Blackfeet Indian Reservation, P.O. Box 850, Browning, MT 59417; 406-338-7521.

A street in Acoma Pueblo, above, displays the traditional architecture of the town. The flat-roofed houses are made of adobe, a building material composed of sun-dried earth and straw.

Rising abruptly from a sandy canyon dotted with juniper trees is a multicolored sandstone mesa nearly 400 feet high. A narrow staircase winds its way precariously up the side, as it has done for centuries. Invisible from the ground, flat-roofed, multistory adobe houses and winding streets adorn the mesa. From the top, the views are spectacular. Golden plains and fields of beans, squash, and corn give way to jagged salmon-colored rock and broken plateaus. In the far distance, silver-tipped Mount Taylor seems to float in a crystal-clear sky.

Also known as Sky City, Acoma Pueblo is considered an ideal site for defense against enemies. Archeologists believe that the occupation of Acoma began about A.D. 1150, making it the oldest continuously inhabited settlement in the nation.

The tortuous stairway, with its narrow toeholds and precarious ladder, was the only ascent to Acoma until the 1930's, when Hollywood came to the mesa to film the movie *African Sunset* and built a rough track to the top of the mesa. It was not until the 1950's that the mesa became accessible to automobiles.

In 1540 the Spanish explorer and soldier Francisco Vásquez de Coronado became the first white man to enter Sky City. He described Acoma as "one of the strongest ever seen, because the city was built on a high rock. The ascent was so difficult that we repented climbing to the top. The houses are three and four stories high. The people are of the same type as those in the province of Cibola [Zuni], and they have abundant supplies of maize, beans, and turkeys like those of New Spain."

After Coronado's visit, Acoma struggled to survive. In 1698 the pueblo rose in rebellion against Spanish forces, which were unable to storm the mesa. The following year, however, Acoma formally submitted to Spanish rule.

Spread by Spanish missionaries who came to the region, Christianity had made inroads by the 1620's. A mission was completed in 1640 under the direction of Friar Juan Ramirez. According to legend, Friar Ramirez gained entry to Acoma after he saved an infant from a fall off the mesa as he was approaching. The people of the pueblo regarded the rescue as a miracle.

Mission San Estevan del Rey remains the most striking feature of the pueblo. All materials used in its construction were hauled up the mesa slopes by hand. More than 60 feet high, and flanked by two square towers, the church probably incorporates more of the original structure than any of the surviving 17th-century churches in New Mexico. Like the pueblo, the mission has been proclaimed a national historic landmark.

DECORATIVE ARTS

Acoma is well known for its pottery, distinguished by its eggshell-like thinness. The pottery's elaborate geometric designs are carefully applied with a single yucca fiber. Pottery making is a family tradition handed down through the generations. Today it is women, for the most part, who continue to practice the craft, and their creations are coveted by collectors. Acoma pottery demonstrates the unique character of the pueblo and its strong relationship with the world around it.

Houses are built with their facades facing south to trap the winter sun. The north-facing back walls shield the houses against the bitter winter winds. There is no electricity or running water on the mesa. Rainfall is collected in three natural cisterns. For 800 years, ownership of the dwellings has been passed from the youngest daughter of one generation to youngest daughter of the next. Most houses are considered family homes, even though only about 30 families live on the mesa year-round. Relatives living off the mesa return to their ancient homeland for ceremonies and dances—most notably the Harvest Dance and Feast of St. Estevan, both of which are held each year in September.

Access to the pueblo is limited. The Acoma people operate a visitor center and provide daily walking tours in the company of guides who recount pueblo history. It is still possible to ascend the ancient stairway to the visitor center, but most visitors today make their way up to the pueblo by means of a shuttle bus.

FOR MORE INFORMATION:
Acoma Tourist Visitor Center, P.O. Box 309, Acoma, NM 87034; 505-252-1139.

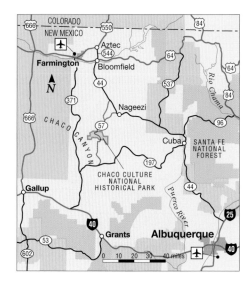

A thousand years ago, a network of arrow-straight stone roads—more than 400 miles in total—crossed the stark sandstone landscape of northwestern New Mexico, the only thoroughfares known to have been built north of Central America before the Spanish Conquest. Impressive even by modern standards, the 20- to 30-foot-wide roads connected approximately 400 villages and towns on the vast desert plain. The largest of these complexes contained multistoried houses and kivas built of sandstone by expert masons. Today crumbling walls and empty rooms are all that remain of the great Ancestral Pueblo center at Chaco Canyon.

Chaco Canyon was a religious and perhaps an economic center for a society that flourished from A.D. 890 until A.D. 1200. Today Chaco Culture National Historical Park preserves hundreds of pueblo sites, including 13 major sites that are open to the public, within a 53-square-mile strip of the canyon. The visitor center near the park's south entrance is accessible by dirt road from Hwy. 57. Its small museum displays artifacts made by the Ancestral Pueblo people, ranging from sandals, cooking utensils, and spearheads to Cibola pottery and turquoise bracelets. From the museum, a short hiking trail brings visitors to Una Vida—a partially excavated 150-room pueblo erected in the 10th century. The masonry is typical of the larger pueblos: its walls are made of closely chinked sandstone blocks set in mortar.

A one-way loop road leads northwest to hiking trails that provide access to other fabled sites. Among the most striking is Pueblo Bonito, the largest Chacoan town. Laid out in a crescent around a central plaza, Pueblo Bonito once covered three acres, stood a staggering four or more stories in height, and contained some 600 rooms and 40 kivas. The structure was a seasonal residence for as many as 1,000 inhabitants. At nearby Casa Rinconada, visitors can explore one of the largest kivas in the Southwest, and then wander up the mesa to Tsin Kletsin, which provides a stunning desert panorama.

MASTER BUILDERS

More strenuous hiking trails lead to the isolated ruins of Peñasco Blanco, Wijiji, and Pueblo Alto, the last of which lies atop the mesa at the junction of several prehistoric roads. Along the way, visitors are constantly reminded of the skill of Chaco's master masons. At Chetro Ketl, built about A.D. 1050, a wall niche sealed with stone was discovered in one of the great circular kivas. Inside archeologists found pendants, shell beads, and copper bells from Mexico, indicating that Chacoans had established extensive trade links.

Out among the scrubby flatlands and yellow sandstone are other great houses with exotic names such as Kin Bineola—a Navajo term meaning "house where the wind whirls"—and Kin Ya'a, or "house rising up high." Both the Navajo and Hopi—the latter with ancestral links to the Ancestral Pueblos—consider Chaco Canyon to be sacred. According to the Navajo, it was here that the legendary Ancient Ones were dispersed by a raging whirlwind when they abandoned their time-honored customs and traditions, and here they haunt the pueblos as ghosts. The Hopi interpret the ruins as the "footsteps" of their forefathers, who migrated to present-day Arizona. The legacy of a sophisticated society, the stones remain behind to tell its story.

FOR MORE INFORMATION:
Chaco Culture National Historical Park, Star Rte. 4, P.O. Box 6500, Bloomfield, NM 87413; 505-786-7014.

A carved jet frog inlaid with turquoise, above, was recovered from Pueblo Bonito in Chaco Culture National Historical Park.

Built between A.D. 850 and A.D. 1130, Pueblo Bonito, right, is one of North America's best examples of monumental public architecture.

The George Gustav Heye Center of the National Museum of the American Indian, above, is housed in an elegant building in Manhattan.

F ew visitors to New York City would expect the city's vast cultural treasures to include dance sticks, purses made of turtle shell, and moccasins decorated with moose hair. Yet these unique objects are part of one of the largest collections of Native American artifacts in the world. They are displayed at the extraordinary National Museum of the American Indian, which is part of the Smithsonian Institution in Washington, D.C.

The museum is the legacy of a wealthy collector named George Gustav Heye, whose great passion for collecting Native American artifacts began during his engineering work on a railroad construction assignment in Arizona in 1897, where he acquired an Apache deerskin shirt. Heye spent his fortune traveling across North America in search of Native American objects, which he bought and shipped back to his Manhattan residence. On one of his visits with the Seneca Indians in upstate New York, Heye was given the name O'owah, or "Screech Owl." In 1922 his huge collection was moved to the Heye Foundation's Museum of the American Indian, located in upper Manhattan.

More than a half-century later, in 1989, the Heye collection itself was acquired by the Smithsonian Institution, and an Act of Congress established the National Museum of the American Indian. Founded with the goal of ending prejudice and misconceptions, the 15th museum of the Smithsonian Institution promised "to change forever the way people view Native Americans of this Hemisphere." Today it is the first and only national museum dedicated to the culture of Native Americans.

The National Museum of the American Indian opened on October 30, 1994, in the Beaux Arts–style Alexander Hamilton U.S. Custom House, which is listed as a national historic landmark. The Heye Center takes up two floors of the building. The openings of two other museum sites, one on the Mall in Washington, D.C., and the other in Suitland, Maryland, are scheduled for the turn of the century.

TREASURED ARTIFACTS

Visitors to the museum can explore hundreds of works gathered from the Arctic Circle to the tip of Tierra del Fuego. An orientation area explains the history of the Lenni Lenape, the Delaware tribe that first inhabited Manhattan Island. Among the museum's highlights are stone, wood, and horn carvings from the Northwest Coast, painted hides produced by the Plains Indians, and pottery and baskets from the Southwest. Also on display are fascinating everyday objects such as Iroquois hair combs, Osage cradleboards, Eskimo kayaks, Huron cigar cases, and a Tlingit wooden telescope box. The museum's resource center includes touch-screen multimedia programs, videos, and unique hands-on discovery boxes that allow visitors to touch drums, wampum belts, Eskimo yo-yos, hide boxes, looms, and other objects.

Throughout the year, Native Americans present programs that highlight contemporary Native artworks, including sculpture, poetry, and music. Such universal themes as creation, sacredness, gender, and the environment are explored through art. Although the point of view is distinctly Native American, the programs enable visi-

From Montana, a Cheyenne mask of a horse's head, above, is now part of the museum's collection.

tors to see the world through the eyes of modern-day Native Americans and to appreciate their unique vision of that world.

Perhaps the true essence of the museum is embodied in its promise of repatriation. Today individual descendants as well as specific tribes can request the return of religious artifacts, funerary finds, and human remains that rightfully belong to them. This policy, like many other aspects of the museum, is rooted in the spirit of Heye's deep respect for Native Americans. It was Heye who set the precedent in 1938, when Hidatsa elders blamed a huge drought in North Dakota on the loss of their sacred medicine bundle, which had been acquired by a missionary and sold to Heye in 1907. Shortly after Heye returned the bundle to the tribe, the rains came. To show their gratitude, the elders of the tribe gave Heye a buffalo medicine horn and bestowed on him the name Isatsigibis, or "Slim Shin." To a man who spent his adult life as a champion of Native Americans, this simple gesture of respect was a greater treasure than even the most valuable artifact surrendered by the earth.

FOR MORE INFORMATION:

George Gustav Heye Center, National Museum of the American Indian, Smithsonian Institution, One Bowling Green, New York, NY 10004; 212-668-6624.

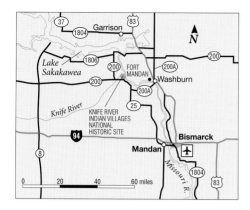

Endless herds of buffalo once roamed the rolling prairies of central North Dakota. A legend recounts how the sound of their thundering bellows rang out across the plains and caught the attention of the spirit world above. Impressed by the bounty of bison, supernatural beings broke through the clouds as arrows, shot down to earth, and founded the 13 clans of the Hidatsa Indians along the Missouri River. They brought with them seed corn and earthlodges, which helped their villages prosper and multiply.

Nowadays mysterious circular rings rising from the flat prairie are the only indication that earthlodges once dominated life along the Upper Mississippi River. Sixty miles north of Bismarck, where the Knife River meets the Missouri, are the only remnants of three villages built by the Hidatsa Indians some 500 to 600 years ago. Recent excavations have uncovered evidence of 11,000 years of human activity in the area, mostly by nomadic hunters. This discovery makes the villages at Knife River some of the oldest inhabited sites in the nation. Today the remains of the Knife River Indian Villages are preserved as a national historic site—the only park of its kind dedicated to the Plains Indians.

The Hidatsa and the nearby Mandan Indians are two of the oldest tribes in North America. These ancient peoples began to settle in semi-permanent villages along the banks of the Knife River some time around A.D. 1300. They lived in round, dome-shaped earthlodges that often measured 30 to 60 feet wide and 15 feet high. The women built, owned, and maintained the lodges, which housed up to 20 people. They also controlled the land, raising squash, beans, sunflowers, and hardy strains of corn to nourish their families.

On display at the visitor center, tepee frameworks, right, reveal how the shelters were constructed.

In 1804, when Lewis and Clark entered the region during their exploration of the West, they marveled at the ordered villages. Typically the communities were located on a river bluff for defense. On later expeditions, artists George Catlin and Karl Bodmer captured village life on canvas. Their stunning paintings showed a society already in transition, marked forever by contact with the Europeans. Ravaged by smallpox and weakened by Sioux raids, the surviving Hidatsa and nearby Mandan tribes moved up the Missouri River about 60 miles and established Like-A-Fishhook Village in 1845. The American Fur Company built Fort Berthold adjacent to the village that same year. In 1862 the Hidatsa were joined by their southern neighbors, the Arikara. In 1885 the Fort Berthold Reservation was established. Today the Hidatsa, Mandan, and Arikara are known as the Three Affiliated Tribes.

LEGACY OF THE LODGES

For a unique journey into the past, visitors can walk to the park's three village sites. They can scan the soil of the Knife River banks and spot the old lodge rings uncovered by erosion. The park is perfect for a leisurely stroll along scenic nature trails that lead through prairie grasses and cottonwood trees. One trail leads from the northernmost Hidatsa village to Sakakawea and Awatixa Xi'e villages in the park's southern section. Here Lewis and Clark met Sacajawea, or the Bird Woman, a former slave of the Hidatsa who accompanied the explorers on their trip across the West. With her one-month baby in tow, the remarkable Shoshone teenager completed the arduous journey, often negotiating with rival tribes for food and horses for the weary party of government explorers.

At the visitor center, a museum exhibits some of the region's most important archeological finds, including hide scrapers, elk-tooth necklaces, and hoes made from the shoulder blades of bison. The center also contains displays that re-create daily life in the villages, as well as detailed information on Lewis and Clark's expedition in this area. Walking tours with interpretive markers lead past the sites of village homes and cache pits, which were used to store food, as well as fortification ditches. The visitor center also sells locally produced Native American arts and crafts.

In July the Northern Plains Indian Culture Fest celebrates the lifeways of the Plains Indians. Descendants of these ancient peoples demonstrate quilting, quillworking, flint knapping, and cooking techniques in remembrance of forebears whose villages are gone, but whose traditions live on.

FOR MORE INFORMATION:
Knife River Indian Villages National Historic Site, P.O. Box 9, Stanton, ND 58571; 701-745-3309.

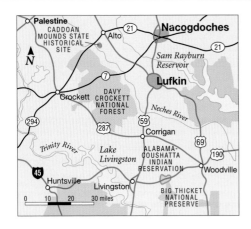

Steps lead to the top of Caddo Mound, above, in Caddoan Mounds State Historical Site.

ALABAMA-COUSHATTA RESERVATION

United for nearly two centuries in the lush timberlands of East Texas, the Alabama and Coushatta Indian tribes have turned their reservation into one of the state's premier tourist destinations. The Alabama-Coushatta tribes, both members of the Muskogean Nations and the Upper Creek Confederacy, settled in the Big Thicket area of Texas shortly after leaving their Alabama homeland at the end of the 17th century. The reservation was created in 1854 by Sam Houston, who purchased 1,280 acres of land and donated it to the tribes.

But the next 74 years proved difficult for these Native peoples, who lived without government assistance on a land entirely unsuitable for growing crops or grazing cattle. Restrictive hunting laws also dealt a serious blow, and malnutrition and sickness whittled the tribal population to fewer than 200. Recognizing the plight of the tribes, the federal and state governments expanded the reservation by 3,071 acres in 1928, and

allocated funds to help improve living conditions. Today approximately 500 tribal members live on the reservation, which is located 95 miles north of Houston and 17 miles east of Livingston.

Set amid the pristine scenery of the Piney Woods region, the reservation receives some 200,000 annual visitors. From March to November, the Alabama-Coushatta Indians host tours and cultural activities. The Indian Chief Train winds through the reservation and into Big Thicket country. A guided walking tour explores the unique wilderness of the Big Thicket area, which contains rare species of trees, plants, and animals. An open-air bus tour enables visitors to see Native homes, campsites, and hunting grounds.

A museum showcases the rich heritage of the two tribes, and the Living Indian Village features demonstrations of basket-making, weaving, beadwork, and traditional cooking methods. Tribal dances are performed on weekends during the spring and fall months, and a powwow is held the first weekend in June.

FOR MORE INFORMATION:
Alabama-Coushatta Indian Reservation, Rte. 3, Box 640, Livingston, TX 77351; 409-563-4391 or 800-444-3507.

CADDOAN MOUNDS
More than two centuries ago, travelers crossing through the heart of East Texas were the first group of people to discover the mounds of this early Indian settlement. In 1779 a Frenchman named Athanase de Mezières recorded the first-known mention of the site during a trip from Louisiana to San Antonio. In 1834 an American traveler named Amos Andrew Parker stopped in the area to investigate the mounds and record his observations in his diary. Since that time, archeologists have continued to study the mounds in an attempt to unravel the mystery as to why they were built.

The Caddo established the most highly developed society among the ancient Moundbuilder peoples, whose culture dominated the Mississippi Valley from 1000 B.C. to A.D. 1500. The partially excavated village at Caddoan Mounds State Historical Site consists of two temple mounds, a burial mound, and a reproduction of a typical beehive-shaped dwelling—testaments to the sophistication, power, and prosperity that the Caddo enjoyed after they settled the fertile woodlands of East Texas in approximately A.D. 800. Here

they found good soil for crops, food in the surrounding forest, and a permanent water supply from the nearby Neches River.

Lured to the lush region by its abundance of wildlife and natural resources in the Neches Valley, the Caddo made this frontier settlement the westernmost ceremonial center of the Moundbuilder culture, providing local native hamlets with social and economic stability that lasted for nearly 500 peaceful years.

Although distanced from their parent group, the Caddoan Mounds people continued to participate in the broad trade network of the Moundbuilders, whose ceremonial centers were scattered along major waterways from Georgia to Oklahoma. Many of the artifacts unearthed at Caddoan Mounds bear a remarkable similarity to objects from as far away as present-day Illinois and Florida. Caddoan artifacts contain shells from the eastern Gulf Coast and copper from the Great Lakes region.

The stability of early Caddoan society rested on its highly structured hierarchy. The elite ruling class, who lived on or around the temple mounds and burial mound in the inner village, conducted the functions of government and religious ceremonies. The common class lived in the outer village and supplied the labor force for food production and community activities—most notably mound building and temple construction. Their circular dwellings, thatched with cane bundles, ranged in size from 25 to 45 feet in diameter, and proved both warm in winter and cool in summer.

The early Caddo erected their mounds in a series of building stages that were associated with important ceremonial events. The ritual destruction of an existing temple, often by fire, was followed by remounding the area with fresh soil, and the cycle was completed with the construction of a new temple on the site. Archeologists can only speculate about the significance of these episodes. Destruction and reconstruction occurred three times at both temple sites. Perhaps coincidentally, the burial mound underwent six stages of ceremonial burial activity during a span of 400 years. Rising to more than 20 feet, the mound held the remains of some 90 individuals of the elite class, who were interred in about 30 pits.

FOR MORE INFORMATION:
Superintendent, Caddoan Mounds State Historical Site, Rte. 2, P.O. Box 85C, Alto, TX 75925; 409-858-3218.

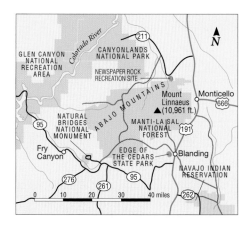

NEWSPAPER ROCK RECREATION SITE

As its name implies, Newspaper Rock Recreation Site offers a story-filled journey within a magnificent natural setting. Nestled at the foot of the Abajo Mountains in the Indian Creek drainage, the walls of Newspaper Rock speak eloquently of the Native Americans' past through a series of approximately 350 petroglyphs.

These figures and symbols, some dating back 1,500 years, were chipped, pecked, and painted onto a portion of the sheer sandstone canyon wall. Over time, the rock face became stained with desert varnish— a dark patina that was formed by the oxidation of minerals on the rock surface.

The Ancestral Pueblo people, or Anasazi, are thought to be responsible for most of the petroglyphs at Newspaper Rock. But the Fremont, Ute, and Navajo peoples, as well as white settlers, also left their marks on the panel that the Navajo called Tse Hane—"the rock that tells a story." The stories behind these markings are only partially understood and still fuel the myths and legends that surround Newspaper Rock. Some of the petroglyphs, such as figures mounted on horseback, are not difficult to decipher. But other etchings remain enigmatic. Some symbols have been recognized as religious icons that are still in use by contemporary Hopi Indians. Others suggest astrological occurrences, the never-ending search for drinking water, or perhaps a safe passage to hospitable land. Still more intriguing are humanlike figures, which some people believe represent extraterrestrial beings.

FOR MORE INFORMATION:
Newspaper Rock Recreation Site, Bureau of Land Management, Moab District, P.O. Box 7, Monticello, UT 84535; 801-587-2141.

EDGE OF THE CEDARS STATE PARK
Lured by the splendor and unobstructed view of the Abajo Mountains from atop a desert rise in southeastern Utah, the Ancestral Pueblo people made this settlement a hub of cultural and ceremonial activity from about A.D. 850 to A.D. 1220. Edge of the Cedars was a prosperous oasis of approximately 75 sandstone dwellings grouped around 10 kivas. The sandstone masonry of the kivas is similar to that found in the ruins of Chaco Canyon, New Mexico: the blocks were held together with clay mortar. The roof of the largest kiva— the site of dances and celebrations—was so large that archeologists think the pueblo may have been a focal point for many clans throughout the Four Corners region.

The museum at Edge of the Cedars State Park displays contemporary rock art sculptures, above.

A portion of the ruins of the pueblo, first discovered in 1905, was excavated and stabilized from 1969 to 1972. Today the site is listed on the National Register of Historic Places. An illustrated guide helps visitors to wander along the pathways of the Indian ruins. A small kiva has been roofed and restored; a wooden ladder enables visitors to climb through the smoke hole and linger awhile in this subterranean chamber.

A museum at the visitor center houses two main exhibit halls, a special exhibits gallery, and a repository wing dedicated to preserving artifacts excavated from public lands in southeastern Utah. A remarkable exhibit of pottery contains everything from simple kitchen vessels to beautiful ceremonial objects. Evening programs and craft demonstrations are held during Utah Heritage Week in May.

Edge of the Cedars is a departure point for the Trail of the Ancients, a 180-mile circuit that excompasses some of Utah's most spectacular scenery. The route crosses the site of the last armed clash between Native Americans and white settlers, which took place in 1923.

FOR MORE INFORMATION:
Edge of the Cedars State Park, P.O. Box 788, Blanding, UT 84511-0788; 801-678-2238.

The unusual animal and humanlike petroglyphs, left, are etched into the sandstone walls at Newspaper Rock State Park.

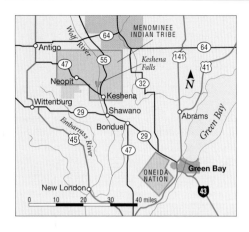

Surrounded by a stockade of poplar stakes, a full-sized replica of a longhouse, above, is located at the Oneida Nation Museum. The house has holes in the ceiling to allow smoke to escape.

MENOMINEE INDIAN TRIBE

Resplendent with hardwoods, virgin pines, and hemlocks, this vast timberland is home to the Menominee Nation, an Algonquian-speaking tribe that has lived in northeastern Wisconsin for more than 5,000 years. The Menominee, whose name means "Wild Rice People," are a federally recognized sovereign nation with their own constitution and bylaws. Roughly 3,900 of the tribe's 8,000 members live on the 234,000-acre reservation. Hunting and fishing are restricted to tribal members, but visitors are welcome to enjoy the untouched beauty of this land of lakes, streams, and wildlife.

From the northern boundary, Wolf River drops 900 feet as it slices through emerald forests to Keshena Falls—site of the 1854 treaty that established the current reservation's boundaries. A footbridge across Smokey Falls, named for its misty waters, offers a superb view of the 40-foot cascade. North of Smokey Falls, a picturesque trail leads past granite walls to Wolf River Dells in the heart of a spectacular canyon. The Annual Menominee Nation Powwow is held on the first weekend in August. During the festival, dancers compete for prizes, a Menominee princess is chosen, artisans display crafts, and cooks serve up fry bread, corn soup, and Indian tacos.

The Menominee Logging Camp Museum is dedicated to the days when logging was Wisconsin's main industry. Thousands of logging artifacts are on display in the museum's buildings. Visitors can tour a cook shanty, bunkhouse, butcher's shop, and blacksmith shop. Logging is still an intrinsic part of the Menominee culture: since 1908, the tribe has operated one of the most modern logging and lumber manufacturing plants in the Great Lakes states, while maintaining a commitment to sustainable forestry practices.

Towering more than 11 feet, a statue of the Menominee Ancestral Bear proudly stands on the reservation. Legend has it that the great bear was created at the mouth of the Menominee River, took human form, and was made an Indian by the Great Mystery. The statue of the bear was carved from the state's largest butternut tree.

FOR MORE INFORMATION:

Menominee Indian Tribe, P.O. Box 910, Keshena, WI 54135; 715-799-5100.

ONEIDA NATION

The Oneida Nation moved from New York State to Wisconsin in 1822, leaving behind the homeland it had shared with the Mohawk, Onondaga, Cayuga, Seneca, and Tuscarora as members of the Iroquois Confederacy. The 64,500-acre Oneida Reservation was established by treaty in 1838. Located just west of Green Bay, the territory is home to approximately 4,900 of the tribe's 12,494 members.

The Oneida are known as the People of the Standing Stone. Before the tribe left New York, they moved every 10 or 20 years, once the soil became barren and hunting was scarce. Legend has it that each time they relocated, a huge rock appeared outside the village gates. In the belief that this large stone was following and protecting them, the Oneida took the rock as their national symbol.

The wolf, bear, and turtle were the symbols of the three clans of the Oneida. Theirs was a matrilineal society, in which the mother determined a child's clan. Women also chose the chiefs and owned the longhouses, where 10 to 30 families of the same clan would live under one roof.

The Annual Oneida Powwow, held every Fourth of July weekend, is a three-day festival in which dancers outfitted in quill- and beadwork dance to the beat of drums. Made of deer, elk, or buffalo hides, each drum is thought to possess its own powerful spirit. Visitors are invited to join in the intertribal dance.

The Oneida Nation Museum, located on the reservation, gives visitors an opportunity to view cultural and historical exhibits relating primarily to the Oneida. Displays of clothing help trace the history of this proud people, as well as demonstrate the impact that contact with the white man had on their everyday life. The Oneida and other Iroquois began trading for cloth in the 1600's, and much of their later attire is of a distinctly European style.

Hands-on displays allow visitors to handle Oneida beadwork or to heft an ominous war club. A reconstructed stockaded village features a full-size replica of a longhouse and a medicinal herb garden. These and other exhibits offer a glimpse of this unique culture, transplanted from its original home, yet still strongly rooted in the land.

FOR MORE INFORMATION:

Oneida Nation, P.O. Box 365, Norbert Hill Center, 3000 Seminary Rd., Oneida, WI 54155; 414-869-2214.

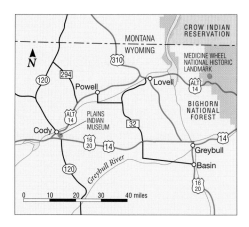

An animal skull offering, above, is attached to the wire fence that encloses Medicine Wheel.

MEDICINE WHEEL NHL

Surrounded by rocky cliffs and deep fissures, a sacred treasure stretches across an alpine plateau in Wyoming's Bighorn Mountains. Medicine Wheel is a prehistoric archeological mystery probably constructed between A.D. 1200 and A.D. 1700. From the hub of the wheel, 28 spokes radiate to the outer rim of the circle. Six cairns lie in small heaps at the ends of six spokes that extend beyond the wheel's circumference.

Medicine Wheel's origins and purpose remain an enigma. Since the number of spokes suggest the days of the lunar month, the wheel may have been connected with celestial observations. Some archeologists liken the wheel to the houses of dawn of ancient sun worshipers and believe the site was built by exiled Aztecs. Other theories attribute the New World Stonehenge to the Lost Tribes of Israel, a vanished people. Whatever its origins, the wheel has been adopted by the Plains Indians as a place of worship. Many Native Americans believe it is a reflection of the essence of life. As an embodiment of this form, the wheel is revered as a place to obtain spiritual power and to commune with the Great Spirit.

FOR MORE INFORMATION:

Medicine Wheel Ranger District, Bighorn National Forest, P.O. Box 367, Lovell, WY 82431; 307-548-6541.

PLAINS INDIAN MUSEUM

Tucked away in northwestern Wyoming, the Plains Indian Museum chronicles the history and culture of Plains Indian tribes such as the Arapaho, Cheyenne, Kiowa,

Medicine Wheel, right, is composed of a circle of stones, 75 feet in diameter, with a donut-shaped central cairn.

Comanche, Blackfeet, Sioux, Shoshone, and Pawnee. The museum is housed in the acclaimed Buffalo Bill Historical Center—often referred to as the Smithsonian of the West—and contains a collection of everyday objects, as well as artworks that range from the Plains tribes' buffalo-hunting days to their contemporary artistic traditions.

The museum focuses on the lifestyles of the nomadic buffalo hunters who tracked the great herds throughout the year, as well as the Plains village tribes who lived along the fertile valleys for half the year, raising corn and other crops. When the buffalo season arrived, they ventured onto the prairies armed for the hunt. The Plains Indians considered the buffalo to be a gift from the Creator, and its carcass was used for tepees, shields, bone and horn tools, robes, and other clothing. The museum's artifacts indicate the prominent role of the buffalo in the daily lives of the people. Hide-working tools used to scrape, tan, and soften the buffalo skins are on display. Moccasins adorned with porcupine quills, painted rawhide bags, and beaded vests illustrate how the Plains Indians transformed buffalo hides into works of art.

After the crops were planted, village tribes performed ceremonies to ensure a good hunting season. Some rituals lasted for days and involved dramatizations of the hunt. Mandan hunters would don buffalo masks and imitate buffalo bulls. One mask decorated with horns, rawhide, and leather is on display at the museum, as well as a Crow ceremonial robe painted with three hunters in pursuit of a trio of buffalo.

The annual Plains Indian Powwow in June brings Native culture out of the museum and into the Robbie Powwow Garden for a celebration featuring dance, music, art, and traditional foods. In September the Buffalo Bill Historical Center hosts the Annual Plains Indian Seminar, a three-day event that showcases the art and history of the Plains tribes.

FOR MORE INFORMATION:

Buffalo Bill Historical Center, Plains Indian Museum, 720 Sheridan Ave., Cody, WY 82414; 307-587-4771.

INDEX

PICTURE CREDITS

ACKNOWLEDGMENTS

Cartography: Map resource base courtesy of the USGS; shaded relief courtesy of the USGS and Michael Stockdale. Shaded relief on pages 10-11 courtesy of Mountain High Maps®. Copyright © 1993 Digital Wisdom, Inc.

The editors would also like to thank the following: Sonia Di Maulo, Lorraine Doré, Dominique Gagné, and Pascale Hueber.